FROM LATIN TO ITALIAN

CW01426109

ALSO FROM TIGER XENOPHON

Grammaire Élémentaire de l'Ancien Français
Joseph Anglade

Kennedy's New Latin Primer
Benjamin Hall Kennedy
Revised by Gerrish Gray
(available in US and UK editions)

Grammar of the Gothic Language
Joseph Wright

A Greek Grammar
William W. Goodwin

ALSO FROM TIGER OF THE STRIPE

The Student's Dictionary of Anglo-Saxon
Henry Sweet

The History of English Handwriting
A.D. 700–1400
Sir Edward Maunde Thompson

FROM LATIN TO ITALIAN

AN HISTORICAL OUTLINE OF THE PHONOLOGY AND MORPHOLOGY OF THE ITALIAN LANGUAGE

CHARLES H. GRANDGENT

TIGER ◪ XENOPHON

This paperback edition
first published in 2008 by
TIGER XENOPHON

TIGER XENOPHON
is an imprint of
TIGER OF THE STRIPE
50 Albert Road
Richmond
Surrey TW10 6DP, UK

ISBN 978-1-904799-23-8

Printed and bound
in the US and UK by
Lightning Source

PREFACE

THIS work, the result of over thirty years' collecting, clas-
sifying, and speculation, after many reconstructions is
at last offered to fellow-scholars in the hope that it may render
service, in America and perhaps in England, to the study of
Romance Philology. It is a source of regret to the writer
that his presentation includes no formal discussion of vocabulary, word-building, syntax, and style; but the addition
of these subjects would have postponed for another decade
or so a publication already long delayed. Incidentally, to
be sure, the main principles of syntax are perhaps adequately
suggested.

What is owed to numerous investigations by other linguists
will be found indicated in the appropriate places. The author
wishes, however, to make a general and conspicuous ac-
knowledgment of his obligation to Professor Wilhelm Meyer-
Lübke, whose *Italienische Grammatik* and *Romanisches Ety-
mologisches Wörterbuch* must ever remain a mine of precious
material for workers in Italian. That the philological theories
set forth in this book are so often and so widely at variance
with those preferred by the master constitutes at once an
excuse for hesitation and a special reason for emphasizing a
really great indebtedness.

The few technical symbols employed will be familiar to any
student of linguistics. An asterisk (*) shows that the word
to which it is prefixed is a conjectural form. The angle > is
a sign of derivation, the source standing at the open, the result at the closed end: as *venit*>*viene* or *viene*<*venit*. An *ü*
stands for the *u* in French *pu*; an *ö* for the *eu* in French *peur*.
Under a vowel letter, a dot signifies the close, a hook the open
sound: as *meno*, *bello*; *molto*, *cosa*. An *s* with a dot beneath
means the sonant or voiced sibilant heard in Italian *caso* or
English *easy*. The signs *š* and *ž* stand respectively for the

sh in English *ship* and the *si* in English *vision*. An accent after a consonant letter indicates a palatal articulation — that is, an arching of the tongue in the middle of the mouth: *ǫn'i, mẹl'o = ogni, meglio; g'is, k'i* would represent English *geese, key*, as compared with *gus, ku = goose, coo*. The Greek β stands for bilabial *v*, as used in Spanish; χ for the *ch* in German *machen;* γ for the corresponding sonant, often heard in German *sagen*. The tailed *ŋ* means the velar nasal of English *long*, or of Italian *lungo = luŋgo;* ð and þ represent the *th* sounds of English *this* and *thin; y* is used for the *y* of English *year*.

Rom. means the *Romania; Zs.*, the *Zeitschrift für romanische Philologie*.

C. H. GRANDGENT

Cambridge, October, 1926

CONTENTS

CONTENTS

FROM LATIN TO ITALIAN

INTRODUCTION

1. Although the subject of this study is the literary and official language of present day Italy, as pronounced by cultivated Florentines, the accepted vocabulary of past centuries will not be left out of consideration, even if now obsolete; and dialect forms will be cited whenever they are of interest in illustrating the development of standard usage.

What is today the national tongue originated in the common speech of Florence. Used by men of letters, it was presently enriched by a multitude of Latinisms, by the adoption of some words from other Tuscan centres, and by the admission of a few elements from dialects or languages outside of Tuscany. Verse was considerably influenced by the parlance of the early " Sicilian School " of poetry (see § 5). Owing to the achievements of Dante, Petrarch, and Boccaccio, not to speak of minor contemporaries who in the fourteenth century used essentially the style of Florence, the Florentine had by the end of that century won preëminence as a literary medium. In the next two centuries the prestige of great Florentine families made it the language of polite society in Rome. Little by little its use was extended through the peninsula; but, as it spread, miscellaneously adding to its store, much of its original tang was lost, until in the early nineteenth century the efforts of Manzoni, Giusti, and other enthusiasts were needed to restore a closer relation between the rather faded conventional language of their time and the racy spoken idiom.

2. The other neo-Latin dialects, which in Italy have been so numerous and so dissimilar, have generally maintained themselves in popular use, and some of them have served, and still serve, as vehicles of important local literatures. Many natives of the peninsula and its islands have scant knowledge of the national tongue. Even among those cultivated people whose only medium is Standard Italian there are differences in pronunciation due in the first place, no doubt, to primitive local habits of speech. The most striking divergences are to be found in the differentiation of close and open vowels, in the use of double consonants, in the sounds of *z*, *s*, *c*, and *g*. In Florence itself, and elsewhere in Tuscany, there are vulgarisms which the better speakers condemn but do not always succeed in avoiding. The refined utterance of Florence has here been chosen as a basis of study, not only because it is by many purists regarded as the norm, but also because it best preserves the nice distinctions inherited from the parent Latin. It may be said in passing that Italian stage usage differs from the Tuscan in some respects, notably in the sound of *s* between vowels.[1]

3. With the exception of a few communities inhabited by foreign colonists (Slav, German, Greek), the present dialects of Italy are all descendants of Latin. But in nearly all regions it was a Latin influenced in its vocabulary and pronunciation by the earlier linguistic habits of the populations that had adopted it. These peoples contained a strong admixture of Ligurian, Gallic, Illyrian, Greek, and Phoenician races, all alien, and of Italic tribes related to the Latin, for instance the Umbrian and the Oscan. The Ligurian strain is found in the northwest; the Gallic in the north; the Illyrian along the Adriatic shore, particularly in the northeast and south-

---

[1] For some of the principal local differences, see O. Hecker, *Zur Aussprache des Italienischen*, in *Archiv für das Studium der neueren Sprachen und Literaturen*, LXIII, 70. For the development of spelling, see G. Hartmann, *Zur Geschichte der italienischen Orthographie*, in *Romanische Forschungen*, XX, i, 199. For the long disputes over the supremacy of Tuscan, see V. Vivaldi, *Storia delle controversie linguistiche in Italia da Dante ai nostri giorni*, 1925– ; Thérèse Labande-Jeanroy, *La question de la langue en Italie*, 1925 (reviewed by P. Rajna in *Marzocco*, Oct. 18, 1925).

east; the Greek in Sicily and the south; the Phoenician on
the coasts of Sicily. With regard to the Etrurians, the chief
predecessors of the present Tuscans, it is not surely known
whether they were Italic or not; at any rate, their own
language seems to have been very different from Latin, they
were at one time the dominant race in Italy, and their civili-
zation antedates the Roman. Who or what the Ligurians
were is a matter of doubt. Gallic, Greek, and Illyrian were
of the Indo-European family; Illyrian has been regarded,
perhaps without sufficient evidence, as the ancestor of Al-
banian. The Phoenicians were a branch of the Semitic race.
Some of the tribes close to Rome offered the stoutest resistance, maintaining their political and linguistic independence
long after outlying countries, such as Spain, had been con-
quered and colonized. In the first two centuries of our era,
hordes of slaves were brought into Italy from Africa, Asia,
and Greece. With the Germanic migrations came a vast
incursion of Goths, Vandals, Longobards. The Western
Empire fell into Gothic hands; a great Lombard Kingdom
was founded in the north. Many noble families in Italy are
of Teutonic origin. Naturally a rich store of Germanic words
was imported into the native stock. In the south, during
and after the seventh century, there was a considerable in-
fusion of Saracen blood, but with little effect on the language.
More important for this territory was Greek, which had long
been there the prevalent tongue. Early Greek colonies had
peopled the shores of Sicily and the southwestern part of the
peninsula; later Byzantine migrations came from the seventh
century to the eleventh; there are still a few Greek-speaking
towns at the end of Calabria. The Norman conquest of
Sicily and southern Italy came in the eleventh century.
At various times there has been some immigration from
Albania and Croatia.[1]

[1] See G. Gröber, *Grundriss der romanischen Philologie*, Vol. I, Part iii,
Abschnitt 1, A *Die vorromanischen Volkssprachen der romanischen*

4. In the northwest of Italy we find the Piedmontese dialects, and, to the south, along the Gulf of Genoa from Monaco to Carrara, the Ligurian; the central north is occupied by the Lombard. These idioms have much in common with the French: they use French *ü*, they simplify double consonants, and they are strong in their inclination to abbreviate words. To the east of Lombardy, in most of Venetia and in Istria, across the Adriatic, is the soft-sounding Venetian, less remote from Tuscan than the Lombard; a part of eastern Venetia speaks Raetian, the Romance tongue of southeastern Switzerland. South of Lombardy and Venetia, slanting across the peninsula northeast of Liguria, Tuscany, and Umbria, is the Romagnole or Emilian territory, embracing Romagna, Emilia, S. Marino, Pesaro e Urbino, and extending up a bit into Venetia and Lombardy. Its principal city is Bologna, and its language is in a way intermediate between north and centre; it possesses the vowel (*ö*) which in French is written *eu*. The central group, which on the whole remains closest to Latin, consists, on the one hand, of Tuscan and of the similar language of Corsica and northern Sardinia; on the other hand, of Umbrian and Roman speech, whose home is the province of Umbria and the Pontifical States, plus the western Abruzzo and Ancona, Macerata, and half of Ascoli Piceno. To the east are the other two Abruzzi, with a style of their own. We come now to the southerly parts. Apulian dialects divide the heel of the boot. In the toe are Calabrian idioms, closely related to the neigh-

Länder; A. Ernout, *Les éléments dialectaux du vocabulaire latin,* 1909; Tenny Frank, *Latin Quantitative Speech as Affected by Immigration,* in the *American Journal of Philology,* XLV, 161; H. H. Vaughan, *The Influence of Non-Latin Elements on the Tonic Vowel in Italian Dialects,* in the *Philological Quarterly,* I, 147; G. Rohlfs, *Griechen und Romanen in Unteritalien,* 1924, and W. Meyer-Lübke in *Archiv für das Studium der neueren Sprachen und Literaturen,* CL, 63, also N. Maccarone, *Romani e Romaici nell'Italia Meridionale, in Archivio glottologico italiano,* 1926. For non-Italian, see M. Bartoli, *Italia linguistica,* 1927.

boring Sicilian; characteristic of these is the use of *i* and *u*
for close *e* and *o* in stressed syllables and for unaccented
final *e* and *o*. The remainder of the peninsula, the region
lying southeast of the Pontifical States, south of the Abruzzi,
southwest of Capitanata, and north of Apulia, contains a
lot of dialects somewhat akin to those just discussed, forming
a group which may for convenience be called Neapolitan;
they are prone to double consonants and to indistinctness of
unstressed vowels. The domain in question consists of Terra
di Lavoro, Napoli, the Principati, Basilicata, Benevento,
Molise. In Sardinia, the central province of Logudoro and
the southern province of Campidano differ markedly from
the mainland in their speech; in fact, Logudoro has features
that distinguish it from any other Romance language — for
instance the retention of " hard *c* " before *e* and *i*.[1]

5. In the thirteenth century, before Dante's time, there
had been apparently two more or less unconscious efforts to
create a national Italian language. At the Imperial court of
Frederick II, the eminent men who there were gathered from
all parts of the country must have felt the need of an intelligibility far beyond that attainable by means of their native
dialects, and an ease of communication greater than was
afforded by the use of their school language, Latin. This
problem they seem to have partially solved by a method of
conciliation, each speaker rejecting those factors of his local
idiom which were most peculiar, while favoring and normaliz-
ing those which were closest to Latin, the mother of all. This
we infer from the verse they produced, the output of the so-

[1] G. Bertoni, *Italia dialettale*, 1916. W. Meyer-Lübke (translated by
M. Bartoli and G. Braun), *Grammatica storico-comparata della lingua
italiana e dei dialetti toscani*, 1906. F. d'Ovidio and W. Meyer-Lübke,
Grammatica storica della lingua e dei dialetti italiani, 1906. P. E. Guar-
nerio, *Fonologia romana*, 1918. P. Savj-Lopez and M. Bartoli, *Altitalie-
nische Chrestomathie*, 1903. B. Wiese, *Altitalienisches Elementarbuch*,
1904.

called " Sicilian School " of lyric poetry, a literature preserved in several great repertory books, adapted to performance in Tuscany. The artificial medium thus brought into existence, becoming still more composite by a process of partial Tuscanization at the hands of minstrels, exercised a considerable influence on the poetic diction of Tuscany and Bologna in the next generation. In Bologna itself, the great university city, a similar need had doubtless already been felt and a similar solution attempted. Dante held that no Italian dialect, as spoken, was quite fit for literary use, but behind them all lurked a common ideal, which the writer should discover and adopt. In practice, Dante wrote Florentine, a sublimated Florentine in most of his lyrics and in his early prose, a rich and vigorous Florentine, with free borrowings from the Latin, in his later prose and especially in the *Divine Comedy*. And thus the Italian language began.[1]

6. In the centuries that have followed, the language has changed but slowly. Pronunciation has remained surprisingly stable; a more important development has taken place in vocabulary, inflections, and syntax, but even that is small compared with the evolution of English in the same years. Between Dante and Manzoni there is no such gap, linguistically, as that between Chaucer and Tennyson. Furthermore, the Tuscan of the fourteenth century is astonishingly close to the ancestral Latin — much closer than are the earliest texts of French or Provençal or Rumanian, closer even than the most ancient Spanish or Portuguese. Italian, from its

---

[1] E. Monaci, *Da Bologna a Palermo*, in L. Morandi's *Antologia della nostra critica letteraria moderna*. G. Cesareo, *La poesia siciliana sotto gli Svevi*, 1894. Dante, *De Vulgari Eloquentia*, I, xi–xix. O. J. Tallgren, *Sur la rime italienne et les Siciliens du XIIIᵉ siècle*, 1909. E. G. Parodi, *Rima siciliana, rima aretina e bolognese*, in *Bullettino della Società dantesca italiana*, XX, 113. G. Bertoni, *Nota sulla lingua dei più antichi rimatori Siciliani*, in *Giornale storico della letteratura italiana*, LXXXVI, 200; also *Seconda nota* in LXXXVI, 392.

beginning to the present day, has shown itself the most conservative of the Neo-Latin tongues.

Our oldest specimens go back to the second half of the tenth century; they consist of a few phrases in southern vernacular, inserted in Latin documents. In the eleventh and twelfth centuries we find more and more pieces of prose in Italian dialects, either alone or mixed with Latin, and a few very poor attempts at verse. There is nothing like a vernacular literature until the thirteenth. Our earliest example of Tuscan prose belongs to the year 1211.[1]

---

[1] E. Monaci, *Crestomazia italiana dei primi secoli*, 1889–1912.

PHONOLOGY

7. The Latin from which Italian, like the other Romance languages, took its start is not the Latin of books, but the popular tongue commonly spoken by the miscellaneous inhabitants of the Roman Empire at its close. This Vulgar Latin of course varied somewhat from place to place, particularly on Italian soil, where it was most at home. Its transformation into the modern types of speech was continuous and gradual, although the movement seems to have been accelerated in the sixth and seventh centuries; at any rate, we may assume, for convenience, that Latin ends and Italian begins at about that time. Before this, certain changes (which affected all the Romance tongues) had occurred in the vernacular, differentiating it notably from the classic idiom of the Augustan writers. Although the most important of these alterations have to do with inflections rather than with pronunciation, the sound-changes in Vulgar Latin are by no means insignificant.

8. In the study of linguistic history it is essential to distinguish " popular " from " learned " or bookish words. The former, having constantly formed a part of the spoken vocabulary, have been subject to the operation of all the phonetic tendencies that have determined the development of the language. The latter class, consisting of words borrowed by clerks or scholars, at various periods, from Latin books and from the Latin of the Church, is naturally exempt from sound-changes that occurred in the vulgar tongue before the time of their adoption. The form of learned words depends, in the first place, on the clerical or school pronunciation of Latin at the date of their borrowing; then, if they came into general use, their form was subject to the influence of any phonetic fashions that were subsequently active. The fate of borrowed terms differs, therefore, according to the date and place of their introduction and the degree of popularity which they afterwards attained.

ACCENT

9. The place of the *primary* accent was in Classic Latin usage determined by quantity, the stress falling on the penult if that was long, otherwise on the antepenult.[1] There is evidence, however, that in an earlier stage of the tongue the accent regularly fell on the initial syllable; and it may be that the first syllable, after losing the main stress, always retained more force than other unaccented syllables. Vulgar Latin, as we know it, generally followed the system postulated for Classic Latin, but we note a few divergences, all of which tend still further to carry the stress away from the beginning of the word.[2]

1. A single consonant between vowels belonged syllabically to the second: *pa-ter.* A group of two consonants was divided in the middle: *por-tus, tem-pes-tas, cur-rus.* But if the group consisted of a mute plus a liquid, there was some uncertainty: *co-lub-ra* or *co-lu-bra.* Hence a short penultimate vowel before a mute followed by a liquid may, in Classic Latin, be stressed or unstressed; the older dramatists treat it regularly as accented; but Quintilian recommends the unstressed penult. In Vulgar Latin, such a vowel seems nearly always to have had the accent, although the consonant combination did not make position in the sense of checking the development of the vowel: *intĕgra* >It. *intéra, tenĕbras*>Sp. *tiniéblas, cathĕdra* >O. Fr. *chaiére.* Italian *ténebre, cáttedra,* then, are presumably learned words.[3]

[1] A syllable was called long if it contained a diphthong, a naturally long vowel, or any vowel plus a consonant, as in *poe-na, pō-no, pon-tem.*

[2] For the nature of Latin accent, see F. F. Abbott in *Classical Philology,* II, 444; R. G. Kent in *Transactions and Proceedings of the American Philological Association,* LIII, 63; and especially E. H. Sturtevant in *Transactions,* etc., LIV, 51. See also T. Fitzhugh, *The Pyrrhic Accent and Rhythm of Latin and Keltic,* 1923.

[3] For some exceptions, see *Rom.,* XXXII, 591; also P. Marchot, *Petite Phonétique du français prélittéraire,* 9. For a theory of double

2. An accented *e* or *i* immediately followed by the vowel of the penult transfers the stress to this latter vowel, and is itself changed to *y*: *arĕŏla* > *aryóla*, *fĭlĭŏlus* > *filyólus*, *mulĭĕrem* > *mulyére*. An *u* thus situated transfers the stress to the *preceding* vowel, and becomes *w*: *battŭĕre* > *báttwere*, *habŭĕrunt* > *ábwerunt*, *tenŭĕram* > *ténwera*. The first of these changes was facilitated by a tendency to stress the more sonorous of two contiguous vowels; but both were primarily suggested, no doubt, by analogy, *battuere* and *habuerunt* and *tenueram* being evidently influenced by *báttuo* and *hábuit* and *ténui*, *filiolus* and *mulierem* perhaps by *fílius* and *múlier* with no stress on the *ĭ* but with a secondary accent on the last syllable.

3. Verbs compounded with a prefix, if their parts were fully recognized, were usually replaced in Vulgar Latin by a formation in which the vowel and the accent of the simple verb were preserved: *infĭcit* > *infácit*, *vendĭdi* > *vendédi*, *decĭdit* > *decádĭt*, *retĭnes* > *reténes*. In *recĭpit* > **recípit* > It. *ricéve* the accent but not the vowel was restored, speakers having ceased to associate this verb with *capio*. In *cólligo*, *cónflo*, *élĭgo*, *érĭgo*, *éxĕo* the composite nature of the word was apparently not appreciated.

4. *Illāc*, *illīc* accented their last syllable, perhaps in conformity with *hāc*, *hīc*, perhaps in memory of their original forms *illáce*, *illíce*. There are some other individual exceptions, such as *ficatum* < *fīcātum* + *sycōtón* +? *hēpar*, and *quarranta* < *quadragínta*.

10. In Italian the primary accent falls on the same syllable as in Vulgar Latin: *bonitātem* > V. L. *bonitáte* > It. *bontáde* *bontà*, *compŭtum* > V. L. *cómputu* > It. *cónto*, *filĭŏlus* > V. L. *filyólus* > It. *figliuólo*, *tenŭĕrunt* > V. L. *ténwerunt* > It. *ténnero*, *retĭnes* > V. L. *reténes* > It. *ritiéne ritiéni*, *illīc* > V. L. *illíc* > It. *lì*.

1. Words borrowed in a literary way from the Greek are generally accented according to the Latin method: καμάρα (short penult) > Lat. *camĕra* > It. *cámera*, κάμῑνος > Lat. *camīnus* > It. *camino*, τάλαντον > Lat. *talentum* > It. *talénto*, φάλαινα > Lat. *balæna* > It. *baléna*, ἱστορία > Lat. *histŏria* > It. *istória stória*, παραβολή > Lat. *parabola* > V. L. *parábula* *pardula* > It. *paróla*, σπασμός > Lat. *spasmus* > It. *spásmo spásimo*.

There are, however, many cases of shifted stress, probably due to forms, quick and slow, in Latin and in other Italic dialects, see K. V. Ettmayer in *Zs.*, XXXIV, 221.

ACCENT: § 10 13

ignorance of quantity: χολέρα > It. *coléra, συκόμορος* > It. *sicomóro;* so in Dante *Ippocráte, Naiáde, Pisistráto,* in Petrarch *Alcibiáde, Antióco.*

In mediæval schools, pupils were taught to accent the last syllable of barbaric words and of Greek nominatives whose oblique cases had a long penult: *Jacób, amén; agathé, Apolló, Calliopé, Eufraté, peán, pentecosté, Pharaó, Titán.* Thus we find in Dante *Cleopatrás, Climené, Clió, Eunoé, Flegiás, Leté, Minós, Semiramís,* in Petrarch *Penelopé,* elsewhere (with some influence of French accentuation) *Andromedá, Ecubá,* and in modern Italian *Agamennón, Davíd, Ettór, Saúl.*[1]

2. Words borrowed from the living Greek speech seem to have generally kept their Greek accentuation: ἄγκῦρα > It. *áncora,* ἀκήδεια > It. *accídia,* βλάσφημος > It. *biásimo,* εἴδωλον > It. *ídolo,* ἔρημος > It. *érmo,* σέλῖνον > It. *sédano,* σίνᾱπι > It. *sénape.*

The Greek ending *ία* sometimes kept its Greek stress, sometimes was assimilated to Latin *-ία:* ἀστρολογία > It. *astrología,* φιλοσοφία > It. *filosofía;* βλασφημία > It. *bestémmia,* ἐκκλησία > It. *chiésa.* The pronunciation *-ía* having prevailed under Christian influence, most new formations show that type: It. *librería* from *librarius* + *ia,* It. *cortesía* from *cohors* + *ensis* + *ia.* In Old Italian the *ía* accentuation was commoner than it is now: *Arménia, Aquitánia, comedía, Germanía, invidia* (in Fr. da Barberino), *Sophía, Soría, tragedía;* on the other hand, we find in Dante *letáne* for modern *litanie.* Συμφωνία gives *sinfonía* and *zampógna.*[2]

Words taken from Middle or New Greek apparently kept their accent unchanged: κορωνίσι? > It. *cornice,* σμερί > It. *smeríglio,* φαρός > It. *faló.*

3. Some Italian forms from the Latin show a shift of stress due to ignorance or to analogy or to both; many of the cases can be explained as changes of suffix: *berbēcem* > *bérbice, exīlem* > *ésile esile, cedrīnus myrtīnus susīnus* > *cedríno mirtíno susíno, trifīlis* > *tréfolo, varīcem* > *varíce.* The older language has many more: *auréo, solforéo, virginéo, Luciféro, simíle, umíle, s'umília, oceáno* (still used in poetry); in Dante *Arábi, collóca, occúpa, perpétra;* in Petrarch *implica;* in Lorenzo *esplica, riplíca;* in Ariosto *esplíco.*

Old *onésta, piéta, podésta* are taken over from Latin nominatives.

---

[1] See E. G. Parodi in *Bullettino della Società dantesca italiana,* N. S., III, 105–107.

[2] See M. De Gubernatis in *Archivum Romanicum,* VII, 27; T. Claussen, *Die griechischen Wörter im Französischen,* in *Romanische Forschungen,* XV, 774. Cf. E. H. Sturtevant, *The Pronunciation of Greek and Latin,* 1920.

Such forms as *Erculesse, Pirusso, Satanasso* in Brunetto Latini seem to show French influence combined with the analogy of Biblical proper names like *Davidde, Giobbe, Saulle.*

4. The name *Pésaro*, corresponding to Latin *Pisaurum*, may owe its accentuation to the adjective *Pésaróse*, assisted by the influence of some other proparoxytonic names, such as *Rimini*.[1]

5. If *dópo* comes from *de póst*, it exhibits a shift due to habitually proclitic position: *de pos' prándiu'* > **de poi pránzo* > *dópo pránzo.*

6. *Nasciéne* for *ne nasce* and *vatténe* for *váttene*, in thirteenth century verse, are southern. *Vatténne* is still used in Naples and Sicily.

Some other inflectional shifts will be discussed under Morphology. The most important of these changes are illustrated by such forms as *credémo* (later *crediamo*) for *crēdĭmus, vedémmo* for *vĭdĭmus, vedéssimo vedéste* for *vidissēmus vidissētis.* The perfect ending *-erunt*, in the vulgar tongue, always had a short *e*, except possibly in the Iberian peninsula.

11. The rhythm of Vulgar Latin, as shown by phonetic changes and by popular late Latin verse, tended to a systematic alternation of stressed and unstressed syllables. The *secondary* accent, then, fell regularly on the second syllable from the tonic, on either side, regardless of quantity: *dólorósa, filiús.* In many cases the intervening vowel (called *intertonic*) either fell out early or lost its syllabic value; when this happened, the two accents were brought together, and the secondary one of course disappeared: *mátutínus* > *mattíno, fábulá* > *fáula* > *fóla, filiús* > *fílyus* > *fíglio, báttuó* > *báttwo* > *bátto.*

When the secondary stress remained, it was apparently stronger in words in which it preceded the main accent than in those in which it followed. At any rate, the vowel thus stressed seems to develop in the former case like an accented vowel, in the latter case like any other unaccented posttonic: *Flórentínus* > *fiorentíno* while *Floréntiœ* > *Firénze, Bónonínus* > *Buologníno* while *Bonónia* > *Bológna, dís-(je)junáre* > *desináre* while *discúrrere* > *discórrere;* on the other hand, *cúrreré* > *córrere* just as *dáre* > *dáre, tépidǽ* > *tiépide* just as *áltœ* > *álte.*

[1] See F. d'Ovidio in *Note etimologiche*, 74.

12. In Latin, as in other languages, there were short, un-emphatic words which, having no accent, were attached as particles to the beginning or the end of another word: *non vénit, te rógo, illum quǽro, áma me, dó illud*. Such words (proclitics and enclitics), if they were not monosyllabic tended to become so; a dissyllabic proclitic beginning with a vowel seems regularly, in Vulgar Latin, to have lost its first syllable: *illum vídet> *lu védet>lo véde, eccum ísta> *(ec)cuésta>quésta*. Proclitics naturally develop like initial, enclitics like final syllables: *se clámat>si chiáma* just as *secúrus>sicúro, dáte 'lu'>dátelo* just as *rótulu'>rótolo*. Words used sometimes independently, sometimes as parti-cles, develop double forms: *illa vídet illam lúnam>ella vede la luna*.

QUANTITY

POSITION

13. In Italian, as in some other Romance languages, posi-tion checked the development of a preceding vowel: *fŏris> fuore fuori* while *fŏrtem>forte*. Mute + liquid, however, did not act as a check: *pĕctus>petto* while *pĕtra>pietra*.

14. In Latin texts there is much confusion of single and double consonants, as in *cot(t)idie, ec(c)lesia, ves(s)ica*, etc. Many words certainly had two forms (doubtless belonging to different Latin dialects), one with a long vowel and a single consonant, the other with a short vowel and a double con-sonant: *būca bŭcca, cīpus cĭppus, cūpa cŭppa;* so perhaps *bāca bǎcca, bāsium *bǎssium* (It. *bascio*), *cāseus *cǎsseus* (It. *cascio*), *lītera lĭttera, lītus lĭttus, mīsi *mĭssi* (It. *messi*). Be-side these two forms there was occasionally a third, a cross between the other two, having both the long vowel and the double consonant: **stēla stĕlla *stēlla* (Tuscan *stęlla*), *strēna strĕnna *strēnna* (It. *stręnna*), *tōta tŏtta *tōtta* (Fr. *toute*).[1]

[1] See A. J. Carnoy, *The Reduplication of Consonants in Vulgar Latin,* in *Modern Philology*, XV, 159.

Vowel Quantity

15. Originally, perhaps, long and short Latin vowels were distinguished only by duration, the vowels having, for instance, the same sound in *lātus* and *lătus*, in *dēbet* and *rĕdit*, in *vīnum* and *mĭnus*, in *nōmen* and *nŏvus*, in *ūllus* and *mŭltus*. However this may have been, long and short *e*, *i*, *o*, and *u* were eventually differentiated in quality, the short vowels being open while the long were close: *vēndo vęndo, sĕntio sęntio; pīnus pinus, pĭper pįper; sōlus sǫlus, sŏlet sǫlet; mūlus mųlus, gŭla gųla.* That is, for vowels which were to be of brief duration the tongue was not lifted quite so high as for those which were to be held longer. In the case of *a*, which is made with the tongue lying flat in the bottom of the mouth, there is no such differentiation: *cārus cănis* > It. *caro cane*.

Later, in most of the Empire, *į* and *ų* were allowed to drop lower still, and became *ę* and *ǫ*: *mĭnus pĭper* > It. *męno pępe*, *mŭlta gŭla* > It. *mǫlta gǫla*. Apparently this last stage had developed by the fifth century of our era. It probably was never reached by Sicily and the greater part of Sardinia, which keep *ĭ*, *ŭ*, as *i*, *u*.

1. Before *j*, a Latin vowel was prolonged by the addition of a glide, but retained its quality: *pĕjus* > *pęijus* > It. *pęggio*.

2. If vowels in late Latin were lengthened before *gn*, as a statement in the sixth century Priscian affirms, it must have been after the differentiation of close and open quality: *sĭgnum* > *signum* > *sįignum* > It. *sęgno*.

3. Vowels originally long seem to have kept their close quality before another vowel, despite the rule that a vowel before another vowel is short: *dĭes* > It. *dì, pĭus* > It. *pio, cŭi* > It. *cui, fŭi* > It. *fui*.

On the other hand, an *ǫ* immediately followed by *u* seems to have been differentiated into *ǫ*: *sŭus* > *sǫus* > *sǫus*.[1] So *ōvum* > **ǫum* > **ǫu* > (with restoration of *v* by the influence of *ova*) **ǫvu* > It. *uǫvo*.

[1] A spelling *sous* occurs, but of course we cannot tell whether the *o* is open or close. See E. Seelmann, *Die Aussprache des Latein*, 216; J. Pirson, *La langue des inscriptions de la Gaule*, 16.

16. When n was followed by a fricative (f, j, s, or v), it regularly fell early in Latin, and the preceding vowel, if short, was lengthened by compensation: $c\bar{e}sor$, $c\bar{o}jugi$, $c\bar{o}ventio$, $\bar{\imath}feri$. Before f, j, and v, however, the n, being always the final letter of a prefix, was usually restored by the analogy of the full forms of the prefixes in question, con- and in-: $infantem$ through $indignus$, etc.; $conjungere$ through $conducere$, etc.; $convenire$ through $continere$, etc. But before s the n was very often a part of the main word, and the fall was permanent, restoration occurring only at the end of a manifest prefix: $\bar{\imath}sula$, $m\bar{e}sis$, $sp\bar{o}sus >$ It. $isola$, $mese$, $sposo$; but $insignio >$ It. $insegno$. Such a word as $pensare$ ('to think') must be a new formation, the old $pensare$ ('to weigh') having become $pesare$.

17. From the second to the fifth century of our era, with a changing population in Italy, the feeling for vowel quantity was disappearing. The old Classic system has left no trace except in the fixing of the accent and in the differentiation of close and open vowels. As it died out, it gave way to a new kind of quantity, not inherent in the vowels but depending on their place in the word, stressed vowels not in position being long, all other vowels short, in the greater part of the Empire: $v\bar{a}l\breve{e}s$, $v\breve{e}nd\breve{o}$, $v\breve{e}(\breve{e}$ long$)n\breve{\imath}s$, $d\breve{\imath}x\breve{\imath}$, $pl\breve{\imath}(\breve{\imath}$ long$)c\breve{a}t$.[1] It is likely that these drawled vowels were pronounced in most regions with a circumflex intonation or a broken stress, which in the transition from Latin to the Romance languages resulted in a diphthongization in most parts of the territory. The vowels most generally affected, and the only ones affected in standard Italian, are $\ee$ and $\oo$: $v\breve{e}n\bar{\imath}s >$ V. L. $v\ee n\dot{\imath}s >$ It. $vi\ee ni$, $t\breve{o}nat >$ V. L. $t\oo nat >$ It. $tu\oo na$.[2]

[1] See J. Brüch in $Zs.$, XLI, 574.
[2] See J. Ronjat in the $Bulletin\ de\ la\ Société\ de\ linguistique$, XXIV, 356. For an interesting theory of Indo-European stress and neo-Latin breaking, with a vast collection of material, see P. G. Goidánich, $L'origine\ e\ le\ forme\ della\ dittongazione\ romanza$, 1907.

The resultant Italian diphthongs (if for convenience they may so be called) are now pronounced *yę* and *wǫ*; nor does there appear to be, as some assume, sufficient reason to believe that they were originally sounded everywhere *íe* and *úo*, although such a stage is evident in a few localities which now so pronounce them and in a few others which have reduced them respectively to *i* and *u* (*priega*>*priga*, *fuori*> *furi*). The more general course may very well have been *tę̄ne tę́éne tę́éne tyęne, sǭle sǫ́óle sǫ́óle swǫle*.

VOWELS

18. In the normal utterance of a vowel the vocal cords pulsate in the larynx, producing a musical note, which then passes through several resonance chambers on its way to the outlet. These chambers are different for the different vowels, their shapes and sizes being determined principally by movements of the soft palate and of the tongue and lips aided by the jaw. Their resonances reinforce different harmonics of the fundamental note issuing from the larynx, and thus one vowel is differentiated from another. For the nasal vowels the soft palate is lowered, admitting the air current to the nose, and a nasal resonance is added to that of the mouth.

Latin had the vowels *a, e, i, o, u* long or short; and, in unaccented syllables before a labial, a short sound similar to German *ü* or French *u* (as in *maxumus, optumus*); furthermore, the groups *æ, au, eu, oe, ui*. Of the simple vowels, *ī, ĭ, ē, ĕ* are formed with the tongue bunched in the front of the mouth cavity and raised to different degrees, *ī* having it highest and *ĕ* lowest. For *ū, ŭ, ō, ŏ* the tongue is hoisted to different elevations in the back of the mouth; and the lips are puckered, making a narrow aperture, smallest for the high *ū*, biggest for the low *ŏ*. The *ü* requires rounding of the lips and forward massing of the tongue. For *a* the tongue is nearly flat and the mouth wide open.

We have already seen (§ 15) that *ē, ī, ō, ū* were pronounced close, and *ĕ, ĭ, ŏ, ŭ* open, while *a* was not affected by quantity; also that the sounds coming from *ĭ* and *ŭ* were further lowered into *ę* and *ǫ*, except probably in Sicily and Sardinia. The primitive *ü*- like vowel became *ĭ*, occasionally *ŭ*: *proxŭmus>proxĭmus*, proclitic *sümus>sŭmus* or *sĭmus*. Early the groups *æ* and *oe* were assimilated respectively into *ę* and *ę*, the latter having doubtless passed through a stage *ö*; later, in Italian, *au* became *ǫ*; *eu* occurs in no really popular Latin word that was kept; *ui* remains as *úi*: *præsto>pręsto, poena >pęna, cui>cui, aurum>*V. L. *auru>*It. *ǫro.*

The Vulgar Latin vowels whose Italian history we have to consider are, therefore: *a, ę, ȩ, i, ǫ, ǫ, u,* and the diphthongs *au* and *ui.*

The principal Classic and Vulgar Latin and Italian stages of accented vowels are shown in this table, a glance at which discloses an interesting symmetry of vocalic developments in Italy:

back vowels		front vowels	
ū>u̧>u̧			*ī>i̧>i̧*
ŭ>u̧>ǫ ⎫			*ĭ>i̧>ę* ⎫
ō>ǫ>ǫ ⎭		*oe>ę>ę*	*ē>ę>ę* ⎭
ŏ>ǫ>ǫ	*au>au>ǫ* *ā* or *ă>a>a*	*æ>ę>ę*	*ĕ>ę>ę*

19. Moreover, as we have seen (§ 17), the Vulgar Latin open vowels *ę* and *ǫ*, when accented and not in position, generally broke in Italian into the diphthongs *ię* and *uǫ*: *tĕpĭdus >tiępido, Fæsŭlæ>Fięsole, hŏmĭnes>uǫmini.*

It is to be noted that the *ǫ* from *au* came too late to participate in this development, except in some of the dialects: *causa>cǫsa* (dial. *cuosa*), *paucum>pǫco* (dial. *puoco*).

1. The unstressed vowels did not break, being pronounced briefly; nor is there in Italian any distinction between the originally long and the originally short unaccented vowels, except in the case of *i*: see § 36.

20. In popular words borrowed from the Greek, *ε* had regularly the close sound (*κέδρος>cędro*), *o* was usually close

but sometimes open (τόρνος > tǫrno, κρόκος > gruǫgo), ι seems
to have been sounded ę (βαπτίζω > battęggio); υ developed
like Latin u in words borrowed early, like Latin i in words
borrowed late (βύρσα > bŭrsa > bǫrsa; γῦρος > gȳrus > giro,
κύμβαλον > cўmbalum > cęmbalo). Greek η, ω were probably
ę, ǫ, the long vowels being open while the short ones (ε, o)
were close: ἧπαρ? > ępa; γλῶσσα > chiǫsa,[1] πτωχός > pitǫcco,[1]
τρώκτης > trǫta. Apparent inconsistencies are probably due to
differences of usage in different Greek dialects; ü, the Ionic
and Attic pronunciation of υ, was a vowel foreign to Latin
at the time when words containing it were borrowed.

In book-words, ε, o, ῑ and ῡ, ῐ and ῠ are treated respectively
like ĕ, ŏ, ῑ, ῐ in Latin book-words: γένεσις > gęnesi, φυσιολόγος >
fisiǫlogo, κατηχίζω > catechízzo, σῡκοφάντης > sicofánte, φιλόλο-
γος > filǫlogo, φῠσικός > físico.

The vowels of words coming from Germanic call for no
special mention. Gręto and spięde seem to correspond to
Old High German words with eo or io, but we do not know
the exact Germanic forms from which the Italian come.

21. In reading Latin, the Italians give the open sound to
accented ē and ō, as well as to ĕ and ŏ, the open quality having
to their ear a more oratorical effect. It is natural, then, that
book-words should have ę and ǫ, in place of ę and ǫ: herēdem
> eręde, glōria > glǫria. Furthermore, inasmuch as all pro-
paroxytones, whether of learned or of popular origin, have
a certain rhetorical ring, suggesting Latin, such words not infrequently open an ę or ǫ into ę or ǫ: σίναπι > sęnape, fŭlĭca >
fǫlaga. In Rome, the open sound is still further extended:
nōmen > Fl. nǫme Rom. nǫme.

Latin au, i, u, and y in book-words are in Italian written
and sounded according to their Latin spelling, y becoming i:
causa > causa, cĭbus > cibo, sŭbĭto > súbito, lyra > lira.

---

[1] For a different etymology of these words, see *Archivio glottologico
italiano*, XVI, 161 and *Zs.*, XLIII, 694.

22. Sicilian has no *ẹ*, *ọ*, because it substitutes *i*, *u* for these sounds: *amọre* = *amuri*, *mẹno* = *minu*. When the Sicilian poets of the thirteenth century adopted Latin or Provençal words containing *ẹ* or *ọ*, they pronounced the vowel open. A word like *amore* may, then, in their verse, rime either with one like *duri* or with one like *cọre*. When their poetry was carried into Tuscany and partly Tuscanized, they seemed (to Tuscan hearers) to have rimed often *ẹ* with *i* and *ọ* with *u*, sometimes *ẹ* with *ẹ* and *ọ* with *ọ*. These confusions led their Tuscan and Bolognese successors into several peculiar practices, notably a disregard of open and close quality in rime, a trait which has persisted to this day.[1]

ACCENTED VOWELS

23. We shall now consider in detail the development of the several Vulgar Latin vowels under the accent.

a

24. V. L. *a* (= Cl. L. *ā* or *ă*) > It. *a*: *altum*>*alto*, *amāre*>*amare, bonitātem*>*bontade bontà, dăt*>*dà, căput*>*capo*.

1. The suffix *-ābĭlis* (as in *amabilis*) was in popular words supplanted by *-ĭbĭlis* (*possibilis*>*possẹvole*): hence *lodẹvole*, beside the bookish *laudabile; -ibile* from *-ibilis* is of course itself bookish (*possibile* beside *possẹvole*).

2. Beside *-aio* and *-aro* (and bookish *-ario*) from *-arius*, we sometimes find *-iero* or *-iere* (as in *cavaliero, cavaliere*), probably borrowed from French and Provençal.[2]

3. Beside Latin *alăcer* there probably was a V. L. **alẹcer *alĭcer*, hence **alẹcrem *alĭcrem*, and, from the latter, It. *allẹgro*, while the former gives central and southern dial. *allẹgro*.

[1] See E. G. Parodi in *Bullettino della Società dantesca italiana*, III, 108 and XX, 113; G. Bertoni in *Giornale storico della letteratura italiana*, LXXXVI, 200 and 392.

[2] For a theory of native development under Germanic influence, see G. Bertoni in *Zs.*, XXXVI, 621.

4. *Gręve* is from *grĕvis*, i.e., *gravis* influenced by *lĕvis*. Beside *mālum* there was a *mēlum* (Petronius), just as Doric and Attic have μᾶλον and μῆλον; from *mēlum* comes It. *męlo*. Beside *cĕrăsus* (Gr. κέρασος) there must have existed **cĕrĕsus*, whence an adjective *cereseus*, whose feminine form gave *ciriegia ciliegia*. *Taglięnte* (for *tagliante* from *tagliare*) shows the influence of *cocęnte, bollęnte*. *Ebbi, seppi* (from *habui, sapui*) may perhaps be explained as follows: when *habui* was added to the infinitive of verbs to form a conditional, *credere* + *habui* (for instance) became *crederabbi*, which under the influence of the perfect *credęi* (*<credędi<crĕdĭdi*) was exchanged for *crederęi*, and *crederęi* + *crederabbi>crederebbi;* hence *ebbi* (and in O. It. also *ei*) for original *abbi* = *habui;* and hence, in the conditional, 1st pers. *crederei* and 3d pers. *crederebbe*. *Seppi* followed *ebbi*, *sapere* being throughout profoundly influenced by *habere*.

5. Beside Latin *vacuus* there existed a popular and probably archaic *vocuus*, and beside *vacare* a popular *vocare* with a perfect participle **vŏcĭtus*, from which comes It. *vuoto*. *Chiǫdo* shows a mixture of *clavum* and *claudere*. *Tǫpo <talpa* and *mǫta <maltha* must have developed outside of Tuscany, in some region where *l>u* before a consonant; of non-Tuscan origin, too, must be Dante's *co* for *capo*. *Quassus*, with a prefix *ex-* would give **squasso;* this appears to have got mixed with the new *mǫsso* from *muovere*, giving *scǫsso*, whence a verb *scuotere* (for *excutere*), *scossi, scosso*. *Nuǫta* from *natat* is unexplained; the word is irregular in most of the languages. *Monco <mancus + trŭncus*. *Fiáccola <facŭla* with metathesis of the *i* which comes from the *l*: **facla> *facchia> *fiacca fiaccola* (for *l>i*, see § 89).

ẹ

25. V. L. *ę* (= Cl. L. *ē, ĭ, oe;* Gr. ε, ŭ) >It. *ę: vērus>vęro, mĭnus>męno, poena>pęna,* κέδρος *>cędro,* κύκνος *>cęcino cęcero.*

1. Final *ę* becomes open in exclamations, proper names, and foreign words: *ahimè, Noè, caffè*.

2. An *ię* coming from *lę* (see § 89) opens its *e* in Tuscany, under the influence of the very common diphthong *ię: blĭtum>biętola, complēta >compięta, flēbĭlis>fięvole, nauclērus>nocchięro, plēbem>pięve, plēnus >pięno.* The same analogy, with a metathesis of *i*, may be responsible for *fięra* ("fair") *< *fięra < *fęria <fēria;* in that case Pr. *fięira* would have to be attributed to the influence of the large class of *-ieira* words.

3. Before a vowel, *ę>i: vĭa>via, prĭus *prĭa>pria, sĭt *sĭat>sia, habē(b)am>avia* (cf. § 202), *haber'(hab)ē(b)am>avria.*

4. In some dialects *i* replaces *ę* before *l'* or *n'*, and many of these forms with *i* have entered the standard language: *consĭlium* > *consiglio*, *Cornēlia* > *Corniglia*, *exĭlium* > *esiglio*, *famĭlia* > *famiglia*; **culmĭneus* > *comígnolo*, *gramĭneus* > *gramígnolo*, *lucĭnium* > *lucígnolo*, *tĭnea* > *tigna*. So *cĭlium* > *cęglio ciglio*, *mĭlium* > *męglio miglio*, *tĭlium* > *tęglio tiglio*, *aurĭcŭla* > *ọrẹcchia origlia*, *strĭgĭlis* **strĭgŭla* > *strẹgghia striglia; benĭgnus* > *benẹgno benigno, Sardĭnia* > *Sardẹgna Sardigna.*[1]

Some dialects of the Centre and South use the *i* if there is an *i* or a *u* in the next syllable.[2] Sicilian uses *i* under all conditions.

5. A following *sky* or *sty* seems to favor *i*: *bestia bistia* (*Studi medievali*, I, 613) > *bẹstia biscia;* so the Italian formations *mischio, vẹschio vischio.*

A combination of *n* + guttural favors *i*: *cĭngo* > *cingo, fĭngo* > *fingo, lĭngua* > *lingua, pervĭnca* > *pervinca, tĭnca* > *tinca, vĭnco* > *vinco;* so *ramingo* (cf. Prov. *ramenc*), etc.

6. Some cases of *i* are due to the substitution of a suffix with *ī* for one with *ĭ*: *capĭtŭlus* > *cavicchio, lentĭcŭla* > *lenticchia, cervĭsia* > *cervigia, servĭtium* > *servigio.* Sometimes *-ēnus* was replaced by *-īnus*: *pullicēnus* > *pulcino, Saracēnus* > *Saracẹno Saracino.*

7. In certain Greek words, *i* represents an *η* that had already changed its sound to *i*: ἀκήδεια > *accídia*, ἐφήμερος > *effímero*, Μεσσήνη > Messina. For earlier *η*, see § 20.

8. Some otherwise unexplainable words would seem to have been borrowed from Sicilian or other Southern dialects that changed *ę* to *i* (§ 25, 4, end): *avire aíre* ("credit") for *avẹre, diritto dritto ritto* from *dīrēctus rēctus, nimo* < *nēmo, racimolo* < *racēmus, riccio* < *erĭcius.*

Can *dito* < *dĭgĭtus* be thus accounted for, or can there be some ancient contamination with the root *dīc* or *deik* ("to show")? Old Perugian has *deto*, Venetian has *ded*.

Are *ditta ditto* dialect forms, or do they go back to original *dīctus*? *Dẹtto*, of course, points to *dĭctus*.

9. Words with *ę* apparently owe their open vowel to some analogy: *baccęllo* < *bacĭllus, suggęllo* < *sigĭllum* show a change of suffix, *-ęllus* for *-ĭllus; adẹsso* (< *?ad id ĭpsum*) probably borrowed from Pr. *adẹs*, would seem to have been influenced in both languages by *aprẹs, prẹsso; balẹstra* < *ballĭstra ballĭsta, canẹstro* < *canĭstrum, capẹstro* < *capĭstrum, maẹstro* (also *maẹstro*) < *magĭstrum, minẹstra* from *minĭstrare* have perhaps come under the influence of *dẹstro* < *dĕxtrum, finẹstra* < *fenĕstra, palẹstra* <

---

[1] See E. Philipon in *Rom.*, XLV, 422.

[2] See A. Camilli in *Zs.*, XLIII, 474.

palæstra; dęve<*dēbet* gets its *ę* from *dębbe*, which gets it from *dovrębbe* (see § 24, 4); *fęnde*<*fíndit, pręnde*<*prēndit,* follow *difęnde, pęnde, ręnde; insieme* shows a confusion of *símul, sěmul,* and *sěmel; prętto*<*purętto* seems to follow *schiętto* (cf. O. H. Ger. *slěht*); *primavęra* (<*prīmus* + *vēr*) may have been attracted by *primięra,* or it may owe its *ę* simply to poetic association; *ręggia*<*rēgia, ręssi*<*rēxi, rętto*<*rēctum* follow *ręggere* <*rěgere.* For *gęsso*<*γύψος* there is no good explanation; outside of Tuscany one finds the regular *gęsso;* can there be an influence of *cęsso?* Pistoiese and Old Sienese *nięve* for *nęve*<*nívem* is not accounted for; cf. Pr. *nięu,* Sp. *nieve. Sęnza sęnza sanza* is peculiar; the basis seems to be *síne* + *absěntia,* with further confusion of the endings *-enza* and *-anza* (as in *stanza*).

10. In learned words, *ē, oe,* ε>*ę*; and *í, ŭ*>*i: crudēlis*>*crudęle, herēdem*>*erędе ręda, rēgŭla*>*ręgola, foetus*>*fęto,* ἔξοδος>*ęsodo; cíbus*>*cibo, rígídus*>*rígido, sítus*>*sito,* λύρα>*lira,* μυρτός>*mirto.* Some words have both a learned and a popular form: *arēna*>*aręna ręna, fidēlis*> *fedęle fedęle, secrētum*>*segręto segręto,* etc. *Dębito*<*dēbítum* has a close vowel in imitation of the popular *dętto.*

In some bookish words, *í* becomes *ę,* doubtless representing a clerical pronunciation of Latin at the time when these words were adopted: *carnífícem*>*carnęfice, discípŭlus*>*discępolo, multíplícem*>*moltęplice, pícŭla*>*pęgola, símplícem*>*sęmplice.* Cf. O. Sp. *contrecion, esposecion.*

11. Proparoxytones, following the fashion of Latinisms, tend to change *ę* to *ę: -ēsímus*>*-ęsimo* (*ventęsimo*), *expíngere*>*spęgnere,* ἔρημος> *ęremo ęrmo* (beside *ęrmo*), *líttera*>*lęttera* (here we may see also the influence of *lętto*), *mínímus*>*męnomo,* σέλινον>*sędano,* σίναπι>*sęnape,* Στέφανος>*Stęfano Stęfano, succēděre*>*succędere,* θύμινος>*tęmolo, vēnděre* >*vęndere* beside commoner *vęndere.*

Similarly, archaic Italian words and foreign borrowings are generally pronounced with *ę: ērígo*>*ęrgo, subínde*>O. Fr. *sovent*>It. *sovęnte.* So perhaps *delíciosus*>*delezioso* whence *lęzio.*

12. A few words offer a strange vowel: *fanciullo* (Old Flor. and Old Emilian *fancello*) <*infantem* + a diminutive ending, is said to be Neopolitan in origin; *ghiqva*<*glēba* + *glŏbus; gǫbbo* is evidently a cross between *gíbbus* and something else; *mándorla*<ἀμυγδάλη, is very much distorted; *mastro,* beside *maęstro,* is generally used proclitically; *trápano*<τρύπανον shows confusion with the prefix *tra-.*

ę

26. V. L. ę (= Cl. L. ĕ or æ) > It. ę, when in position:
bĕllus > bęllo, cĕrtus > cęrto, mæstus > męsto, præsto > pręsto.

1. Before *n* + dental, there is in Tuscany a growing tendency to
substitute ę: *męnte, męnto, -męnte, -męnto, antęnna, scęnde, semęnta, tor-
męnta;* in *Firenze, rende, tende* one may hear both vowels. There seems
to be a conflict of fashions.[1] Many words have thus far escaped: *gęnte,
sęnte, spęnto, talęnto,* present participles in *-ente* and gerunds in *-endo.*
Siena has *faccęnda, meręnda.*

A few words show the close as well as the open vowel before nasal +
labial or guttural: *giovenco, grembo (<grĕmium), rimembra, tempie,
tempio.*

2. Some words have an ę due to analogy: in *carętto <carĕctum* and
cutręttola <cauda trĕpĭda there is the influence of the ending *-ętto;
cicęrchia <cicĕrcŭlum* follows *cęrchio.* Why *cęspo* beside *cęspite <cæspĭ-
tem, tęschio* beside *tęschio <tĕstŭla?* Cf. § 27, 2. The *-ęi* and *-ę* of the
perfect of the third conjugation have become *-ęi* and *-ę,* following the
imperfect and the other persons of the perfect: *credédi > credęi, credidĭsti
>cre(d)dęsti, credĕdit > credę, credidĭmus > *credędmo credęmmo, credi-
dĭstis > cre(d)dęste.*

3. A few words have *i. Dispitto* and *rispitto* are French, and so
perhaps *accisma (accismare <O. Fr. acesmer), profitta, registro;* while
gitta < (e)jĕctat may be Provençal. Unexplained are *ischio* beside *ęschio
<æsculum, minchia <mĕntŭla;* likewise *rischia* (also *risica*) if it comes
from *rĕsĕcat.*

In such a word as *macia* corresponding to *macĕria,* we might seem to
have a reduction of *iei* to *i,* as in Old French (*macęrya > *macęia >
macięya >macia), for *-ry-* in Italian regularly gives *y;* similarly the
-io of *calpestio, mormorio,* etc., might appear to come from *-ĕrium.*[2]
Direct evidence, however, is lacking. The alternative would be a new
formation in *-ia,* and in *-io* constructed on the model of *-ia.*

27. When not in position, ę breaks into *ię:* [3] *bręve > brieve,
cæcus > cieco, cælum > cielo, gĕlus > gielo, hĕre > iere ieri, prĕco
>priego, Sæna > Siena, sæpes > siepe, tĕnet > tiene; Dĕcĭmus >*

[1] See *Rom.,* XXIX, 570.

[2] See E. G. Parodi in *Miscellanea linguistica in onore di G. Ascoli,*
457.

[3] In Naples, *ie* is pronounced *ię: vięnə* for *vięni.* This sound is heard
even in some central dialects.

*Diecimo, fĕrīre > *fĕrĕre > fiedere, Fœsŭlœ > Fiesole, lĕvātus *lĕvĭ-
tus > lievito, lĕpŏrem > lievore, mĕtĕre > mietere, Nœvŭlœ > Nie-
vole, pĕdĭca > piedica, postĕrŭla > postierla, quœrĕre > chiedere,
tĕpĭdus > tiepido, trĕmĭtus > triemito.*[1] But the vowel remains
intact before *l', n', ddž,* or *ttš: mĕlius > męglio, vĕtŭlus > vęglio,
tĕnĕo > tęgno, vĕnĭo > vęgno, lĕgit > lęgge, rĕgit > ręgge, fœcem >
fęcce fęccia.* In *gręmbo* (also *gręmbo) < grĕmium, vęcchio <
vĕtŭlus,* position perhaps developed too early for the growth
of a diphthong.

In modern standard Tuscan the *i* of *ie* has disappeared
after *dž, tš,* and consonant + *r: gęlo, bręve, pręgo;* so *cielo,
cieco,* in which the *i* is silent. On the other hand, some Tuscan dialects (like some in Umbria and in the Abruzzi) early
reduced *ie* to *i: priega > priga, insieme > insime.*

In hiatus, *ie* remains before *i,* but is reduced to *i* before the
other vowels: *mĕi > miei, mĕus > *mieo > mio, mĕa > ?*miea >
mia, mĕœ > ?*miee > mie, dĕus > dieo > dio, crĕat > ?*criea >
cria, ĕ(g)o > *ieo > io.*[2]

1. Words often used as proclitics have *ę* intact: *bene venuto > benvenuto,* etc.; hence *ben-;* hence *bęne* employed independently with
stress. (Cf. Umbrian *biene.*) Originally Latin *ĕrat* gave *iera* accented,
era proclitic, of which pair only the latter has survived; so V. L. **sĕs*
for *ĕs* and **sĕtis* for *ĕstis* gave *siei,*[3] *siete* and *sei,*[3] *sete,* from which with
apparent inconsistency the language has chosen *sęi* for the singular,
sięte for the plural. From *sĕx* we have only the proclitic *sęi.* V. L.
illœi for fem. dat. *illi* may similarly have given rise to double forms,
liei and *lei;* the former was preserved in Siena, but not in Florence;
lęi, moreover, is now used only as a stressed form, the unstressed use
being restricted to *le* (from *illœ = illi*). On the model of *lęi* we have
colęi, costęi. For *-ei* in verbs see § 26, 2.
    Why have we *lępre* (beside *lievore*) from *lĕpŏrem?* From *lepratto?*

[1] In Arezzo, judging from the usage of Guittone and Petrarch, both
e and *ie* were in vogue: see *Zs.,* Beiheft XV, 20.
[2] A Lat. form DIEO has been found: C. I. L., VIII, 9181; see *Zs.,*
Beiheft V, 160–162. In O. It. we have *die, mie,* apparently reductions
of *dieo, *mieo.*
[3] The final *i* of *sei, siei* comes from the *-s:* see § 94, *s.*

2. There are some cases of ę, most of them unexplained: *Cæsărem* >
Cęsare (N. and S. dialects, and also Sienese, have ę); *ĕbŭlum* > *ębbio;*
grĕgem > *gręgge* (possibly influenced by *lęgge* < *lēgem*?); *hĕdĕra* > *ędera*
ęllera; ingĕnium > *ingęgno,* perhaps attracted by *dęgno, lęgno, sęgno;*
intĕgrum > *intęro* (also *intiero*) under the influence of *sincęro, vęro (integro* beside *intęgro* follows *intęro*); *lĕpra* > *lębbra; mĕta* > *męta* and *męta*
with different meanings; *nĕbŭla* > *nębbia* (Pr. has forms with *e* and with
i); *nĕgo* > *nęgo* (O. It. also *niego*); *prægnans* > *pręgna.*

3. Latin book-words keep ę unbroken: *dęcimo, impęro, lęva (lięva* in
Dante), *spęra* (< *sphæra*), *tęnebre.* So a few popular proparoxytones,
which perhaps suggested a Latin rhythm: *pęcora, ręcere* (< *rĕĭcere*),
rędina (connected with *rĕtĭneo*?), *tęnero;* on the same principle, *Vĕnĕris*
dĭe > *venerdi.*

In poetry we often find such forms as *crea, dea, deo, eo, meo, reo* (for
rio); also *fęro, lęve, męle, possęde,* etc., under the influence of Latin,
Provençal, and the Sicilian and Aretine poets. *Eu* for *io* is still current
in Sicily.

i

28. V. L. į̇ (= Cl. L. ī and Gr. v̄) > It. i̯: *audīre* > *udire,*
dīcĕre > *dícere, dīxit* > *disse, rīdet* > *ride, vīnum* > *vino,* γῦρος >
giro.

1. Greek ι, as we have seen (§ 20), had a very open sound, which in
Italian apparently became ę and in proparoxytones ȩ: βαπτίξω > *batteg-
gio; ἀρθρῖτικός* > *artętico,* σίναπι > *sęnape,* χρῖσμα > *cręsima.*

2. Varro, *De Re Rustica,* I, 48, 2, speaks of a rustic *speca* for *spīca.*
If there was, in Latin times, a country dialect that could substitute *ē*
for *ī,* we may look to it for an explanation of a number of odd forms:
carīna > *caręna* (now poetic), *īlĭcem* > *ęlce,*[1] *līntea* > *lęnza* (now rare),
*mītiare > *mezzare męzzo, orīgănum* > *ręgamo* (proparoxytone), *rīxa* >
ręssa (old, for *rissa*), *sīcīlis *sīcŭla* > *sęgolo, stīva* > *stęgola,*[2] *trībŭla* >
trębbia, vītĭcem > *vętrice;* perhaps also *bięco* < ? *oblīquus, lętica* < *lītĭgat,*
and even the mysterious *freddo* < *frīgĭdus.* An ę vowel occurs in this
last word in Gaul as well as in Italy (Pr. and O. Fr. *freit,* Mod. Fr.
froid); it has sometimes been attributed to the influence of *rĭgĭdus.*

---

[1] *Elice* occurs in MSS. of Gregory of Tours. Cf. Pr. *euze.* An *ĭlĭcem*
might perhaps be explained by the analogy of *fĭlĭcem, sĭlĭcem;* an
ēlĭcem would have to be classed as an old rustic form with *speca.*

[2] The interchange of *v* and *g* is not uncommon: see § 103, 1.

3. *Se*<*sī* (cf. O. Fr. *se*) was influenced at some stage by *e*<*et*, *che*< *quid*. The influence is attested by the alternative O. It. form *sed*, created, for use before vowels, on the model of *ed* and *ched*.

4. *Pręnce*, a poetic word, was probably borrowed from French at a time when Fr. *in* had begun to alter its vowel by nasalization. The It. representative of *prīncipem* is *príncipe*. Cf. *prencessa* for *principessa*. *Pręncipe* may be a cross between *príncipe* and *pręnce*.

ǫ

29. V. L. ǫ (= Cl. L. ŏ and ŭ, Gr. o and old ŭ)> It. ǫ:
hōra>*ǫra*, *nōs*>*nǫi*, *pōnĕre*>*pǫrre*; *diŭrnum*>*giǫrno*, *mŭlier* >*mǫglie*, *mŭltum*>*mǫlto*; κόλαφος>*cǫlpo*, ὄργανον>*ǫrgano* (*ǫrgano* in Siena); θύννος>*tǫnno*, θύρσος>*tǫrso*.

Greek ω, in really popular words, was probably open; but the evidence is extremely slight: πτωχός>*pitǫcco* (cf. § 20).[1]

1. When It. ǫ is or becomes final, it is opened to ǫ: *dǫ, stǫ; nōn*>*nǫn nǫ, prō(dest)*>*prǫ* (whence, no doubt, the ǫ of *prǫde*). *Lǫ* and ǫ are of course proclitics.

2. Before a vowel, we find *u* instead of ǫ: *dŭœ*>*due, dŭo*>*duo, grŭem*>*grue, tŭa*>*tua*.[2]

3. Before *n* + guttural or palatal, there was a strong tendency to use *u* in central and west Tuscany, while east Tuscany preferred ǫ; hence an inconsistency in the standard language: *axŭngia*>*sugna*, **dŭmque*?>*dunque* (*donque* in Domenico Cavalca), *fŭngus*>*fungo*, *ĭŭngo*>*giungo, jŭngit*>*giunge*, σπογγιά>*spugna, ŭngo*>*ungo, ŭngĕre*> *úngere, ŭngŭla*>*unghia, ŭnquam*>*unqua*; but γόγγρος> *grǫngo*, κόγχη >*cǫnca, pōno*>*pǫngo* (*g* perhaps late), *trŭncus*>*trǫnco, ūncia *ŭncia*> *ǫncia*.[3] Cf. the treatment of ǫ before *n* + gutt. (*lungo*): § 30, 2.

Whatever the following consonant, some dialects have *u* for *o* when there is a final *i* in the next syllable (cf. § 25, 4, end). Sicilian uses *u* under all conditions.

[1] E. H. Sturtevant, in *Transactions and Proceedings of the American Philological Association*, LVI (1925), 24, expresses the opinion that by the middle of the second century B.C. Greek ω and o were alike in quality. For an explanation of It. *mǫlo*<*mōles* through a Greek **μῶλος*, see *Rom.*, XXXV, 141.

[2] See *Zs.*, Beiheft V, 160–162.

[3] See *Zs.*, Beiheft XV, 15.

4. There are some other cases of *u*. The attraction of analogy is responsible in *agucchia* < *acŭcŭla* influenced by *aguglia* < *acūlea*, and in *giuso* (W. and S. Tuscan *giọso*) < *deōrsum* plus *suso* < *sūrsum*. Other words probably reveal a difference of dialects: *butto bọtto* < ?Ger. *bŏtan*, *corruccio* < **corrŭptio*, *cucio* < *co(n)suo*, *gubbia cọppia* < *cōpula*, *ligusta locusta* < *locŭsta*, *prua* < *prō(r)a*. *Vui* for *vọi* is Sicilian. Perhaps the much discussed *u* of *tutto* comes originally from a dialect which changes *ọ* to *u* when there is a final *i* in the next syllable: *tōtī* > (§ 14) *tōttī* > *tutti*, hence *tutto*.

Uscio is from *ūstium*, a V. L. form of *ōstium*, perhaps due to the effect of the following *sty*. *Urla* < **ūlŭlat*, an onomatopoetic form of *ŭlŭlat* (cf. Fr. *hurler*). *Paúra* (*pavōrem*) shows a change of suffix. *Sur* is not from *sŭper*, but from *su* (< *sūrsum*) probably influenced by the prefix *sor-*.

5. There are many examples of *ọ* or *uo*. In some the open vowel goes back to Latin times. *Truova trọva*, if it comes from τρόπος, proves that in this word the *o* was open; cf. Pr. and Fr. Beside Lat. *plŭĕre*, there existed an old *plŏvĕre*, whence It. *piọvere;* there must have been also a **plŏvia*, whence *piọggia*. *Fọssa* postulates, beside *fōssa*, a **fŏssa* with the *ŏ* of *fŏdere*. For *nŭrus* there was a **nŏra*, influenced by *sŏror* and *nŏva*. An *ọ* before *u* in late Latin became open, apparently by dissimilation (§ 15, 3): *ō(v)um* > *ọu(m)* > (by analogy with *ova*) *ọvu* > *uovo; sŭus sọus* > *sọus*, whence pl. **sọi* > *suoi*.[1]

In certain cases the analogical cause is easy to guess. *Calọtta* < καλύπτρα, *gọtto* < *gŭttus*, *grọtta* < κρύπτη, *lọtta* < *lŭcta lūcta*, *mọtto* < *mŭttum* betray the attraction of the suffix *-ọtto*, to which *ghiọtto* < *glŭttus* and *sọtto* < *sŭbtus* did not yield. *Cọsta* < *cō(n)stat*, *sọsta* < *sŭbstat* have perhaps been affected by *accọsta*, *pọsta*. *Ginọcchio* < **genŭcŭlum*, *nọcchio* < *nŭcleus* seem to owe their *ọ* to *ọcchio*. *Mọro* < *mōrum* + *maurum*. *Piọppo* < *pōpŭlus* has felt the influence of *ọppio* < *ŏpŭlus*. *Sọffre* < *sŭffert* has followed *ọffre* < *ŏffert*. *Trápano* < τρύπανον is associated with the prefix *tra-*. *Tremuoto* < *terræ mōtus* evidently follows *muovere*.

A few are foreign: *bọlgia* < *bŭlga* is Fr., *dọge* < *dŭcem* is Venetian, *giọstra* (ultimately from *jŭxta*) is Pr.

For others no explanation suggests itself: *cọnio* < *cŭneus*, *cọppa* < *cŭppa*, *crọsta* < *crŭsta*, *mọia* < *mŭria*, Palermo < Πάνορμος, *stọggio* < ?*stŭdium*, *zavọrra* < *sabŭrra*.

In non-Tuscan dialects there are many more cases of *ọ*. The Roman *nọme* < *nōmen* is heard even in Lucca.

---

[1] This seems to be the most generally accepted explanation of the curious plural forms, *suoi, tuoi*.

6. In book-words, Lat. *ō* and Gr. *ο* appear as *ǫ*, Lat. *ŭ* as *u*, Gr. *ŭ* as *i*: *dōtem* > *dǫte*, *glōria* > *glǫria*, *mōbĭlis* > *mǫbile*, *mōtus* > *mǫto*, *nōbĭlis* > *nǫbile*, *nōnus* > *nǫno*; λογική > *lǫgica*, χορός > *cǫro*; *cŭmŭlus* > *cúmulo*, *dŭbius* > *dubbio*, *fŭlmen* > *fúlmine*, *lŭpus* > *lupo* (beside rare *lovo*), *nŭmĕrus* > *número*, *sŭbĭto* > *súbito*; κρύπτη > *critta* (cf. popular *grǫtta*), σύνθεσις > *síntesi*.

Some words have both a popular and a learned form: *nōdum* > *nǫdo* in Tuscany, *nǫdo* outside. When a learned word has an ending that is common in popular words, the *o* of the ending follows the popular style: *abbǫndo*, *divǫra*, *facǫndo*, *pavǫne*, *pavǫre*.

7. Proparoxytones, even though they be of popular origin, tend to open their *o*, especially (it would seem) before or after a labial: *amŭrca* *amŭrcŭla* > *mǫrchia*; *bŭxus* *bŭxŭlus* > *bǫssolo*, hence *bǫsso*; *cōpŭla* > *cǫppia*; *cŭbĭtus* (+*incŭmbĕre*) > *gǫmito*; *fŭlĭca* > *fǫlaga*; *hŭmĕrus* > *ǫmero*; *jŭvĕnis* > *giǫvane* *giǫvane*; καρυόφυλλον > *garǫfano*; *mŭccus* *mŭccŭlus* > *mǫccolo*; *nŭmĕrus* > *nǫvero* (cf. *número*); *recŭpĕrat* > *ricǫvera* (cf. *ricúpera*); *scrōfa* *scrōfŭla* > *scrǫfola*, hence *scrǫfa*; *sŭffōcat* > *sǫffoca*; *tŭnĭca* > *tǫnaca*; *vōmĕrem* > *vǫmere*.

Archaic and poetic words are apt to have *ǫ*: *prōra* > *prǫda*, *vobiscum* *vōscum* > *vǫsco*. Perhaps *angǫscia* < *angŭstia* belongs here.

ǫ

30. V. L. *ǫ* (= Cl. L. *ŏ* and probably Gr. ω) > It. *ǫ*, when in position: *cŏrpus* > *cǫrpo*, *fŏrtem* > *fǫrte*, *nŏctem* > *nǫtte*, *pŏst* *pŏs* > *pǫi*, *tŏstus* > *tǫsto*; *ecce hŏc* > *ciò*, *per hŏc* > *però*; γλῶσσα > *chiǫsa*.

1. There seems to be a tendency to substitute *ǫ* before nasal + labial or nasal + dental: *cŏmplet* > *cǫmpie*, *cŏmpŭto* > *cǫnto* (and *cǫmputo*), *cŏnflat* > *gǫnfia*; *abscŏndĕre* > *nascǫndere*, *cŏmĭtem* > *cǫnte*, *cŏntra* > *cǫntra*, *fŏntem* > *fǫnte*, *frŏntem* > *frǫnte*, *mŏntem* > *mǫnte*, *ŏmnem* > *ǫnne* *ǫgne* *ǫgni* *ǫgni*, *pŏntem* > *pǫnte*, *respŏndet* > *rispǫnde*, *sŏmnium* > *sǫgno*, *somnum* > *sǫnno*.[1] But *dŏmĭna* *dŏmna* > *dǫnna*.

---

[1] Rome and Naples have *cǫnte*, *fǫnte*, *pǫnte*. Velius Longus cites the Latin forms *frundes*, *funtes*; Priscian mentions *funtes*, *frundes*, *grungum*, *huminem* as old forms kept in rustic parlance. It may be that there were in ancient times two pronunciations, one favoring *o*, the other *u*. In that case, the *u* type was preserved in Rumania and central Sardinia, the *o* type in Gaul and Spain, both types in Italy (*u* in northern dialects, *o* in southern).

2. Before *n* + guttural or palatal, we find *u* in *lŏngus>lungo* (in Siena and Arezzo *longo*), *lŏnge>lungi*, ἀγωνιάω>*agugno agogno*.

3. In *scǫrtica*<**excŏrtĭcat* we may suspect the influence of *cǫrto*< *cŭrtus;* in *sǫrdido* (also *sǫrdido*), that of *lǫrdo* and *sǫrdo*<*sŭrdus*. The ǫ of *quattǫrdici* (ǫ in Rome and Naples) represents a fusion of the Latin *uo;* for the ǫ, cf. § 29, 7.

31. When not in position, ǫ breaks into *uǫ: cŏrium>cuoio*, *fŏcus>fuoco*, *lŏcus>luogo*, *mŏrit(ur)>muore*, *vult *vŏlet>* *vuole; hŏmĭnes>uomini*, *mŏvēre *mŏvĕre>muovere*, *sŏcĕrum>* *suocero.*[1] But the vowel remains intact after *y* and before *l'*, *n'*, *ddž*, or *ttš: cŏma *clŏma* (for *cŏmŭla?*)*>chiǫma*, *glŏmus* *>ghiǫmo*, *pluit plŏvit>piǫve; cŏllĭgit *cŏljit *cǫl'it>cǫglie*, *fŏlia>fǫglia; cŏngius *cŏnjus *cǫn'us>cǫgno cǫnio; hŏdie>* *ǫgge ǫggi*, *fŏvea>fǫggia*, *pŏdium>pǫggio; nŏceo>nǫccio.*

In hiatus, it would seem, the *uo* remains before *i*, but is reduced to *u* before other vowel sounds: *bŏ(v)es>buoi*, *bŏ(v)em>bue; *sŏi>suoi*, **sŏa* (or *sŭa*)*>sua*. See § 29, 5.

In modern Tuscan the *u* of *uo* disappears after consonant + *r: gr(u)ǫgo*, *pr(u)ǫva*, *tr(u)ǫva*. Indeed, modern Tuscan is returning to ǫ under all circumstances, ǫ and *uǫ* being used interchangeably in the whole series: *b(u)ǫno*, *c(u)ǫpre*, *m(u)ǫve*, *n(u)ǫvo*, *r(u)ǫta*.

On the other hand, some Tuscan dialects (like some in Umbria and the Abruzzi) early reduced *uo* to *u: fuori>furi*, *pǫi *puoi>pui*. Such forms are occasionally used in the rime by Florentine poets.

1. *Pǫsi* (for earlier *puosi<pŏsui*) has ǫ borrowed from the present, *pǫne<pōnit;* hence *pǫsto* for *pǫsto<pŏsĭtum*. Why have we ǫ in *fǫra<* *fŏrat*, *lǫglio<lŏlium*, *vǫla<vŏlat? Saldo<sŏlĭdus* + *salvus. Uggio* (<?*ŏdium*) may come from *uggioso<?odiōsus.*

2. *Nǫve* (also *nuove* in dialects)*<nŏvem* seems to have kept its ǫ because of proclitic use.

---

[1] In Arezzo both *o* and *uo* seem to have been current in such words: see *Zs.*, Beiheft V, 160–162.

3. Latinisms have simple *ǫ*: *attǫnito, bǫve, mǫdo, tǫnico*. So, no doubt, have some popular proparoxytones: *cǫfano* <*cǒphǐnus, crǫnaca* <*chrǒnǐca, mǫdano* <*mǒdǔlus, mǫnaco* <*mǒnǎchus, ǫpera* <*ǒpera, pǫpolo* <*pǒpǔlus, vǫmita* <*vǒmǐtat*. Poetic words and forms, through Latin, Provençal, Sicilian, and perhaps Aretine influence, often have *ǫ*: *foco, loco, move, novo*. *Rǫsa*, an essentially poetic word, always has the simple vowel (cf. the other languages).

ṳ

32. V. L. *ṳ* (= Cl. L. *ū*) > It. *ṳ*: *adjūtat* >*aiúta, flūmen* >*fiume, frūctus* >*frutto, lūmen* >*lume, mūrus* >*muro, ūsus* > *uso, ūtǐlis* >*útile, virtūtem* >*virtude virtù*.

1. Some Latin words seem to have had two forms, one with *ū*, the other with *ǔ* (or *ō*): *lūcta lǔcta* >*lǫtta* (see § 29, 5 for the *ǫ*), *lūrǐdus* *lǔrǐdus?* >*lǫrdo* (cf. Fr. *lourd*), *pūmǐcem* *pōmǐcem* >*pǫmice* (see Zs., XXVI, 617–618), *sūber* *sǔběrum* >*súghero sǫvero* (see § 103, 1, for the *gh*). *Nūptiæ* (by the analogy of *nǒvius* " bridegroom " <*nǒvus*) became *nǒptiæ*, whence *nǫzze* (cf. Fr. *noces*). *Sǫso* beside *suso* <*sūrsum* follows the analogy of *giǫso* <*deōrsum*. Sienese *ǫnto, pǫnto* for *unto, punto* <*ūnctus, pūnctus* are evidently from *ǫngere, pǫngere* <*ǔngěre, pǔngěre* (cf. § 29, 3).

2. Bologna seems to have used *o* for *u*, and some of these Bolognese forms were borrowed by Tuscan poets. Guittone d'Arezzo has many of them; Guido Cavalcanti has *costome, fiome, lome*, etc.; Dante has *lome*. Dante's *brollo* for *brullo* may be a word of this type, but its origin is uncertain.

au

33. V. L. *au* (= Cl. L. *au, avⁱ, abᵘ, abᵃ*) >It. *ǫ*[1]: *audit* > *ǫde, causa* >*cǫsa, claustrum* >*chiǫstro, fraudem* >*frǫde, gaudet* >*gǫde, pausat* >*pǫsa; amāv(i)t* >*amò, av(ǐ)ca* >*ǫca; fabǔla* > *faula* >*fǫla, parabǒla parabǔla* *paraula* >*parǫla; gabǎta* *gabǔta* *gauta* >*gǫta*.

In some central and southern dialects, including some of those of southern Tuscany, the ending *-aut* from *-avit* remained dissyllabic, and gave *-ao* instead of *-ò*: *amavit* >*amò amáo*.

---

[1] In Lucca and Arezzo this *o* is pronounced *ǫ*.

1. In some dialects the *au* was reduced to *ǫ* early enough to break into *uo* like original *ǫ*: *cuosa, puoco*, etc. These forms never became literary, although some of them crept into some Tuscan dialects.

2. Learned words introduced at different times and in different places show different results. The greater part show *au* retained as *au*: *causa, laude, lauro*. A few, perhaps originating in the south, have *avo* from *au*: *caulis* > *cávolo*, ναῦλον > *návolo* (cf. *nǫlo*), *Paulus* > *Pávolo* (cf. *Páolo, Pǫlo*). Some change *au* to *al*, doubtless at first with a *u*-like sort of *l*: καῦμα > *calma*, σάγμα **sauma* > *salma* (cf. *sǫma*), σμάραγδος > **smaraudus* > *smeraldo*. In some old texts the spelling *al* for *au* is very common: *fralde, lalde, palmento* (< *paumentum pavimentum*).[1]

3. In the perfect of the first and fourth conjugations, *-ávǐmus* and *-īvǐmus*, which might have given *-aumus* and *-iumus*, were changed in Italy and elsewhere to *-āmus* and *-īmus* under the influence of *-āstis* and *-īstis*. Later, in Italy, came a doubling of the *m*, which probably started with such words as *credǐd'mus* > *credęmmo, stět'mus* > **stęmmo stęmmo*. The forms with *mm* had the advantage of differentiating perfect from present: *credemmo, credemo*, etc.

ui

34. V. L. *ųi* (= Cl. L. stressed *ui*, however it was pronounced) > It. *ųi*: *cui* > *cúi, fui* > *fúi*, *illui* (= *illi*) > *lúi*.

Italian Falling Diphthongs

35. In Florence, in the thirteenth century or earlier, *ai, ei, oi* in the interior of a word lost their *i*: *accǫgli-lo* = *accǫi-lo* > *accòlo, andrai-ti* > *andràti, diręi-lo* > *dirèlo, recai-mi* > *recàmi, vuǫi-mi* > *vuòmi*. Similarly *che i fanti* > *che fanti* in early prose. Such forms lasted into the sixteenth century and later: e.g., *parlàne, vorrène*, in Machiavelli.

[1] H. Schuchardt, in his *Vokalismus des Vulgärlateins*, II, 496, notes *palcis* for *paucis* from A.D. 345. Virgilius Maro Grammaticus, in his *Epitomæ* (probably of the eighth century), has *palculis* (p. 8, line 12). Such forms as Lat. *palcis*, It. *fralde* may be due to a reaction against the tendency, strong in many regions, to turn *l* to *u* before a consonant; in the effort not to say *auto* for *alto*, one may have said *fralde* for *fraude* (cf. § 49, 5).

34 PHONOLOGY

So *aĕrem>áere aire>are, cōgĭto>cóito>coto, fragĭlem>
fraile* (orginally N. dial.?) *>frale*, Ger. *laiδ>laido>lado,
placĭtum>*(N. dial.) *piaito>piato, repatriat>*Pr. *repaira>
ripara, vŏcĭtus* (see § 24, 5)>(N. dial.) *vuoito>vuoto.*

1. The S. Tuscan dialects apparently either kept the *i* after the *a*,
e, o, or transferred it to the next syllable: *laido* or *ladio;* thus Siena
has *votio* for *v(u)oto.* Some of these forms with transferred *i* were
adopted in Florence: *aere aire aira>aria, bajula baila>balia.*

Secondary Tonic

36. Vowels under the secondary accent *preceding* the main
stress (see § 11) seem to have developed like accented vowels,
as long as their accent persisted; but the evidence is scanty:
blásphemáre>biasimare, cf. *blasphémia>bestęmmia;* **Bóno-
nínus>buolognino* (Florence, 1211), cf. *Bonónia>Bologna;
comínitiáre (from *ĭnĭtium*)*>comenzare* (also **comenciare
cominciare*); **déretránus* (from *rĕtro*)*>deretano,* cf. *depéndet>
dipende; *dís(je)junáre>desinare,* cf. *discúrrit>discǫrre;
Flórentínus>fiorentino,* cf. *Floréntiæ>Firenze; júdicáre>
giudicare, lúnæ díe>lunedì,* cf. *ūrína>orina; *míxtulare
*mísculáre>mescolare; négligéntem>negghiente; *néglectósus
>neghittoso; *nívicáre>nevicare; pígritári>peritare;* Pr.
sérventés (also *sírventés*)*>serventese; símiláre>sembiare sembrare; víctuália>vettovaglia.* Many of these examples signify
little or nothing, because the forms may be simply analogical
— *névicáre,* for instance, following *névica<*nĭvĭcat.*

More convincing are such combinations as *dé (i)lla dómina
>della donna,* beside *de dómina>di donna; mihi illud dicit
>mé (i)llu dícit>me (l)lo dice,* beside *me vídet> mi vede; sé
(i)nde vádit>se ne va,* beside *se stát>si sta.* Following the
pattern of these, we have *ét me vídet>e mmi vede, néc me vídet
>ne mmi vede, sí me vídet>se mmi vede, quíd me vídet>che
mmi vede.*

Desnore<*díshonórem probably comes through a stage
*desonore. Scuriata<excóriáta, sdrucciolare<*exróteoláre seem

to belong to some dialect that reduces *uo* to *u* (§ 31, end). *Bunaffè* (apparently from *Buonaffe*) and *bulognini* (beside *buolognini*) are found in Florence in 1211. The old names *Dietajuti* and *Dietisalvi* contain a remnant of earlier *dieo* from *deus* (§ 27, end).

Some early learned words show a change of *ĭ* to *ę* under the secondary accent, a change which in a number of learned words occurred under the main stress (§ 25, 10): *commessione* (Sacchetti), *fermamento* (beside *firmamento*), *oppenione* (Passavanti), *partecipare*, *scomenicare* < **excomĭnicare* for *excommūnicare* under the influence of *mĭnari* or *mĭnus*.

1. There are some examples of special alteration of the secondary tonic: *fĭstulare* > *fischiare* (onomatopoeia); *lŭsciniola* > *lusignuǫlo usignǫlo* (why?); *mĕlanchŏlĭcus* > *malinconico* (influence of *malincorpo, malincuore*); *mīrabĭlia* *mĭrabīlia (a clerical mispronunciation) > *meraviglia* and *maraviglia* (cf. Sp.); *oboedire* > *ubbidire obbedire* (why *u*?); *rōs marīnus* > *ramerino* (association with *ramo*?); *satisfacere* > *soddisfare* (*satis*- being understood as *sub-dis*-); *vespertĭlio* > *vespistrello pipistrello* (onomatopoeia, with suffix *-ello*). *Scilinguágnolo* looks like a mixture of *sublinguaneus, *sciogliere*, and *sciliva*. *Gracidare* and *lamicare* represent unknown combinations. *Leonfante* for *elefante* shows contamination with *leone*, perhaps in association with *leopardo pardo*. *Diciannove*, *diciassette* < *déce' ac nóve'*, *déce' ac sépte'* seem to follow *diciotto* < *dece'ócto*. *Mercoledì*, from *Mercŭrī dīe*, suffered a shift of accent under the influence of *Vĕnĕris dīe* (§ 27, 3), becoming probably at one stage *Mercŏris die.

2. Book-words have in general the same vowel that they would have had under the main accent: *dędicare*, *dęcimale*, *sitibondo*, *nǫminare*, *mǫvimento*, *accumulare* (and *ammucchiare*).

UNACCENTED VOWELS [1]

37. Because of their comparative inaudibility, unaccented vowels are less stable than accented, and more exposed to external influences. They show little trace of original Latin quantity; in Italy, the once long and the once short seem to

---

[1] Unaccented *e* and *o* in Italian have sounds intermediate between the close and the open, but nearer to the former than to the latter. The open *i* and *u* of English *pit* and *put* are lacking.

have developed alike, with the exception of $\bar{\imath}$, which held itself aloof from $\breve{\imath}$. Their fate depended largely on their position in the word. We must consider them separately as they stood in the first, the last, the intertonic, or the penultimate syllable.

Before starting on this examination, it is well to look at certain cases involving the adjacent vowels of two consecutive syllables. In these cases the two syllables coalesced, either by the change of the first vowel into a consonant or by a fusion of the two vowels.

1. *E* and *i*, unaccented and followed by another vowel, became *y;* a *u*, similarly situated, became *w*: *ĕāmus* > **jamus* > *giamo*, *fīlĭus* > **fĭljus* > *figlio*, *paruit* > **parwit* > *parve*. But *suavis*, a poetic word, retained its trisyllabic pronunciation: *soave* (cf. O. Fr. *soef*, Pr. *su-au*). In *fŭĕrunt*, *fŭĕrat*, etc., the V. L. accent regularly fell on the *fu-*, and these forms became on Italian soil **furunt* > *foron*, **furat* > *fora*.

2. After a consonant, *ye* was contracted to *ē*, *wo* to *ō*, *wu* to *u*: *facĭēbam* > **facjeba* **faceba* > *facęva*, *mulĭĕrem* > (§ 9, 2) **muljére* *mul'ere* > *moglięra* (with *ę* by analogy with the common suffix *-iera*), *parĭĕtem* > **parjéte* *parete* > *paręte*, *quĭētus* > *quetus* > *chęto;* *dŭōdĕcim* > **dwōdece* **dōdece* > *dǫdici*, *quattuŏrdĕcim* > **quatwórdece* **quattōrdece* > *quattǫdici* (also with *ǫ*: see § 29, 7); *cŏquus* > *cocus* > *cuǫco*, *mŏrtuus* > *mortus* > *mǫrto*.[1]

3. The group *eé* seems to have fared like *ye*, and *oó* like *wo*: *prehendere* (*h* silent) > *prēndere* (Terence) > *pręndere* (*ę* by analogy with *ręndere*), **dĕ-ĕxcĭto* > **dēscito* > *dęsto;* *cŏŏperire* > *cōperire* **cŏperire* (analogy of *cŏ-* and of *ŏp-*) > *coprire*. *Coagulare*, which presents a different combination, gives *cagliare* and *quagliare*, the first of which may have been borrowed from the French.

4. With the compounds *eccu' illúi*, *eccu'íllu'*, *eccu' illóru'* (§ 182), the outcome depends on the accentuation: *u* + *ĭ* > *wę*, while in unaccented *u* + *i* the first vowel simply absorbs the second. Thus we have *colúi*, *quéllo*, *colóro;* similarly (from *iste*) *costúi*, *quésto*, *costóro*.

---

[1] For a different theory, see O. J. Tallgren in *Mémoires de la Société néo-philologique à Helsingfors*, VII (1924), 243.

First Syllable [1]

38. Here *a* long or short remains as *a*, *ī* remains as *i*, *e* long or short and *ĭ* give *i* (sometimes *e*), *o* and *u* long or short give *o* (sometimes *u*); *au*, under different circumstances, gives *a* or *u* (sometimes *o*): *mājālis* > *maiale*, *ămōrem* > *amore*; *cīvitātem* > *città*; *sēcūrus* > *sicuro securo*, *nĕpōtem* > *nipote nepote*, *mĭnōrem* > *minore menore*; *prōmĭssa* > *promessa prumessa*, *jŏcāre* > *giocare giucare*, *frūmentum* > *formento frumento*, *scŭtella* > *scodella scudella*; *augustus agustus* > *agosto*, Pr. *ausberc* > *usbergo osbergo*.

In the inconsistent examples of *i* or *e*, *u* or *o*, we see now a conflict between popular and bookish forms, now a mixture of dialects, now an imitative turn.

1. Latinisms naturally tend to keep the Latin letter, changing only *y* to *i*, *æ* and *oe* to *e*: *sēbaceus* > *sebaceo*, *sĕcare* > *secare*, *mĭcantem* > *micante* *prōponere* > *proponere*, *pŏliticus* > *politiço*, *crūdelis* > *crudele*, *rŭina* > *ruina*; *tȳrannus* > *tiranno*, *præsæpe* > *presepe*, *phoenicem* > *fenice*.

2. In popular words, as between *i* and *e*, Florence displays a decided preference for *i;* but its development from *e* seems to have taken place rather late, perhaps not before the thirteenth century, and the tendency to change did not last long. Western Tuscany (Pisa, Lucca, Pistoia) has *i* oftener than *e*; southern Tuscany (Siena) shows a slight preponderance of *i*; in eastern Tuscany, Arezzo inclines to *e*, but Valdichiana is strong for *i*. Outside of Tuscany, we find northern Italy, Umbria, and Rome favoring *e*, while Romagna and the south have *i*.

Mixed conditions exist also for *u* and *o*, the latter prevailing in Florence and Lucca, *u* in Siena, Arezzo, and Valdichiana, while the outside dialects, except some in the south, generally show *u*.

3. Among prefixes, it is to be noted that *præ-* *pre-* is always *pre-*. *De-* and *re-* should give *di-* and *de-*, *ri-* and *re-* in popular words, and *de-*, *re-* in learned; but some bookish words take over the popular forms with *i* (*dilicato* for *delicato*, *ripulsa* for *repulsa*). So *sub-*, in some learned words (such as *sotterraneo*) assumes the popular form. *Es-* from *ex-* is always learned, the popular form being *s-* (*expensa* > *spesa*). *In-* *im-*

---

[1] See E. B. Schlatter, *The Development of the Vowel of the Unaccented Initial Syllable in Italian*, 1913 (in *Transactions of the Wisconsin Academy of Sciences, Arts and Letters*, XVII, ii).

remains; but changes to *em-* in *empire* < *implēre*, under the influence of *émpiere*.

In Lucca, Siena, and Arezzo, *re-* sometimes changes to *ar-*, the vowel being doubtless obscured by a strong trill (*armanere, arliquia*); in some words *ar-* or *a-* is simply prefixed (*aracogliere, arrendere, arritornare*).

4. Occasionally one prefix is exchanged for another: *affogare* < *offocare, amendare* < *emendare, annacquare* < *inaquare, annoiare* from *in odio* (perhaps through the French), *asciolvere* < *ex-solvere, assedio* < *obsidium, assemplo* (beside *esempio*) < *exemplum, soddurre* (beside *sedurre*) < *seducere*. In *ritondo* the prefix *re-* was substituted, in Latin times, for *ro-*. *In-* replaced the *hi-* of *hibernus* > *inverno*. *Sub-* entered into *sigillum* > *suggello*. *Anguinaia* seems to get its *a-* from a plural *illa inguina* with elision of the *i-, arete* (beside *rete*) from a feminine *illa rete* with false division of the words; so *ancudine* for *incudine;* so *alloro* from *illa laurus* with an unexplained doubling of the *l* (possibly *il loro*).

39. To *s* + cons., a vowel, *i* or *e*, was prefixed from the second century on, probably because *s* thus situated had a long, almost syllabic utterance, as *s* still has in Italian before a consonant (*pa-s-to*). So, when Italian began, such words as *scala, spoglia, stende* were usually pronounced *iscala, ispoglia, istende* (cf. Sp. *escala*, Fr. *échelle*). This *i*, however, was absorbed by a preceding vowel (*la 'scala*), until gradually the prevalent form came to be once more the one with initial *s-*. Nowadays the *i-* remains only after a consonant: *per istrada, in iscuola, non istà,* etc.[1]

40. Frequent is the loss of any initial vowel through elision with the article or some other word: *la abbadia, la'bbadia, la badia* from *abbatia.* So *bottega* < *apothēca, cagione* < *occasionem, chiesa* < *ecclesia, dificio* for *edificio, lezzo* for *olezzo, limọsina* for *elemosina, lọdola* from *alauda, Magna* for *Alamagna* (twice curtailed), *mándorla* < *amygdăla, morosa* for *amorosa, nemico* < *inimīcus, pẹcchia* < *apĭcŭlus, rabesco* for *arabesco, ragna* < *aranea, rame* < *æramen, riccio* < *erĭcius, Rímini* < *Arīmĭnum, rọndine* < *hirŭndĭnem, sala* < **axalis, scuro*

[1] For conditions in early Italian, see W. Meyer-Lübke in *Behrens-Testschrift*, 24–31.

for *oscuro, sparago* for *asparago, spedale*<*hospitale, Taglia* for *Italia, vangęlo*<*evangĕlium, vęscovo*<*epĭscŏpus.*

In the future of *essere* and in its old perfect participle, from **esser'ho* and **essūtus*, the *e-* was lost probably by elision: *sarò, suto.*

1. An original vowel before *s* + cons. was very often lost with the prosthetic *i-* described in § 39, from the fourteenth to the sixteenth century. When *istato* (<*status*) became usually *stato, istanotte* (<*ista nocte*) became *stanotte*. So *stamane*, on the model of *stanotte;* so *sciame* <*exāmen, Spagna*<*Hispania, state*<*œstatem;* thus *stesso*<*ist' ĭpsum stimare*<*œstimare, storia*<*historia, strumento*<*instrumentum.* From words like *schiudere*<*exclūdere* developed a prefix *s-*, with a negative sense, which was voiced before a sonant: so *nodare, snodare. Dis-* was probably understood as *di- s-:* hence *dispiace* side by side with *spiace.* § 53, 1.

2. The prefixes *de-* and *re-* generally elide their *e* before a vowel in popular words: **de-undulare*>*dondolare, *re-ad-colligere*>*raccogliere.* But in the primitive *deōrsum* from *devorsum* the *de* became *dy,* then *y* (see § 78): *gioso.*

3. In **eccu' illorum, *eccu' istui,* the first vowel absorbed the second: *coloro, costui.* But in Arezzo we find both of them kept, the second prevailing and the first reduced to *w: quelui, queloro.*

4. Some words have lost their whole first syllable, in most cases because the syllable in question seemed like a useless prefix: *bilico* for *umbilico, corbezza*<**cucurbitia, fante* for *infante, fondo* for *profondo, gnorsì* for *signor sì, mentre* for *domentre, nestare* for *innestare, ritto* for *diritto, tondo* for *ritondo, tavia* for *tuttavia, vaccio*<*vivacius, verno* for *inverno.* Many proper names are thus shortened: *Vanna* for *Giovanna.* The prefixes *infra-, intra-* become *fra-, tra-: frattanto, travedere.*

41. In a few cases the medial vowel of an initial syllable disappears, being swallowed up in the roll of an *r* or the hiss of an *s: crollare*<**corrotulare, dritto*<*dīrēctus, gridare*< *quĭrītare, scure*<*secūris, staccio*<**setacium, staio*<*sextarius, stu = se tu, trivello*<*terebellum.* For *sor, monna,* etc., see § 148, 3. The syncopation in **corrotulare, directus, quiritare* is very old: cf. Fr. *crouler, droit, crier.*

42. In the speech of Florence, secondary *ai, ei, oi, ui* lost their *i: aitare* (<*adjutare*) >*atare, Guillelmo* (found in Boccaccio and in a Florentine document of 1211)>*Guglielmo*, *meitd* (<*medietatem*)>*metd*. The group *che i* ('that the'...) often appears in early Florentine texts as *che*.

Words like *egli*, pretonic before a consonant, reduced *gli* to *i* (see § 59, 1), and then fell under this tendency: *begli*> *bei*>*be'*, *cogli*>*coi*>*co'*, *dagli*>*dai*>*da'*, *degli*>*dei*>*de'*, *egli* >*ei*>*e'*, *quegli*>*quei*>*que'*. Similarly *voglio*>*voi*>*vo'*.

Accented *rex, tres, magis, nos, vos* regularly give (§ 94, *S*) **rei, trei, mai, noi, voi*, which, used before the accent, become *re, tre, ma, no, vo;* under the influence of *me* and *te, no* and *vo* then changed to *ne* and *ve* (later *vi*). Pretonic *dopoi (from *de post*) is supposed to be the origin of *dopo*.

1. In Siena the *i* seems either to have been retained or to have been transferred to the next syllable: *meità* or *metià*.

43. Generally in Tuscany, the groups *ia, ie, io, iu*, lose their second element: *io* pretonic>*i'*, *Fiorenze*>*Firenze*, (*piuma*)*piumaccio>*pimaccio*, *pluvialis*>*piuviale piviale (also, in a different sense, *piviere*), (*pieve*) *pieviere>*piviere*. For *Giuseppe, Giseppo* occurs, as do *sciliva* for *scialiva*<*salīva*, *scigatorio* for *sciugatorio*. German *thiudiskô* gives both *tedesco* and *todesco*.

Pietà piatà is perhaps too closely associated with Latin to follow the rule. In the numerous cases represented by such forms as *chiedete, chiudeva, fiutò, pianura, pienezza, pietroso, piuttosto*, the second vowel is saved by the influence of *chiede*, etc., in which that vowel has the accent. The *ma*- of *madonna* is probably not from Italian *mia*, but from an old Latin popular *ma* for *mea*. *Bestemmia*<*blasphemia* seems to have been influenced by *bestia*.

1. In colloquial speech, *ua, ue, uo* lose their second vowel: *la su' moglie, la su' casa, la tu' povera mamma; du' franchi, du' mesi, du' posti; su' padre, il su' cane.*

a

44. V. L. *a* (Cl. L. *a* long or short)>It. *a*: *mājōrem*>*maggiore, căpĭllus*>*capello*. So bookish words: *analysis*>*analisi*.

1. Exceptions are few. *Lacerta* (still used in Naples) > *lucertola*, being associated with *luce*. *Maitino*, used by Sicilian and early Tuscan poets for *mattino*, is not accounted for. *Ottone* seems to come from *lattone* < Ger. *latta*. From Ger. *warjan* we find occasional *gherire* (as in Fr.) beside *guarire*. Some other words have a by-form with *e* for *a* before *r*: *garofano gherofano* (< καρυόφυλλον), *sarmento sermento*, *variegato vergato*; *smeraldo* < σμάραγδος has *e* in the other Romance languages. For *bestemmia* see § 43.

e

45. V. L. *e* (Cl. L. *e* long or short, *ĭ*, *œ*, *oe*, *ȳ*) > *i*: *prehensionem* > *prēsiōne > *prigione*, *sēcūrus* > *sicuro*; *mĕliōrem* > *migliore*, *nĕpōtem* > *nipote*; *mĭnōrem* > *minore*, *cĭcāda* > *cicala*; *cæsōria > *cisoie* (also *cesoie*); *phoenīcem* > *finice* (oftener *fenice*); *tyrannus* > *tiranno*. So proclitics, such as *di, mi, si, ti*. For the prefixes *de-, prœ-, re-*, see § 38, 3.

Before *r* + cons., however, *e* remains: *berbice, cervello, cervigia, mercante, mercè, pernice, sermone, serpente, vergogna, verrina* < *veruina, verruca*. So always *per* as prefix or proclitic: *perfetto, per me*. Such words as *cercare, serbare, servire, terzuolo* follow the same principle, although here the *e* might be attributed to the influence of *cerco*, etc. *Firmare* (beside *fermare*, differentiated in meaning) and *virtù* are evidently bookish. *Birbone* follows *birbo*, whatever be the origin of the latter. A few words change *er* to *ar*: *parlato* for *prelato*, *phreneticus* > *farnetico*, Eng. *sterling* > *sterlina starlino, sternūtat* > *starnuta*; cf. Fr. *marchant, parfait*, Eng. *Clark, sergeant*.

Before *r* + vowel, we find both *e* and *i*: *pĕrĭculum* > *periglio, Perŭsia* > *Perugia, sĕrēnus* > *sereno, vēre ūnus* > *veruno; cĕrēsea* > *ciliegia; Hĭĕrōnymus* > *Girolamo Gerolamo*.

Book-words show *e* for *e* long or short, *œ*, *oe*; *i* for *ĭ*, *ȳ*: *detesto, reprimere, questura, penale; sinistro, fisico*. But even here the Tuscan *i* occasionally intrudes: *diciferare* for *decifrare, finice* for *fenice, quistione* for *questione*. On the other hand, the earliest poetic language seems to have favored the Latin form of proclitics such as *me, te, se*.

1. Many words have *e* under the influence of forms in which the *e* is accented: *bellezza, bevanda, entrare* (also *in-*), *essuto* (also *is-, s-*), *fedele, megliore* (beside *mi-*), *peggiore* (also *pi-*), *pedata, pescare, preghiera, prestare, sedere* (also *si-*), *seguire, serbare, servire, settanta, vedere, venire,* after *bello, beve,* etc. *Serò* (= *sarò*), found in the thirteenth century, apparently succumbed to the analogy of *starò* too early to become **sirò*. Dissimilation may be responsible for *nemico* < *inìmīcus, reina* < *rēgīna* (cf. bookish *regina*); then *reame* (also *ri-*) may follow the lead of *re, reina*.

The proclitics *nec* and *sī* early came under the influence of *et* and *quìd* (see § 184), which became before vowels *ed* and *ched,* before consonants *e* and *che;* hence we have in early Italian *nè ned, se sed* (*se* occurs, indeed, in late Latin), which, like *e ed* and *che ched,* kept their *e,* perhaps following the analogy of such combinations as *de llo, ne llo, me lo, te lo, se lo,* in which the first member always had a secondary stress (§ 36). *Neuno* (also *ni-*) and *nessuno* (also *ni-*) keep the vowel of *nè.*

2. Certain words have come into the standard language from dialects in which the *e* is kept (§ 38, 2): *età* < *ætatem, legume, segreto, tesoro, veleno* < *venēnum.* Some have been used in literature with both forms: *cesoie, felice, festuca, mestieri, secondo, spedale* < *hospitale, tenore,* beside *cisoie, filice, fistuga,* etc. Such words as *dettaglio, etichetta* are late borrowings from the French.

3. In some Tuscan dialects, especially the Florentine, *e* before labials tends to become labialized into *o* or *u;* this change apparently occurred while *v* was still bilabial (see §§ 77; 83; 103, *B*): *da de vero* > *daddovero, debere* > *dovere, demandat* > *domanda* (also *di-*), *de mane* > *domani* (also *di-*), *de pòst* > *dopo, *deventat* > *doventa* (also *di-*), *ebriacus* > *ubbriaco, eremita* > *romito, exire* > *uscire* (here we have both the labial *š* and the influence of *uscio*), *gemelli* > *giumelli* (also *ge-*), *peponem* > *popone, rebellis* > *rubello* (also *ribelle*), **reversius* > *rovescio, *similiat* > *somiglia;* so, no doubt, *æqualis* > *uguale,* the *q* being labialized by the following *u.* The whole phenomenon is due to a premature partial closure of the lips, in anticipation of the coming labial; *i* and *e,* thus modified, sound as *ü* and *ö,* and these latter vowels, being unfamiliar, were replaced by the nearest Italian substitutes, *u* and *o.* Cf. Pr. *prümier* from *primarium.* Why the labialized vowel is sometimes *o,* sometimes *u,* is not apparent.

Arezzo, like Umbria and Rome, does not share in this tendency.

In an undiscriminating reaction against the habit of labializing, there sometimes arise such forms as *dimestico* for *domestico, diminio* for *dominio, rimore* for *romore* or *rumore.*

4. Several Tuscan dialects occasionally turn *e* to *a* when there is a stressed *a* in the next syllable: *aguale* for *iguale* (= *uguale*), *piatà* for *pietà*, *sanato* for *senato*, *tanaglia* (also *te-*) < *tenacula*. *Danaro* for *denaro* < *denarium* passed into general use. Although *salvaticus* for *silvaticus* is common to all the Romance group, Italian *salvaggio* is less common than *selvaggio*, which maintains contact with *selva*. *Travaglio* < **trepalium* is doubtless borrowed from Provençal or French, but in any case shows a substitution of the prefix *tra-* (= *trans-*) for the syllable *tre-*. *Avorio* < *eborius* seems to be Provençal.

5. There are a few peculiar cases. *Bieltate*, common for *beltà* in the *Vita Nuova* and other early texts, is probably a borrowing from Old French. *Rognone* (cf. Fr. *rognon*) < **rēniōnem* is obscure. *Suggello* < *sĭgĭllum* shows the influence of the prefix *sub-*. *Zampogna* < *symphonia* seems to have been associated with *zampa;* in some parts of rustic Italy musical pipes are still made of the shin-bones of sheep.

Ne, from *inde*, owes the preservation of its *e* to its prevailing use as an enclitic: *datene, mene dà*, etc.; hence *ne parla*. In the early language, moreover, there was a strange confusion of this word with the preposition *in*: *indel, indella* were used for *nel, nella* (so still in Lucca and Arezzo); conversely, *nel, nella* may have influenced *inde, 'nde*.

Ciascuno, if it be not French or Provençal, would seem to be a fusion of *cescheduno* < **quisquid unum* or **cescuno* < *quisqu' unus* with *catuno, caduno, cadauno*, all from *cata unum*. The Greek distributive preposition κατά was carried by merchants around the Mediterranean, and entered into the Romance tongues, becoming in Spanish the adjective *cada*. It must be assumed that the first *qu* of *quisquis*, like the first *qu* of *quinque*, was simplified to *c* by dissimilation.

i

46. V. L. *i* (Cl. L. *ī, ȳ*) > It. *i*: *cīvitatem* > *città, clīnare* > *chinare, fīlum* > *filanda, mīrare* > *mirare; gȳrare* > *girare*. Also, of course, in book-words: *filiale*.

Before labials, *i*, like *e*, is sometimes labialized into *o* or *u*: *dīvīnat* > *in-dovina, dīvĭtiæ* > *dovizie, līmacem* > *lumace* (association with *lume?*).

1. Peculiar cases are: *chīrūrgĭcus* > *cerúsico* (why?), *sīrēn* > *sirena serena* (influence of *serenus*), *vīndēmia* > *vendemmia* (influence of *vēndere?* Cf. Fr. and Pr.) *Sī* > *se* was discussed in § 45, 1.

o

47. V. L. *u, o* (Cl. L. *u, o*, long or short) > It. *o: pōnentem* >
ponente, sponsare spōsare > *sposare; cŏndūcere* > *condurre*,
dŏctōrem > *dottore, jŏcare* > *giocare; frūmentum* > *formento, in-*
strūmentum > *stromento stormento, rūmōrem* > *rumore romore*
(Machiavelli), σκίουρος > *scūrius* > *scoiattolo, ūrīna* > *orina*;
eccŭ' sīc > *così, rŭīna* > *rovina, sŭbtrahere* > *sottrarre*.
Book-words generally follow the Latin spelling: *crudele,
frumento, futuro, politico, ruina*. Prefixes, however, even in
learned words, are sometimes influenced by the analogy of
the popular vocabulary: *sotteraneo*.

1. Many words have *u* by analogy with forms in which the vowel
is accented: *buttare, furioso, fumare, giudizio, pugnale, unire, urlare,
usare*.

2. Most of the Tuscan dialects outside of Florence prefer *u*: thus
cusì in Pisa and Pistoia, *cumune* and *cuprire* in Siena. Vulgar speech,
also, in all districts favors *u*: *cultello, prumessa, uguanno* < *hōcqu'anno,
usatto* < Ger. *hosa*. So we find *giucare* beside *giocare, nudrire* beside
nodrire (*nutrire* probably is literary), *pulire* beside *polire* < *pŏlire,
scudella* beside *scodella* < *scŭtella, strumento* beside *stormento*. It is
natural, then, that the standard language should have many cases of *u*:
budello < *bŏtellus, cucchiaio* < *cŏclearium*, early *u* < *ubi, uggioso* < *ŏdiosus*.
Rather curiously for Tuscan, which is not addicted to *umlaut*, the examples seem to show a preference for *u* when the next syllable contained
a stressed *i*: *cucina* < *cŏcīna coquina, cugino* < Fr. *cousin, cuscire cucire*
< ?*consŭĕre,*[1] *fucile* < *fŏcile, fuggire* < *fŭgĕre, mulino* < *mŏlīnus, nudrire* <
nūtrire, pulcino < *pŭllicēnus, pulire* < *pŏlire, ruggire* < *rŭgire, ufficio* <
ŏffĭcium, ulivo < *ŏlīvum, unire* < *ūnire*.

3. In Neapolitan and some Sicilian dialects, *o* becomes *au* (as in
auliva for *uliva*); hence the old poetic forms: *aulente, aunore, auriente*,
etc.; so probably the old *caunoscere*, which, however, early developed
an unexplained *canoscere*, still alive in the Montagna Pistoiese.
For *occīdĕre*, V. L. seems to have substituted, for unknown reasons,
aucīdere, which gave regularly It. *uccidere*, Sic. *aucidere*, Rum. *ucide*,
Pr. *aucire*, Fr. *ocire*. From *aucidere* grew up *alcidere* (cf. § 49, 5) and,
strangely, *ancidere* (Venetian *ançir*). *Aucidere, alcidere, ancidere* were
freely used by the early poets.

[1] See F. d'Ovidio, *Note etimologiche*, 52.

4. There are a few special cases. *Bifolco*<*bŭbulcus*, *filiggine* for *fuliggine*<*fūlīgĭnem*, *ginepro*<*jūnĭpĕrum*, *ligusta*<*lŏcusta*, *sirocchia* (also *se-*)<*sŏror* + *-cula*, *squittino*<*scrūtĭnium*, *vilume* for *volume*< *vŏlūmen* have for one reason or another substituted *i* for *u* or *o*. For *dimestico*, *diminio*, see § 45, 3, end.

V. L. used (why?) a new *tortūca for *testūdo*: Fr. *tortue*. Italian has, however, *tartaruga* (Sien. *tartuca*), thanks to some obscure association.

au

48. Cl. L. *au*>V. L. *a* if there was **an** *ú* in the next sylla-ble; and this *a* remains in Italian: *A*(*u*)*gústus*>*agosto*, *a*(*u*)*scúlto*>*ascolto*, *ex* + *a*(*u*)*gurium*>*sciagura*. Learned words, however, keep the *au*: *augusto*, *augurio*.

49. When there is no *ú* in the following syllable, Cl. L. *au* >V. L. *au*>It. *u*: *audire*>*udire*, Pr. *ausberc*>*usbergo*, *avi-cellus* *aucellus>*ugello* *uccello*, Ger. *bausi* + *-ía*>*bugia*, *flavitare *flautare ?>*fiutare*, Ger. *laubja* + *-one*>*lubbione*, Pr. *lausenga*>*lusinga*, Ger. *raubon*>*rubare*. Learned words keep the *au*: *autoritá*, *tautologia*.

1. In a few words we find *o* by analogy with forms in which the vowel in question is accented: *godẹre*, cf. *gọdo*; *orẹzzo*<*aurĭtium, cf. *ọra*<*ọura*. So perhaps *boccale*<*baucalis*, cf. *bọcca*<*bucca*.

2. *Orecchio* probably comes, not from *aurĭcula*, but from a Latin *oricula* used by Cicero, Pliny, Festus (also in *Appendix Probi*: *oricla*); so *o* from V. L. *ot for *aut*. Old Florentine *urecchio* and *u* may come from *auricula* and *aut*.

3. From the south the literary language gets some forms with *au-*: *audire*, *augello*.

4. Among the Tuscan dialects, only the Florentine seems to prefer *u*. Pisa, Lucca, Siena incline to *o*, while Aretine texts show a confusion of *au*, *o*, *u*. It is possible that *orbacca*<*lauri bacca*, *orbaco*<*lauri bacus*, *orpello*<*auri pellis*, *osbergo* for *usbergo* come from an *o* dialect.

5. In some old Tuscan texts we find *al* for *au*: *alcidere* for *aucidere* = *uccidere*, *algelli* for *augelli* = *uccelli*, *laldare* for *laudare*. Occasionally there occur such mixed spellings as *auldace*, *lauldare*.

The *al* is used not only in Italian but in medieval Latin. It probably came into Tuscany from other regions, more northerly, where there was a tendency to vocalize *l* before a consonant, and represents an undiscriminating reaction against that tendency: in the effort not to say *auto, autro* for *alto, altro*, people said *altentico, altorità, galdere*. Cf. § 33, 2.

Last Syllable

50. Unlike the sister languages, Italian kept all the vowels of final syllables — *a* long or short as *a; e* long or short and *æ* and *ĭ* as *e; ī* as *i; o* and *u*, long or short, as *o: fŏrās>fuǫra cantăt>canta, fŏliă>fǫglia; pūrē>pure, lūmĕn>lume, placĕt >piace, lūnæ>lune, cŭrrĭt>cǫrre, fŏrĭs>fuǫre; bŏnī>buǫni, cantāstī>cantasti, fŏrīs>fuǫri, vēnī>vǫnni, vĕnīs>vieni, v(ig)-ĭntī>vęnti* (see § 106); *de rĕtrō>dietro, ŏctō>ǫtto, plangŏ> piango, illæ manūs>*Old It. *le mano, cŏrpŭs>cǫrpo, fŏcŭs> fuoco.*

1. There is a little evidence, from words borrowed in German, that *-um* became *-o* at a time when *-us* still retained *u*: see *Zs.*, XLI, 429.

2. In some Italian dialects the development of the stressed vowel differs according as the Latin final vowel was *u* or *o*: see § 25, 4, end.

3. Sicilian pronunciation turns *-e, -o* to *-i, -u*. The literary Italian language retains a few traces of this local usage.

51. When the syllable was not really final, but formed an element within a phonetic group, its vowel was accordingly treated not as final but as medial. In *puǫte fare*, for instance, the first *e* is really intertonic, and falls (§ 59); then the *t* is assimilated to the *f: púote fáre>puot' fare>puo ffare*, hence *pù*. So *cencinquanta* for *centocinquanta, fi' Pietro* for *figlio Pietri, fra Marco* for *frate Marco, gran che* for *grande che, me' fatto* for *meglio fatto, Or* (for *Orto*) *S. Michęle, Por* (for *Porta*) *S. Maria, vo'* (for *voglio*) *dare. Ver' me* for *verso me* may have felt the influence of *per*.

Such fall is particularly common after *l, m, n, r*. Here, in connected speech, *e, i, o* regularly disappear before any sound except *s* + cons., although the *-e* and *-i* of plurals are usually kept for syntactic reasons: *bel tempo, quel paese, talvolva;*

andiam via, uom grande; buon giorno, Can Grande, man mano, pian piano, vien qui; amor mio, far fare, signor padre, venerdì; but *belle figlie, cani piccoli.*

1. *Rima tronca,* or the employment of similarly truncated forms in the rime (therefore at the *end* of a phrase), is probably a practice imitated from the Provençal, which had an abundance of monosyllabic rimes: *invan-stan, lor-amor,* etc.

2. *Gioi* beside *gioia* is Provençal (borrowed from French). The existence of this pair led to *noi* for *noia* and the early practice of counting as monosyllabic such combinations as *-oia, -oio, -aia, -aio.*

52. *Piede* and abstract nouns in *-de* form a class by themselves. At an early stage of the language, such phrases as *alli piede de Deo, la mercede de Deo, la fede de Deo, la bontade de Deo* (or similar combinations ending in another word) seemed to contain a needless repetition, and one of the *de* syllables was cut out; hence *piè, mercè, fè, bontà.* Thus all the *-ade* and *-ude* abstract nouns lost their *-de: caritd, virtù.* But for several centuries the longer forms in *-ade* or *-ate, -ude* or *-ute* were used also; and for the *-ede* words the complete form is still the commoner.[1] *Mo* for *modo* probably arose in similar fashion.

Die' for *diede* seems to follow both *pie, piede* and *fe', fece.* The latter apparently shapes itself on *fa, face,* alternatives in the present indicative, *fa* modeled on *da* and *sta, face* coming regularly from *facit.* We find also *sie'* for *siede. Tie', vie'* for *tiene, viene* fall in with the same pattern. *Tie', tiene* and *vie', viene* in turn afford a starting point for such forms as *fane, saline* for *fa, sali;* the *-ne* is sometimes extended even to pronouns, as in *mene = me, ciòne = ciò,* and to adverbs, as in *piùne = più, quine = qui.* Cf. Calabrian *sini, cchiuni, ohimeni* for *sì, più, ohimè,* etc.

1. From *sūrsum, deōrsum* come *suso, giuso* (§ 29, 4), which have been generally shortened to *su, giù,* the abbreviation doubtless starting

[1] See P. G. Goidánich, *Le origini e le forme della dittongazione romanza,* 1907, pp. 213–215.

with *suso* (or earler *susu*) which sounds like a reduplication. Possibly their example reduced *testeso* to *testè;* the make-up of *testeso* itself is unknown.[1] *Sur* for *su* before vowels shows some kind of contamination, see § 29, 4.

53. In early Italian the principles of elision were not identical with those of to-day. At present, when the first of two adjacent vowels belongs to an unstressed *word*, that is the one to fall, if either is suppressed: *l'amóre, l'aspéttano, t'ascólto* or *ti ascólto, vien incóntro* or *viene incóntro*. In the older language it was the vowel of the weaker of the two adjacent *syllables* that fell: *lá istória, ló ingégno, ló impéro*, with a slight secondary stress on the article, became *la 'storia, lo 'ngegno* (still common in parts of Tuscany), *lo 'mpero;* whereas *la árte, ora óra, viene óggi*, where the first of the contiguous vowels has no stress, became *l'arte, or ora, vien oggi*, as to-day. When, however, the two vowels formed a combination familiar in the interior of a word, they probably both remained, as a diphthong: *li usci, ti amo, tu odi, vi esce* (cf. *rifiuto, piano, tuono, viene*).

1. From *or ora*, no doubt, arose *or*, and then the poetic *allor, talor, tuttor*. Through the elision of *i* before *s* + cons., as in *la Ispagna> la 'Spagna, lo isciame>lo 'sciame*, we have the modern forms beginning with *s* (cf. § 39 and § 40, 1).

2. For *quello colui coloro, questo costui costoro*, see § 37, 4.

54. To a final accented vowel before a pause, an indistinct *e* or *a* sound was formerly added: *àe* (= *ha*), *amòe, cantòe, èe* (= *è*), *foa* (= *fu*), *piùe, prestòa, tùe* (= *tu*), *virtùe*. When a word beginning with a consonant followed one of these, the *e* or *a* was assimilated to that consonant: *àe lo>a llo, amòe mi>amommi, piùe tosto>piuttosto, tùe sai>tu ssai*. In modern Italian this doubling of the initial consonant is preserved (though not always written): *dammi, dille, treppiede; tu ssei.* But the echo vowel, in general, is no longer heard: *amò, verrà, virtù, più* (vulg. *piùe*).[2] Cf. § 88.

[1] See P. Skok in *Rom., L.,* 228.

[2] Perhaps these phenomena can be better described by saying that

1. To the final consonant of borrowed words, an *e* was and still is added, a single final consonant being then doubled: *Davidde, enne* (name of the letter *n*), *este* (Lat. *est*), *Saulle*. Thus *Cavour, frac, idem, lapis, omnibus* are often pronounced *Cavorre* or *Cavurre, fracche, idemme, lapisse, onnibusse*. Sometimes the word was partially Latinized by the substitution of *o* for *e*: *Daniello, Joseppo*, used by Dante and others.

55. Corresponding to the verb and noun endings *-ās, -ēs*, we now find in great measure *-i*, and some philologists have regarded this as a phonetic change. For a considerable number of the cases, however, the shift to *i* has occurred since the twelfth century; and, bearing in mind what has happened in French, Provençal, and Rumanian in the way of inflectional assimilation, we can best explain the *i* in all such instances as a morphological substitution. Ex.: *amās = ami, amēs = ami, amabās = amavi, amassēs = amassi, vidēs = vedi, canēs = cani, matrēs = madri*.[1]

As far as nouns and adjectives are concerned, the masculines of the third patterned themselves on the second, the great masculine declension. Pl. *padre* became *padri*, like *figli;* this occurred mainly before the thirteenth century, although Dante still used such m. pl. forms as *presente* (*Par.*, XVII, 93), *sospire* (*Per una ghirlandetta*). Then the *i-* plural was extended, very slowly, to feminines, *madre* following *padri;* this process, which may well have begun with adjectives (such as *forte*) having only one form in the singular, seems to have started in the thirteenth century or before, and is not yet entirely completed. Pl. *padre* is still regular in the Abruzzi, pl. *matre* in Calabria, and pl. *chiave, gente, parte, torre* may still be heard in parts of Tuscany. Such first

the energy of a final stressed vowel is so intense that it cannot check itself with that sound, but expends itself on the next consonant if there is one, or on an echo murmur if no consonant follows.

[1] For a discussion of the problem see J. Bacinschi, *zur Pluralbildung im Italienischen und Rumänischen*, in *Archiv für das Studium der neueren Sprachen und Literaturen*, CXLIX, 258. See also Elise Richter in *Zs.*, XXXIII, 147; and C. H. Grandgent in *Mélanges Thomas*, 187.

declension forms as *le porti*, which occasionally turn up in the old language, are probably to be attributed to the infection of the long conflict between -*e* and -*i* in feminines of the third declension; some scholars, however, have regarded *porti* as a descendant of the ablative *portīs*. In Rumanian the substitution of -*i* for -*e* in third declension feminines was early completed, and the incursion of -*i* into the first declension went much further than in Italian.

In the present indicative of verbs, a regular phonetic process would have made the second and the third person singular identical in all conjugations but the fourth: *amo*, **ama, ama; vedo, *vede, vede; credo, crede, crede; odo, odi, ode* (the last two from *audīs, audīt*). In this emergency, speakers very early borrowed for the first conjugation the second person endings of the second and third and the fourth conjugations, and for the second conjugation the ending of the fourth, saying *tu ame* or *ami, tu vedi, tu crede, tu odi;* later they began to say *tu credi*, like *tu vedi*, and finally came the triumph of *tu ami*. This *ami*, once introduced into the indicative, made its way into the present subjunctive, where it supplanted original *ame* in all three persons, and turned *amen* to *amin*. The imperfect indicative and subjunctive, *cantava and *cantasse*, were subjected to the powerful influence of the perfect, *cantasti;* in the subjunctive the example of the perfect brought an -*i* even into the first person. The imperative of nearly all verbs shaped itself on the indicative.

1. A factor in the change to -*i* for the second person was the phonetic development of *das, stas* into *dai, stai*, with the imitative forms *fai, hai, sai, vai*.

2. The question has been raised whether, in the third declension, the Latin *i*- stem accusative plurals in -*īs* can have influenced the result. It seems unlikely that in current speech this type was sufficiently common to affect materially the Italian development.[1]

[1] A. Carnoy, *Le latin d'Espagne d'après les inscriptions*, 2d ed. 1906, p. 219, says the -*is* endings were never popular; but E. Bourciez, in

3. Some names of places end in an -*i* that comes from the Latin locative, the form being either that of the genitive singular or that of the ablative plural: *Agrigentī* > *Girgenti*, *Arīmĭnī* > *Rimini*, *Clūsī* > *Chiusi;* *Aquīs* > *Acqui*, *Parisiīs* > *Parigi* (whence *Tamigi?*), *T'arvisiīs* > *Trevigi;* but *Tĭbŭrī* > *Tivoli* is an ablative singular. Hence by analogy such names as *Capri*, *Luni*, *Semifonti* (also -*te*). *Firenze* is from locative *Florentiœ*.

4. Men's names in -*i* are probably for the most part of Sicilian origin (§ 50, 3): *Dionigi*, *Gottifredi* (= *Goffredo*), *Rinieri*, *Ruggeri* and *Geri;* so *Luigi* and *Gigi*, perhaps *Giovanni* (old *Gioanne*, *Giovanne*) and *Vanni*. For this last name, and some others, one must consider the possible influence of a genitive dependent on *chiesa* understood [1]: *(Chiesa)* S. *Pietri*, ' St. Peter's '; hence ' St. John's '; so Machiavelli's S. *Chimenti;* cf. *Buorgo Salorenzi* in Monaci, 20, line 27. Sicilian are also presumably *cavalieri*,[2] *sembianti*, *siri*, used as singulars. *Mestieri*, on the other hand, appears to be a genitive: *est ministerii* > *è mestieri*.

5. Lat. *ĭlle* became *ĭllī* under the influence of *quī*, and *ĭllī* became before a consonant *ęlli*, before a vowel *ęgli*. On the model of *egli* we have *quegli* as a masculine singular; then *questi* and *altri;* then various forms subsequently discarded, *ciascuni*, *iguali*,[3] *nissuni*, *qualcheduni*, *simili*, *stessi*, all masculine singular, and the feminine *la quali*. From *omnem* comes Old It. *onne*, which before a vowel became *onni*, *ogni*. *Pari* and *dispari* may be ablatives, preserved by the use of *parī* with *mente: parimente* (see § 55, 6). *Dieci*, for older *diece*, seems to have followed the lead of *venti* < *vigintī; undici*, *dodici*, etc., follow *dieci*. Ariosto regularly used *diece* and *due* as feminine forms of *dieci* and *duo; due* really was by origin a feminine form,*duœ*. Old It. *dui*, which goes back to V. L., substitutes the plural -*i* for the dual -*o; duo* is still a common form in Naples. The preference for *due* in the standard language is probably attributable to *tre*.

6. A number of common adverbs regularly inherited final *i: sīc* > *sì*, *illīc* > *lì*, *hīc* > *i*, *ecc' hīc* > *ci*, *eccu' hīc* > *qui*, proclitic *ĭbĭ* > *vi; ad satis* + *magis* > *assai; bocconi* is plural,[4] and so perhaps is *di fatti* < *de factĭs; quasi*, *fuori*, *ieri* probably retain the old Latin long *i* (QVASEI, *forĭs*,

Revue critique d'histoire et de littérature, XLI (1907), p. 221, declares they were extensively used in Gaul and Italy.
[1] See C. Salvioni in *Rom.*, XXXV, 205.
[2] For the ending -*iero*, -*iere*, see § 24, 2.
[3] *Iguali* belongs to east and south Tuscany.
[4] So *carponi*, (*in*)*ginocchioni*: see S. Pieri in *Zs.*, XXX, 337.

herī). From *eccu' ĭbĭ*, under the influence of *qui* and *vi*, we get *quivi;*
so from *ĭbĭ + i + vi* we have *ivi. Eccu' hīnce* and *illīnce*, influenced by
ci, give *quinci, linci;* hence *lici, laci* and *quici, quaci.* Thus -*i* came to
be felt as a distinctively adverbial ending (as was -*s* in French and Provençal), and was attached to other adverbs: *forse, forsi; ogge, oggi;
domane, domani; ante, anti; avante, avanti; anzi; tardi; volentieri;
parimente, parimenti,* whence *altrimenti* for *altramente.* In some of these
cases there were, no doubt, contributory causes: in *oggi* the example
of *dì*, in *volentieri* the analogy of *mestieri*, in *parimenti* the attraction of
the vowel of the second syllable (from *parī*); *anzi* is for **anza<antea,*
perhaps understood as *anz'a.* See W. Meyer-Lübke in *Zs. für französische Sprache,* LIII, 485.

56. Some peculiarly conditioned developments result in
irregular vowels other than -*i.* The ending -*unquam,* for
instance, gave regularly -*unqua,* which was generally superseded by -*unque*: *chiunqua, -que; ovunqua, -que; qualunqua,
-que;* on the other hand, we occasionally find *dunqua* for
dunque, whatever be the origin of this word. Possibly the
substitution of -*e* for -*a* is due to the thought of *qualche,* originally perhaps a syntactic combination: *qual che (sia).*

The pronoun *nulla* may have been affected by *ogna<omnia.*

Ultra>oltra, which becomes *oltre,* perhaps under the influence of *mentre<dum interim. Ore* for *ora* doubtless comes
from *tuttore,* a plural. *Prius* and *postea* made in V. L. an exchange of endings, which resulted in the pairs *prĭus *pria,
pŏstea *postius;* hence It. *pria, pŏscia,* and Perugian *poscio*
(cf. Fr. *puis*). *Prŏpe>pruovo* under the influence of the
synonyms *presso* and *vicino.*

Quōmŏdo, which came into great popular vogue, for some
reason lost its -*do* in late V. L.; *quōmo* then gave It. *como,*
which was kept in Siena and Lucca (cf. Spanish). In the
old language, especially in poetry, we find *como* often reduced to *com', con, co* (cf. § 51). A combination *com' e* (=
quomodo et, 'as also') was understood as one word, *come,*
which generally supplanted the original form. So Fr. *comme,*
Pr. *coma* started as *com a.*

1. A puzzling word is *anche*, with its cognates in the other languages. If the etymology tentatively proposed by W. Meyer-Lübke [1] is correct (interrogative *an* + *que*), or the one recently put forward by J. Brüch [2] (*denique* with a substitution of *a-* for *de-*), the *-e* is regular.

2. A few nouns have a peculiar *-e*. *Cŭlcĭta cŭlcĭtra* > *coltre* (of French origin?), also *colcitre*, both fem. sing. *Fĭmus* gives *fimo*, *fime*, perhaps with thought of *concime*, which also means 'manure.' Why is there a *pome* beside *pomo* < *pōmum*?

Intertonic Syllable

57. That is, the syllable that follows the secondary and precedes the primary accent. In the rhythm of the phrase, such a syllable has a position not unlike that of a final syllable, and is exposed to similar influences, but, having no inflectional value, its tendency to syncopation is stronger: *béllitátem* becomes *beltáde* just as *béllo témpo* becomes *bel tempo* (see § 51); but while *mátutínum* is reduced to *mattíno*, the phrase *fáte tútto* retains its intertonic vowel, which, with its inflectional function, is needed for intelligibility; so *cérebéllum* gives *cervéllo* while *sére bélle* neither loosens its *b* to *v* nor discards its *e*, because the collocation of intertonic *e* and *b* is in the one case permanent, in the other transient and fortuitous, and the *-e* of *sere* is the sign of the plural.

58. It is a general practice of language to drop such portions of familiar words as are not required to make them recognizable. This proclivity is much stronger in some peoples, in some social strata, in some epochs, than in others. Various factors contribute to this difference: habits of breathing, short or deep; indoor or outdoor life; education or ignorance; a careful or a heedless disposition.

In Tuscany (as in most places) there was evidently a conflict between the vulgar and the cultivated or clerical speech: the former, from late V. L. times to well along in the Italian period, inclines to drop the intertonic vowel, except under the

---

[1] *Romanische Grammatik*, III, 495.   [2] *Zs.*, XLI, 582.

influence of allied forms in which the vowel in question was regularly kept; the latter, being in close touch with Latin, likes to preserve the vowel in all words resembling Latin and even to restore it in words that had lost it. The language represents, then, a compromise between two opposite tendencies, the popular one prevailing in common words.

59. Examples of fall: *albergo* < Gothic **háribérgo, alcuno* < **áliqu' únus, beltá, bontá, cervello, cittá* < *cīvitātem, comenzare* < **cominitiáre* (from *initium*),[1] *costura* < *consūtūra, crollare* < **corrótuláre, destare* < **de-éxcitáre, dottare* < *dúbitáre, mattino, parlare* < **párauláre, sembrare* < *símiláre, strillare* < **stríduláre, umiltá, vedestu* = *vedesti tu.*

So it fares with the commonest futures in all the conjugations: *andrò, avrò, corrò* (from *cogliere*), *dirò, morrò, parrò, potrò, vedrò, verrò.* In the thirteenth and fourteenth centuries the syncopation was regular whenever the stem ended in *r: liberrà* for *libererà, sospirrà* from *sospirare.*

1. Intertonic *gli* or *glio* became *i: degli padri* > *dei padri, egli tace* > *ei tace, vuogli dare* > *vuoi dare, voglio fare* > Old It. *voi fare, figlio mio* > *fi' mio.* Thus we have *bei, coi, dai, quai, quei,* etc. Then all these diphthongs, standing just before the stressed syllable, in Florentine regularly lost their *i* (§ 42): *de' Medici, e' parla, vo' dire.*

The *gli* in such cases first developed before a vowel, and subsequently was used also before a consonant: *delli anni* > *degli anni,* then, instead of *delli mesi,* presumably *degli mesi,* whence *dei mesi, de' mesi.* So *elli ode* > *egli ode,* then *egli dice* > *ei dice, e' dice* (although in modern literary Italian the older *egli* has prevailed).

2. For a change of *a* to *e* between *i* and a consonant (*siano* > *sieno*), with a subsequent shift of accent (*sièno*), see § 204, 2.

60. Examples of vowels kept by analogy: *aiutare* (beside *aitare atare*) < *ádjutáre,* by the influence of *aiúta* < *adjūtat; coglierò* and *correrò* (beside *corrò*), thanks to *cógliere* and *córrere; disonore* (beside *disnore, desnore*), *onorato* and *onorevole* (beside *orrato* and *orrevole*), after *onóre; dondolare,* following

1 With a change of ending (*-iciare* for *-itiare*) this verb became also *comenciare* > *cominciare,* which prevailed.

dóndola; udirò (beside *udrò*), after *udire*. So *cálzatúra, cóntadíno, fínirò, fiórentíno, póssedére, rímanére, tróvatóre,* etc.

1. Adverbs in *-mente*, originally two words, were treated as such: *bélla ménte, bréve ménte*. But final *e* of the adjective has fallen after *l* or *r*: *facilmente, regolarmente*. Cf. § 51, end. Nouns in *-mento* apparently followed the model of adverbs in *-mente*: *inténdi-ménto*.

2. Evidently the names of the days of the week were regarded as two-word phrases: *lūnæ dīe* > *lúne-dì, Martis dīe* > *márte-dì, Jŏvis dīe* > *gióve-dì, Vĕnĕris dīe* > **vénere-dì,* then *vénerdì* (§ 51, end). *Mercŭrī dīe,* under the influence of *Vĕnĕris dīe,* became **Mércŭris* (or *Mércŏris*) *dīe* and by dissimilation **Mérculis dīe,* which gave *mércole-dì;* it is odd that the *-e* should not have fallen as in *venerdì*.

61. Examples of vowels preserved by Latin influence: *cápitáno* beside *cattano* from *capitanus; benedetto; dómeneddío* < *Domine Deus,* whence *Iddío; nobilità* beside *nobiltà;* etc.

62. When the vowel was preserved or restored, either through analogy or through Latin influence, it tended to become *e* before *r, i* before other consonants; *anderò* for *andrò, canterò* for **cantarò,* etc.; *venderò,* etc.; *comperare* < *comprare* < *comparare, sceverare* < *scevrare* < *separare; coperire* for *coprire* < *cooperire; giocheria* < *jocus* + *arius* + *-ia, libreria* < *lĭbrarius* + *-ia; laberinto* < *labyrinthus, margherita* < *margarīta; biasimare* < *biasmare* < *blasphemare, caricare* < *carcare* < **carricare* (from *carrus*), *coricare* < *corcare* **colcare* < *collocare, desinare* < *desnare* < *dis(je)junare, manicare* < **mancare* < *manducare, manimettere* for *manomettere* (Latin *manu-*), *neghittoso* < **neglectosus, nevicare* < **nivicare, ubbidire* < *oboedire*.

In Siena and Lucca *a* was preferred before *r*: *cantarò, vendarò*. Both in Siena and Lucca and in Florence, however, the fourth conjugation kept its *i*: *sentirò*.

An extra vowel was inserted in *sopperire* < *supplēre*.

1. The choice of *e* when *r* follows, and *i* elsewhere, is probably a phenomenon of association, *e* being in the whole mass of words the commonest intertonic vowel before *r, i* the commonest before other con-

sonants. The Sienese preference for *a* may show the assimilative power of the first conjugation or simply the natural tendency of *r* to open a preceding vowel.

63. Pure book-words generally preserve as closely as possible the Latin spelling, *æ* and *oe* becoming *e*, *y* becoming *i*, *u* appearing as *o* or *u*: *Amarílli*<*Amaryllis*, Old It. *cómedia* <*comoedia, mánoscrítto, órológio, páleógrafo, póliglótto, pórtuláca.*

Penult

64. Here, as in the intertonic syllable, there was a difference between popular and cultivated speech, although the incentive to omission was not so strong in the penult as in the syllable between accents. The vulgar tendency to suppress the vowel goes back, in the main, to the Latin period and lasts only into the very first stage of Italian; it is generally confined, moreover, to a vowel in one of several specific consonant settings. The cultivated taste was inclined to keep all the vowels, and began, early in the development of Italian, a process of restoring vowels that had been dropped. Both types of pronunciation are represented in the stock of the present standard language.

1. In some words in which the vowel might otherwise have fallen it seems to have been kept for morphological reasons: so in many infinitives, as *scrivere*, and in such perfect forms as *diedero*.

2. In a few Italian words the syncopation is disguised by subsequent metathesis of a consonant: *fabula*>*fabla* (cf. Sp. *hablar*)>*flabla*> *flaba*>*fiaba;* so *pópulus* (' poplar ')>*poplus*>*poppio*>*pioppo;* so perhaps *cŏma *cŏmula*>*comla*>*clomla*>*cloma*>*chioma.*

65. The vowel positions that invite syncopation are these: (*a*) between labial and consonant, as in *cŏmĭtem*>It. *conte;* (*b*) between consonant and liquid, as in *ŏcŭlus*>*oclus;* (*c*) between liquid and consonant, as in *ērĭgit*>It. *erge;* (*d*) between *s* and a voiceless stop, as in *pŏsĭtus*>*postus;* (*e*) between two dentals, as in *nĭtĭdus*>It. *netto.* These classes will now be discussed.

1. A few sporadic cases do not enter into any of these categories: *anima > anima alma,* while there was no fall in the similar word *Girolamo; maríttima > maremma,* whereas the penult vowel stays in *attimo < atomon, ottimo, ultimo,* etc.; *pantĭcem > pancia,* but cf. *piedica, sedici.*

66. In common words in V. L., the vowel tended to fall between a labial (*p, b, m, v*) and any consonant: *avĭca > auca > ǫca, cŏmpŭtus > cǫnto, crĕpĭtus > crĕtto, dēbĭta > dĕtta, dŏmĭnus dŏmnus > dǫnno, dŭbĭto > dǫtto, hŏspĭtem > ǫste, navĭtat > *nautat > *nǫtat?> nuota, parabula > *paraula > parǫla, rapĭdus > ratto, *vŏlvĭtus > vǫlto.*

1. A good many words that seem popular keep the vowel: *agĭbĭlis > agĕvole,* etc.; *arbŏrem > albero, cŭbĭtus* (+ *cŭmbere) > gǫmito, *lĕvĭtum* (for *levatum) > lĭevito, mespĭlum > nĕspolo, *nĭvĭcat > nĕvica, nūbĭlus > nuvolo, pĭper *pĭpĕrem > pĕvere* (cf. *pĕpe < pĭper), rōbur *rōbĕrem > rǫvere, sūber *sūbĕrem > suvero sughero, thÿmĭnus > tĕmolo, tĕpĭdus > tiĕpido, ūvŭla > ugola, hŏmĭnes > uǫmini.* Some words have double forms: *fabula > *faula > fola* beside *fiaba* (§ 64, 2) and the bookish *favola.*

2. Other words that keep the vowel are probably late or learned: *amabile,* etc.; *possibile,* etc.; *amÿlum > amido; comico, debito, dubito, favola, fǫmite < fōmĭtem, frivolo < frĭvŏlus, rapido, ripido, stipite, strĕpito, tavola, vimine < vīmen, vǫmita,* etc.

67. In common words in V. L., the vowel fell between any consonant and a liquid: *altera altra > altra, aspera aspra > aspra, βούτυρον > burro* (why *rr?), cūna *cūnula *cūlla* (cf. *corōna corōlla) > culla, ŏculus ŏclus > ǫcchio, spathula *spatla > spalla, spĕculum spĕclum > spĕcchio, spīna spīnula *spīnla > spilla, *strīdulat *strīdlat > strilla, tŏllere *tŏlre > tǫrre, vĕtulus vĕclus > vĕcchio, vigĭlat *vĭglat > vĕgghia.* In this last case the *i* of the penult must have fallen very early, before the palatalization of *g. Altra, aspra* are good classical forms.

1. It did not fall, however, if the first consonant was a palatal: *cóll'gere > cogliere, ér'gere > ergere, lĕggere > leggere, plangere > piangere, sŏcĕrus > suocero, tollere + coll'gere > togliere.* See § 71. *Corre* for *cogliere* follows the analogy of *torre < tollere* (§ 67).

2. The law of the fall between consonant and liquid apparently ceased to operate before the end of the Latin period, and failed to affect many words; these kept their vowel even in Italian, having preserved it either through learned influence or because of late introduction into common speech: *arbŏrem* > *albero*, *cĭthăra* > *cętera*, *chŏlĕra* > *cǫllera*, *dactўlus* > *dattero*, **d'ŭndŭlat* > *dǫndola*, *hĕdĕra* > *ęllera*, *facula* (+ *flamma*) > *fiaccola*, *Fœsulæ* > *Fiesole*, *fragum* + *ula* > *fragola*, *mūgio* *mūgĭlo *mūgŭlo > *mugolo*, *pĕcŏra* > *pęcora*, *pĭcula* > *pęgola*, *spīculum* > *spigolo*, etc. Some words existed in both shortened and unsyncopated form: *lĕpŏrem* > *lępre lievere lievore*, *macula* > *macchia macola*, *ŏpĕra* > *ǫvra ǫpera*, *tēgula* > *tęgghia* ('pan') *tęgola* ('tile'). A few popular forms attested for V. L. were not preserved in Italian: *anglus*, cf. *angolo*; *maniplus*, cf. *manipolo*.

68. Throughout the V. L. and the earliest Italian period, in common words, the vowel fell between a liquid and any consonant: *accŏrrĭgo > *accǫrgo*, *calĭdus caldus* > *caldo*, *carrĭcat > *carca*, *clērĭca* > *chięrica chięrca* (§ 25, 2), *ērĭgit* > *ęrge* (§ 25, 11, end), ἔρημος > *ęrmo*, *ex* + *cŏrrĭgit* > *scǫrge*, *fallĭta > *falta*, *fĭlĭcem* > *fęlce*, *īlĭcem* *ēlĭcem (or *ilĭcem: § 28, 2) > *ęlce*, κόλαφος > *cǫlpo*, *larĭdum lardum* > *lardo*, *mĕrĭto mĕrto* > *męrto*, *ōrulum* > *ǫrlo*, πολύπους > *pǫlpo*, *pŏrrĭgo* > *pǫrgo*, *salĭcem* > *salce*, *sĭlĭcem* > *sęlce*, *sŏlĭdus sŏldus* > *sǫldo*, *sōrĭcem* > *sǫrce*, *varĭcat* > *valica varca*, *vĭrĭdis vĭrdis* > *vęrde*.

On the model of *calĭdus caldus* was formed from *frīgĭdus* a *frĭgdus* (with unexplained *ĭ*); this syncopation occurred earlier than the palatalization of *g*. From *sǫrci*, plural of *sǫrce*, were formed apparently the new singulars *sorcio* and *sorco*.

1. In many words the vowel was kept by learned influence: *angelico*, *cattolico*, *colica*, *corrigo*, *navigo*, *orafo* < *aurifex*, *orrido*, *pallido*, *solito*.

A very few apparently popular words preserved the vowel: *fŭlĭca* > *fǫlaga*, σέλινον > *sędano*.

69. Between *s* and a voiceless stop, in common words, a vowel probably began to fall in V. L. and the tendency to disappear continued through the transition period: -*assētis* *-*assĭtis* (§ 10, 6, end) > -*aste* (so -*este*, -*iste*), *persĭca* *pessĭca > *pęsca*, *pŏsĭtus pŏstus* > *pǫsto* (for *ǫ* see § 31, 1). There seems to be no example of *s-p*.

1. In some words learned influence maintained the vowel: *fisico, musica.*

70. There seems to have been a tendency, perhaps going back to V. L. or to transition times, to drop a vowel between two dentals (*t, d, n*): Frankish *hauniþa* > *ǫnta, nĭtĭdus* > *nętto, pūtĭdus* > *putto,* *vanĭto > *vanto.* Yet several apparently popular words keep the vowel: *anătem anĭtem* > *anatra anitra,* *andĭtus > *andito,* *rĕtĭna > *rędina.*

71. When a vowel stood between a palatal (*c', g', y*) and any other consonant, it seems regularly to have maintained itself, although some striking cases appear to point in the direction of fall when the palatal was intervocalic: *fracĭdus* > *fracido fradicio, frīgere* > *friggere, bajulus* > *baggiolo; placĭtum* > *piato, farragĭnem* + *ferrum* > *ferrana, bajula* > *balia.*

1. Let us first consider the cases of apparent fall. *Dire* and *fare,* beside Old It. *dicere* and *facere,* do not count, because they come from V. L. *dire and **fare,* derived from *dīc* and *fac* under the influence of *audire* and *dare. Dure,* beside *ducere,* is built similarly on *dūc,* but became *durre* under the influence of *tǫrre* (§ 67). *Dicere, facere, ducere* were popular forms in Old It.; to be sure, they may have been reconstructed from *dice,* etc., but nothing forbids our regarding them as direct descendants of the Latin infinitives. *Trarre* comes from *trahere* influenced by It. *torre,* while the representative of V. L. *tragere is *traggere. Cǫrre* and *scęrre* and *sciǫrre,* for *cǫgliere* and *scęgliere* and *sciǫgliere,* likewise show imitation of *torre.* The imperatives *accòlo, tòti* (§ 35) are probably reduced not from *accǫglilo, tǫgliti,* but from *accoi-lo, toi-ti,* to match the infinitives *accǫrre, tǫrre,* the *accoi* and *toi* being modeled on *fai* < *fac, dui* < *duc, di* < *dic* (cf. *di* = *dici*). *Coto,* ' thought,' is a post-verbal noun from *cotare* < *coitare (§ 42) < **cójitáre cōgitāre.*

The rest of the examples are probably foreign. *Balia,* in its older form *baila* (§ 35, 1) from *bajula,* may have been borrowed from Provençal. Possibly *madia* (from *magida*) represents a dialect borrowing (cf. Sic. *maidda*). *Frale, futa* come from *fragilis,* *fugita through O. Fr. *fraile, fuite. Ferrana* may come from a dialect (?Sardinian) *ferraina* < *farraginem. Piato, vuoto* (§ 24, 5) seem to be taken from N. It. forms *piaito* < *placĭtum, vuoito* < **vŏcĭtus.*

2. On the other side may be arrayed more numerous examples, few of which can be dismissed as bookish: *acero* <*acer, acido, ácino* <*acĭnus, agnolo* <*angĕlus, bággiolo* <*bajulus, búcine* <*būcĭna, cęcino* <*cўcĭnus cycnus, cǫgliere* < **coll'gere, cuocere* <*cŏcĕre cŏquĕre, Diecimo, durácine* < *duracĭnus, facile, figgere* <*fīgĕre* (and six others in *-ggere*), *fiǫcine* < *flŏces* + ending, *fradicio fracido* <*fracĭdus, giugnere* <*jŭngĕre* (and ten others in *-gnere*), *gracile, lęcito* <*lĭcĭtum, mácine* <*machĭna, mucido, muggine* <*mūgĭlus, nuǫcere* < **nŏcĕre nŏcĕre, piantaggine* (and nine others in *-ggine* <*-gĭnem), ręcere* <*rēĭcĕre, scęgliere* < **ex-ēl'gĕre, sollęcito, sudicio sucido* <*sūcĭdus, suǫcero* <*sŏcĕrus.*

72. At an early period of Italian there was a tendency to insert a vowel between two consonants one of which was a liquid, and also between *s* and *m,* perhaps owing to an impression that proparoxytones, being closer to Latin usage, were more elegant. The vowel inserted before *r* was *e,* before other consonants *i* (cf. § 62, 1, and § 73): *cętera cętra* < *cĭthăra, fǫdero* <Ger. *fōdr, gambero *gambro* <*gammarus cammarus, maghero magro* <*macrum, mitera mitra* <*mĭtra, ricǫvero ricǫvro* <*recŭpero, scęvero scęvro* <*sēpăro, sgǫmbero sgǫmbro* < Low Lat. *combrus; biasima biasma* <*blásphēmat, carico carco* < **carrico, chięrica chięrca* <*clērica, cǫrico cǫrco* <*cŏllŏco, fantasima fantasma* <*phantasma, męrito męrto* <*mĕrĭtum, pǫllice* <*pŏllĭcem, salice salce* <*salĭcem, sirima* <*syrma, sǫrice sǫrce* < *sōrĭcem, spasimo spasmo* <*spasmus, tǫssico tǫsco* <*tŏxĭcum, valica varca* <*varĭcat.*

Of course it is sometimes impossible to tell whether a given form belongs to this class or to the following category.

73. When the vowel was preserved from the beginning, it usually kept close to its original form, *u* becoming *o,* and *y* becoming *i: ǫrfano, cǫllera, subito, pęcora; rǫtolo* <*rŏtulus, pǫlipo* <*pŏlўpus.* In book-words of the purest type, even *u* is unchanged: *sillaba, paręntesi, nǫbile, sincope, cǫpula, analisi.*

In many cases, however, when a word came into general use, its vowel was altered, probably by auditive association with other words of similar, but not identical, termination.

Before a nasal or a guttural, *a* is common, following the type of *ŏrfano, mŏnaco: attamo attimo < atŏmon, cŏfano < cŏphĭnus, crŏnaca crŏnica < chrŏnĭca, fŏlaga < fŭlĭca, giŏvane* (also *giŏvine*) *< jŭvĕnem, Girŏlamo < Hierŏnўmus, indaco indico < indĭcus, pampano < pampĭnus, sĕdano < σέλινον, sindaco < syndĭcus,* etc. Before *r,* we find *e,* after the fashion of *credere, pŏvero,* etc.: *albero < arbŏrem, dattero < dactўlus,* etc. Before *l,* we have *o,* as in *pĕntola, ragnolo,* etc.: *agĕvole* (and others in *-ĕvole < -ĭbĭlis), nĕspolo < mĕspĭlum, nuvolo < nūbĭlus, sĕmola < sĭmĭla, utole utile < ūtĭlis.* Cf. § 62, 1, and § 72. For other alterations, such as *ŏrafo < aurĭfex,* there are no doubt special analogies.

1. *Undici, dodici,* etc., may have felt the influence of the numerous plurals in *-ici,* such as *cŏmici, fradici, pratici, salici, sudici,* etc. Or it may be that in these words and some others, such as *giŏvini,* the penult vowel was harmonized with the plural ending. For *giŏvine* one might think also of the attraction of *grandine, fulmine.*

2. Siena and Arezzo prefer *a* before *r* (cf. § 62) ,as in *albaro, chiĕdare; lĕttara.*

3. Pisa and Lucca have *ul* for *ol: discepuli, Napuli, populo.*

74. In final *-ŭa,* a *v* is generated between the *u* and the *a*: *contĭnua > contĭnova, Gĕnua > Gĕnova, Patavium = *Padua > Padova, vĭdua > vĕdova.* So *contĭnovo, continovamente. Mŏr-tuus* had become *mŏrtus* in V. L.; hence *mŏrta.*

CONSONANTS

75. Consonants are sounds produced either by closing some part of the vocal passage and then opening it with a faint pop, or by forcing the current of air through a channel so narrow as to cause audible friction. The result in each case is modified by the resonance of chambers in the mouth or in the mouth and nose. Some consonants are made with the glottis wide open, as in breathing, others with the cords pulsating close together, as for vowels.

Of the consonants with which we shall have mainly to deal, the following are voiceless, or surds, being made without vocal vibration: *p, t, t', k', k, s, š, h*. The others are voiced consonants, or sonants: *b* is the sonant corresponding to *p*, *d* the sonant of *t*, *g* the sonant of *k*, *z* the sonant of *s*, *ž* the sonant of *š*. The signs *ž* and *š* are used to denote respectively the sounds of *si* in *vision* and *sh* in *ship*.

P, b, t, d, t', d', k', g', k, g are stops: that is, they are made by stopping the current of air that issues from the glottis. For *p, b* the stoppage is made by contact of the two lips; for *t, d*, by contact of the front rim of the tongue with the teeth or gums; for *k, g*, by contact of the back of the tongue with the soft palate. If *k, g* be carried forward to the hard palate, by lifting the middle instead of the back of the tongue, we get *k', g'*, as in *keep, geese;* if we draw them still further to the front, retaining the same formation with the point of the tongue down, we reach a point where they sound closer to *t, d* than to *k, g*, and then they may be called *t', d'*, which some speakers use in *itch, edge*. *K', g', t', d'* are called specifically " palatal "; but Latin and Italian *t, d* are in a way palatal also, as compared with English, the upper surface of the tongue being convex, although the actual contact is made at the teeth.

If while forming *b, d, d', g* we drop the soft palate and allow the air to escape through the nose, we get respectively *m, n, n', ŋ; ŋ* being the sound of English *ng* in *song*, and *n'* that of French and Italian *gn* in *agneau, sogno*. These are nasals.

Starting with *d*, draw in the sides of the tongue, allowing the air to escape between the two rows of back teeth on either side (or on one side), and the result is *l*. Similarly from *d'* one gets *l'*, the sound of Italian *gli* in *figlio*. Taking again the *d* position, and holding the thin rim of the tongue very loosely against the gums, so that it flutters in the current of breath, we obtain *r*. It will be noted that *d, l, r* are in formation very close to one another; they are not infrequently interchanged.

Now, instead of making a close contact of the lips, as for *b*, bring them loosely together, so that the air buzzes through, and one has Spanish *v*, or *β*, the bilabial fricative. If the loose touch is made, not between the two lips, but between the lower lip and the upper teeth, the sound is the dentilabial or labiodental *v*, which we have in Italian and in English; the corresponding surd is *f*. Air forced out between the upper front teeth or through the little notches at their edge produces þ and ð, the English *th* of *thin* and *then*. A narrow channel made between the rim of the tongue and the upper front teeth gives the sibilants *s* and *z*. A much wider channel a little further back produces š and ž. A *g'* formed with imperfect closure is the *y* of *ye*, whose surd mate is the *ch* of German *ich*. So a *k* made without full contact is χ, or *ch* in German *ach;* the corresponding sonant may be written γ. *H* is mainly the hiss of air passing through a partially closed but not quivering glottis. The simultaneous utterance of γ and *β* gives *w*, as in *woo*, which has two narrow passages, one in the back of the mouth and one at the lips.

76. Not all these sounds existed in Latin. The classic tongue of the later Republic had the stops *p, b, t, d, k', g', k, g,* the nasals *m, n, ŋ,* the so-called "liquids" *l* and *r*, the fricatives *f, y, w, s, h.* There seems to have been no *z*, the letter *s* between vowels being pronounced voicelessly as in English *mason:* so *nasus, causa.* Early Latin *z* had long since become *r: *flosem > florem.* The *f* was probably bilabial, but became dentilabial under the Empire: so earlier *comfluo* came to be sounded *confluo.* The *w* was of course written *u*, as the *y* was written *i: uado, amaui; iocus, maior. H*, although purists tried to keep it, had vanished from the speech of the people: so *prehendo* had become *prēndo* and *cohors* was pronounced **cōrs;* there is no trace of any Latin *h* in Romance utterance except a school pronunciation of intervocalic *h* as *k*, which in Italy still persists (*mihi* = *michi*, *nihil* = *nichil*). The sound *ŋ* was given to an *n* before *k* or *g*, as in *longus* (compare English *longest*). The dentals were formed with the top surface of the tongue arched slightly up, not hollowed as in English; the *l*, particularly after a consonant, must have had a distinctly palatal quality: *clarus*, almost *cl'arus*.

K and *g* followed by *i* or *e* were doubtless already drawn forward into the *k'* and *g'* position, *feci* and *gentem* being sounded *fec'i* and *g'ente*.

Final *m* and *n*, except in monosyllables, had generally ceased to be heard in popular speech. Indeed, the fall of -*m* must have begun very early, since -*m* does not prevent elision of the preceding vowel in Latin poetry. *N* before *s*, as we have already seen (§ 16), was regularly silent, having probably vanished through nasalization of the preceding vowel (the soft palate being prematurely lowered), as in French; but the vowel must quickly have lost its nasal quality: *censor* > *cēsor*, *consul* > *cōsul*.

R, in certain words, was early assimilated to a following *s*: *dŏrsum* > *dŏssum*, *deōrsum* > **deōssum*, *sŭrsum* > *sŭssum*, *retrōrsum* > *retrōssum*. Then, early in the Empire, *ss* after a long vowel was reduced to *s*, and **deōssum*, **sŭssum*, **retrōssum* became **deosu*, *susu*, **retrosu*, while *dŏssum*, with its short *o*, retained its *ss*.

Qu and *gu* before *u* or *o* had probably begun to be sounded *k* and *g*, the *w* element fusing with the similar vowel that followed: *coquus* > *cocus*, *distinguo* > **distingo*. This simplification was carried through in the Empire.

The group *ks* (written *x*), either at this time or soon after, began to lose its *k* element before a consonant, as in *sextus* > *sestus*, and at the end of a word of more than one syllable: *senex* > *senes*; but *sex*.

Final *s* was always rather weak in Rome. It sometimes did not count in verse: e.g., *infantibu' parvis* in Lucretius.

77. Some rather important developments occurred during the first centuries of our era. Latin *w* (written *u*) became *β*, and Latin *b* between vowels also became *β*, so that the middle consonants of *vivit* and *bibit*, for instance, were identical. This happened probably by the first century. Then any *β* followed by stressed *u* or *o* seems to have been absorbed by that vowel, in some regions, but not in all: *pavonem* > It. *pavone paone*. Moreover, the groups *aβu aβa, aβi* before a consonant were in popular usage condensed into *au: fabŭla* > **faula* > It. *fǫla, gabăta* > **gauta* > It. *gǫta, amavit* > *amaut* > It. *amò* or *amdo, avica* > *auca* > It. *ǫca*. From *fabula* we have three forms, *fola, fiaba, favola*, representing three chronological or social strata.

An *iβu* or *iβi* before a consonant apparently became *iu* in some dialects but not in others: *rivus* > *rius rivus* > It. *rio rivo, nativus* > It. *natio nativo, civitatem* > Sp. *ciudad* It. *cittá; finivit* > **finiut* > It. *finìo* (*finì* is from **finìt = finìit*).

A new *w* later develops out of unaccented *u* before a vowel: *habuit* is pronounced *aβwit, eccum ìsta = *eccu-ìsta* > It. *quęsta*. This *eccum*, a synonym of *ecce*, was much used in Vulgar Latin as a prefix to demonstratives. Cf. § 9, 2 and § 37, 1.

78. Latin had a *y* sound, written *i* (in later ages *j*): as in *jam, pejor*. In the vulgar tongue the prevalence of this consonant was greatly increased by the development of other sounds or groups into *y*.

An unaccented *i* or *e* in hiatus lost its syllabic value and thus became *y* (cf. § 9, 2 and § 37, 1): *diŭrnus* > **djurnus, fīlia* > **filja, ratiōnem* > **ratjone, deorsum* > **djosu* (§76, *R*), *eāmus* > **jamus, tĕneat* > **tenjat*.

Later the group *dy* between vowels, while preserved for a while in school usage, became *y* in popular speech: *mĕdius* > **mejus* or **medjus* > It. *meio* or *mezzo, radius* > **rajus* or **radjus* > It. *raggio* or *razzo*. Late formations had the *dy*

pronunciation: e.g., *olĭdiare (<olĭdus<olēre) = *oledjare
>It. olezzare.[1] Cf. § 106. Initial dy seems to have been re-
duced to y: as diŭrnum *djurnu *jurnu>It. giọrno.
*Gy, too, was reduced to y: as *Georgius (= Georgicus)>
Jorjus>It. Giorgio, fageum>*faju>It. faggio.

Moreover, any g' (§ 76, K) regularly opened into y, which
developed like original y, unless it was intervocalic and the
following i or e was stressed, in which case the y was generally
absorbed by that vowel: gĕlu>*jelu>It. gielo then gẹlo,
gypsum>*jissu *jessu>It. gesso, argentum>*arjentu>It.
argento and ariento; pagensis (<pagus)>*pajésis>It. paése,
magĭstrum > *majéstru > It., maéstro, regīna > *rejína > It.
reína (regina is learned). For lg', ng', rg', however, see § 130.

But that is not all. The Greek ʒ, however it may have been
pronounced on its own soil, was sounded dz in the Roman
schools, while popular usage, in borrowed Greek words, made
it dy: βαπτίζειν>baptizare = *baptedzare or *baptedjare>
It. battezzare or batteggiare, ʒῆλος>zelosus = *dzelosus or
*djelosus>It. zeloso or geloso. It is extremely probable that
this dy, like native Latin dy, passed through a stage of simple
y: just as mŏdius>*mojus>It. moggio (cf. majus>maggio),
so -ίʒω, which came to be a fairly common ending in late
Vulgar Latin, was popularly treated as -edjo, then as -ejo, then
in Italian became -eggio or -eio (also -eo and -io[2]). For the
y stage in Latin there is considerable direct evidence.[3]

79. The ʒ, just discussed, was not the only Greek consonant foreign to the Romans. The explosives, θ, φ, χ, consisted,
in Classic times, of a stop followed by a strong puff, much
as in the Irish pronunciation of tin, pin, kin. Borrowed Greek

[1] Cf. A. J. Carnoy, *Some Obscurities in the Assibilation of ti and di
before a Vowel in Vulgar Latin*, in *Transactions of the American Philological Association*, XLVII (1916), 145.

[2] See E. G. Parodi, *Il tipo italiano aliáre aléggia*, in *Miscellanea
linguistica in onore di G. Ascoli*, 1901.

[3] See C. H. Grandgent, *An Introduction to Vulgar Latin*, p. 141.

words containing θ or χ were written by careful spellers with
th or *ch*, but were evidently pronounced by the masses with
Latin *t* or *c*: θύρσος > *thyrsus* = **tursus* > It. *torso*, χορδή >
chorda = **corda* > It. *corda*. In early medieval schools, θ
came to be pronounced *ts*: hence It. *zio* from θεῖος. As to
φ, whose pronunciation early in our era changed to *f*, we find
in borrowed words two types, according to the date of borrowing; early loans have *p*, late ones *f* (generally spelled *ph*):
πορφύρα > *purpŭra* > It. *pórpora*, φάντασμα > *phantasma* > It.
fantásima, φάσηλος > *fasēlus fasĕŏlus* > It. *fagiŏlo*.

The Greek κ, whose explosion must have been very faint,
evidently sounded to the Roman ear between *k* and *g*, and
the Romans reproduced it by both these consonants in their
loan words: κάμμαρος > *cammărus gammărus* > It. *gámbero*,
κυβερνῶ > *guberno* > It. *governo*, κατά > *cata* > It. *cata-* (in
cataúno), κρύπτη > It. *grotta*. So π doubtless lay between
Latin *p* and *b*: πύξος > *buxus* > It. *bosso*, πυξίδα (from πυξίς)
> It. *bússola*, πατάσσειν > It. *batassare*. There seems to be
no evidence of a similar confusion for τ.

80. Popular Latin and early Romance took from Germanic
dialects a number of words which had a few consonants de-
manding special notice.

German *b*, it would seem, did not become *v* between vowels:
rauba > *rọba*, *raubon* > *rubare*. German *k* apparently was not
palatalized in Italy by a following front vowel. Longobard
skĭna? > It. *schiena;* cf. Lat. *scœna* > It. *scena*. *G*, however,
seems to have succumbed to *i* in Old High German *gīga*, It.
giga. Examples are very scarce.

Germanic ᵽ, or *th*, was rendered by *t*: so *trescare* corresponding to Gothic *thriscan*.

W, probably toward the end of the Vulgar Latin period
became *gw* through reinforcement of the velar element,
which led to a momentary closing of the narrow passage in
the rear of the mouth (see § 75, end): *wardan* > It. *guardare*,
warjan > It. *guarire*, *wīsa* > It. *guisa*. This *gw* pronunciation

was for some reason substituted for β in a few Latin words beginning with *v*: *vagīna* > It. *guaina*, *vadum* > It. *guado*, *vŭlpes* > It. *golpe* (where the *w* has been absorbed by the *o*). Occasionally one can plausibly conjecture contamination of the Latin with a particular Germanic word: *vastare* + *wōstjan* > It. *guastare*.

Borrowings from Germanic took place at a time when Latin popular speech had no *h*. Germanic *h*, then, was something new. At the beginning of words it was simply omitted, except in northern Gaul, where it remained as *h* until modern times: Frankish *hardjan* > Fr. *hardir* > It. *ardire*, *hauniþa* > Fr. *honte* > It. *onta*, *hanka* > Fr. *hanche* and It. *anca*. Between vowels, in Italy, it either fell or was replaced by *cc*: *spehon* > *spiare*, *jehan* > *gecchire*. The group *ht* became *tt*: *slahta* > It. *schiatta*.

81. The Latin, then, which we must take as our basis, had these consonants: *b*, β (from *v* and from intervocalic *b*), *d*, *f*, *g*, *k*, *k′*, *l*, *m*, *n*, *p*, *r*, *s*, *t*, *w* (derived from Lat. *u*; or contained in Lat. *qu* and *gu* followed by a vowel other than *u* or *o*; or contained in V. L. *gw* from Ger. *w*), and *y* (representing *e* or *i* in hiatus, *g′*, *j*, *dj*, *gj*, ʒ).

The history of the consonants differs according to their position in the word, or in the speech unit that was felt to be a word. We shall consider first the initial consonants, next the final, then the medial. Single consonants, moreover, must be distinguished from consonant groups.

Generally speaking, consonants tend to remain unchanged at the beginning of a word (where the speaker's attention is concentrated), to disappear at the end (where attention is relaxed), to be influenced by environment in the middle.

INITIAL

82. Under initial consonants we must include those which, after a recognized prefix, began the second part of a compound: such are the *b* of *ribattere*, the surd *s* of *disegno*.

Single Initial Consonants

83. Among the labials we note the change of β to *v*, as in *vento, voce*. The V. L. *gw* from Ger. *w* remains unaltered, as in Longobard *waidanjan* > It. *guadagnare:* see § 80, *W*.

1. Many southern dialects change initial β, not to *v*, but to *b*. A few such forms have crept into literature, as *boglio* for *voglio, botare* (Machiavelli) for *votare*. *Boce* and *bociare*, which seem to be really Tuscan, were probably influenced by *bocca*.
Why should we have *gomire* (Abruzzi) and *bomire* from *vŏmĕre*?
Why *avvoltoio* from *vŭltŭrius*? Analogy of *avvolgere* (spiral flight)?
Pipistrello is an onomatopoetic word, with *vespertilio* as a basis.

2. *Nẹspolo* < *mespĭlus* shows an early cross with some unknown word; the *n* is found in other languages. *Nicchio* < *mītŭlus* has apparently combined with *nicchiare*, a derivative of *nīdus*.

3. For *b* from Greek π, see § 79.

84. The dentals regularly do not change; but *l*, *n*, *d*, suffer a few accidents. *Labellum* > *avello, lauri bacca* > *orbacca, lusciniola* (from *luscinia*) > *lusignolo usignolo*, the *l* being taken for the definite article; cf. Fr. *lendemain* for *l'endemain*. So in *alauda* (+ *-ŭla*) > *lodola* the *a-* is lost by mistaken division of article and noun. By false separation from the *indefinite* article, Persian *narang'* becomes *narancio arancio* (cf. Fr. *orange*) and *Nanchino* gives *anchino* (' Nankeen cambric '), as in English *a nadder* becomes *an adder*. Confusion of *d-* with the preposition *di* accounts for *amoscino* ('Damascus plum ') from *Damascenus*.
S, which ordinarily maintains itself (*sapere, sè, sotto*), becomes in some words *š*, in others *ts: salīva* > *scialiva, separare* > *sceverare, sīmia* > *scimmia, sĭmplex* *sĭmplus* > *scẹmpio, sipare* > *scipare, supare* > *sciupare; saburra* > *zavọrra, sambū-cus* > *sambuco zambuco, sŭfflare* + *sībilare* > *zufolare, sŭlfur* > *zọlfo*, Ger. *suppa* > *zuppa*.

1. From *simia, saburra, sulfur* the forms are peculiar in Spanish also: *jimia, zahorra, azufre*. For a suggestion that *zappa, zoccolo, zolfo, zufolo*

may be of Faliscan origin, see *Zs.*, XL, 647. *Scirocco, sciroppo* come from Arabic words that begin with *š*. For *zampogna* see § 45, 5.

2. Vulgar Tuscan has a certain tendency to palatalize *s-* into *š-*: *sciabbia, sciala, sciringa* (also *scilinga*), *sciubboto* (for *subito*), *sciguro* (for *sicuro*). See S. Pieri in *Studj romanzi*, I, 52.

3. *Ciciliano* for *Siciliano*, which occurs in Boccaccio and is still occasionally heard, seems to show a curious type of backward assimilation. *Ciucciare ciocciare* for *succiare* < **suctiare* is probably onomatopoetic. For *singularis* > *cinghiale* (cf. Fr. *sanglier*), association with *cinghia* (< *cingula*) has been proposed, despite the remoteness of meaning.

4. Unexplained are *giglio* < *līlium*, *gioglio loglio* < *lŏlium*, and the opposite change in *Julius* > *giuglio luglio*. See S. Pieri, in *Studj romanzi*, I, 42.

5. *Gnuno* comes from *niuno* = *nè uno* < *nec unus*. So from *nocchio nocchi* apparently comes by metathesis **niocchi gnocchi*. For *nocchio* itself, *nŭcleus* and *nōdŭlus* have been proposed.

6. A mispronunciation of *l* as *r* is found in *ligusticus* > *rovistico*, which seems to show also a metathesis of the first two vowels.

7. *R* is lost in *oleandro* < *rhododendros* + *oleum*. *Bruire* seems to be a fusion of *rugīre* with **bragire* or *bragĕre* (It. *braire*, Fr. *braire*). *Granocchio* (cf. Fr. *grenouille*) for *ranocchio* has apparently been influenced by *crocitare*. *Gracimolo* and *graspo* show similar contamination of *racimolo* < *racēmus* and *raspo* < Ger. *raspon* with *grappolo* < Ger. *krappa*.

85. The palatals underwent most change. *K'*, which in Vulgar Latin advanced to *t'*, then developed its explosion into a perceptible *š*, *centum* being sounded successively *kentum*, *k'entu, t'entu, t'šento*. The sound, still written *c* (*cento*), was in Old Italian often spelled *ci* (*ciera*), and one cannot be sure whether the *i* represents an audible glide or is simply a sign carried over from the notations *cia, cio, ciu*, where it was needed to mark the " soft " type of *c*; modern Sicilian pronunciation seems to support the former conjecture. The same problem presents itself for medial *c* (O. It. *pacie, piaciere*), and for *g* initial and medial (O. It. *giente, correggiere, piangiere*).

1. After a vowel, in closely connected discourse, the stop element of
tš is lost in the current speech of Tuscany, Umbria, and Rome, the *c*
being pronounced *š*: e.g., *cena* = *tšẹna*, but *la cena*>*la šẹna;* cf. *cento*
and *duecento.* See § 106. This reduction of course does not occur after
a particle that causes doubling (§ 88): *dicci, vacci, che cerca* = *ke
ttšerka.*

86. A V. L. *y*, from whatever source, regularly becomes
dž, spelled *g* before *e* and *i*, *gi* before other vowels: *eāmus*>
*jamus>*giamo, iambus*>**jambus*>*giambo, gĕlu*>**jelu*>*gẹlo,
jŏcus*>*giuoco, deōrsum*>**josu* (§ 76, *R*)>*giuso* (*u* by analogy
of *suso*), *diŭrnum*>**jurnu*>*giorno, *Georgius*>**Jorjus*>
Giorgio, zelosus>*geloso.* For the old spelling *giente,* etc.,
see § 85.

1. After a vowel, in closely connected discourse, the stop element of
dž is lost in the current speech of Tuscany and Umbria: *gente* = *džẹnte,*
but *la gente*>*la žẹnte* (Rome, *la džẹnte*). See § 106. This reduction
of course does not occur after a particle that causes doubling (§ 88):
da gente = *da ddžẹnte.*

2. In popular Tuscan the combination *dža-* is often pronounced
dya: jacēre>*giacere* = *dyašẹre.* Hence *iaspis*>*diaspro.*

3. In book-words, *g* is treated as in popular words, Cl. L. *di* and *ge*
retain their spelling and are sounded accordingly, *z* keeps its spelling
and is pronounced *dz: gelsomino, diurno, geometra, zelo.* As to *i* and *j*,
they generally become *dž*, as in folk-words, but occasionally retain their
original spelling and sound: *gerarca, geroglifico, giacinto, giurisdizione,
giocondo;* but *iota, iato, iattanza.*

87. The velar *k* regularly remains unchanged (*caro, colle,
cura*), but in certain words it is voiced into *g: cavea*>*gabbia*
(cf. Fr. *cage*), *cattus*>*gatto* (cf. Fr. *chat*), *cŭbĭtus* + *cumbere*
>*gọmito* (cf. Fr. *coude*), *conflare.*>*gonfiare* (cf. Fr. *gonfler*),
castigare>*gastigare, ex-*combrare?*>*sgọmberare.* This change
must have started in combinations where a vowel immediately
preceded the *k:* as *lo catto* >*lo gatto.* It is commoner in colloquial Tuscan than in the standard language: e.g., *gattivo.*
Cf. § 90. See S. Pieri in *Archivio glottologico italiano,* XV,
369 and *Studj romanzi,* IV, 167. Some occur in the south.

72 PHONOLOGY

Pieri gives a list of twenty cases of *g-* for *c-*, seven of them with alternative *c-*; also fourteen cases of *gr-* for *cr-*, with no alternative forms.

1. In Vulgar Tuscan, *c* between vowels is opened into χ, which generally becomes *h*: *causa>cosa*, but *una cosa = una hǫsa*. Cf. § 108. This development does not occur after a particle that causes doubling (§ 88): *e come = e kkǫme*.

88. At the beginning of a phrase, an initial consonant is often held to double length in emotional utterance: *bbello! Ddio! vvile!* Immediately after a vowel, *Dio, Maria*, and *Santo* always double their initial sound: *solo Ddio, addio, Domineddio* (which became *Iddio*), *Ognissanti, avemmaria.*[1]

In the interior of a phrase, any initial consonant is doubled: (*a*) after an accented vowel, through assimilation of the final echo sound (§ 54), as in *amòe + mi>amommi;* (*b*) after a proclitic ending in a consonant, through assimilation of that consonant, as in *et pure>eppure;* (*c*) after certain proclitics ending in vowels, through the analogy of the preceding class, as in *soprattutto.* Examples: (*a*) *dammi, dà ssempre, dillo, farotti, fummi, piuttosto, stavvi, tre vvolte, vattene;* (*b*) *accanto, checchessia, che vvuole, e cciò, giammai, laggiù, nemmeno, ovvero, siccome, siffatto;* (*c*) *daccapo, frattanto, ma ssenti, trattiene, tu ssai.*[2] In modern spelling, of course, the doubling is indicated only where the two words are joined into one.

This protraction is far less common in Siena and Arezzo than in Florence. Outside of Tuscany, doubling is much favored in the south but not practised in the north.

1. Between vowels, the consonants *l', n', š* and the groups *dz, ts* are always sounded long in central Italy west and north of the Tiber: *daglielo, far lo gnorri, la scesa, la zona, lo zio.*[1]

[1] See A. Camilli in *Archiv für das Studium der neueren Sprachen und Literaturen*, CXXXI, 170.

[2] For a list of the proclitics that cause doubling, See F. d'Ovidio in Gröber's *Grundriss der romanischen Philologie*, I (2d ed.), p. 644. For doubling in Roman dialect, see M. Porena in *Italia dialettale*, III.

Initial Groups

89. The most important are those ending in a liquid. Groups made up of cons. + *l* keep the first consonant but change the *l* to *y* (written *i*). The palatal quality which was always in the *l* was emphasized, in such combinations, by substituting a small air passage over the tongue for an outlet at the sides. The alteration doubtless occurred first in *kl* and *gl*, which are rather hard to manage with their bilateral (or unilateral) explosion of the stop; then it was extended to other groups. The change was probably not complete before the thirteenth century. Examples: Ger. *blank*>*bianco*, *blasphemare*>*biasimare*, *clamo* > *chiamo*, *reclūdit* > *richiude*, *flōrem*>*fiore*, *flūmen*>*fiume*, *glacies glacia*>*ghiaccia*, *glŭtto*> *ghiotto*, *placet*>*piace*, *plūs*>*più*, *ex-plĭcare*>*spiegare*.

Stl, which occurs in the word *stloppus*, became *skl* (just as *tl* became *kl* in the middle of a word: § 113) and then changed to *sky:* *scloppus>*schioppo* and by metathesis *scoppio*.

Sl, a group unfamiliar to Latin, developed a *k* between the *s* and the *l*: Ger. *slahta*>*schiatta*, *slavus sclavus*>*schiavo*, Longobard *slĭht*>*schietto;* an exception is O. H. G. *slito*> *slitta*.

1. In popular Tuscan the groups *gya-* and *skya-* are often pronounced *dya* and *stya: ghiaccio = diaccio, schiacciare = stiacciare.* Cf. § 113, 3.

2. Such forms as *chiù* for *più* are southern, especially Neapolitan. *Ciù* is Genoese.

3. *Giaggiǫlo*<*gladiŏlus* seems to show the regressive assimilation which we find in *Ciciliano* (§ 84, 3). *Cherica, cherico* for *chierica chierico* possibly owe the loss of *y* to dissimilation in the plural *chierici* or *chierci*.

4. Book-words keep the *l: claustro* (cf. popular *chiostro*), *flebile* (pop. *fievole*), *gloria, plebe* (pop. *pieve*), *splendido.* Similarly in medial position, *exemplum* gave *esemplo*, which the influence of the popular *scempio* turned into *esempio*.

90. Cons. + *r* regularly suffered no alteration: *crēdo*> *credo, crīnis*>*crine, crŭcem*>*croce, frēnum*>*freno, gravis*> *grave, prīmus*>*primo, strata*>*strada, tres*>*tre.* A few words, however, changed *kr* to *gr* (cf. § 87): Ger. *kripja*>*greppia*, *quirītare*>V. L. *c'rītare* (§ 41)>*gridare*, *crypta*>*grotta*. *Grasso* is from *crassus*, which, contaminated by *grossus*, became *grassus*.

1. *Brina* seems to combine *pruina* and *bruma*.

2. *Coccodrillo* shows metathesis, *squittino* <*scrutinium* shows popular distortion, in an unfamiliar word.

3. *Sr* developed a transitional *d* in *sdraiare* < *ex-radiare*, *sdrucciolare* < *ex-roteolare;* but not in later formations with *s-*, such as *sradicare*, *sragionare*.

91. There are three groups ending in *w*: *dw*, *kw*, *gw*. The last of these, which developed out of the single consonant *w*, was discussed in §§ 80, 83. *Dw* occurs apparently in Longobard *dwerh*>*guercio*.

There remains *kw*, which is of two kinds: (*a*) Latin *qu*, pronounced *kw;* (*b*) Latin syllabic *cu* in hiatus, which lost its syllabic value and became *kw*. The original *qu* was reduced to *k*, except before *a*, where it remained *kw*: *quem*> *che*, *quī*>*chi*, *quĭd*,>*ched che*, *quod*>*co;* *qualis*>*quale*, *quantum*>*quanto*, *quartus*>*quarto*. The secondary *kw* from *cu* remained unaltered before an accented vowel, and absorbed a following unaccented vowel, becoming *ko* (cf. § 40, 3): *eccu' ĭlla*>*quella*, *eccu' ĭstum*>*questo*, *eccu' hīc*>*qui; eccu' illūi*>*colui*, *eccu' illōrum*>*coloro*. Arezzo, however, treated these latter words like the former: *quelui*, *queloro*.

1. The particle *ca*, which in early Italian had the functions of *che*, seems to be of southern origin, coming apparently from three Latin sources: (1) *quia*, which in late Latin often became *qui'* before vowels, *qu'a* before consonants; (2) the conjunction *qua;* (3) the conjunction *quam*.

2. *Quinque* by dissimilation became in V. L. *cinque*, which gave It. *cinque*, Sp. *cinco*, Fr. *cinq*, Rum. *cincĭ*, etc.

3. *Cagliare* for *quagliare*<*coagulare* is probably from the Fr. *cailler*.

92. Groups beginning with *s* — except *sk'*, the *sl* discussed in § 89, and the *sr* mentioned in § 90, 3 — remain unchanged, save that the *s* is voiced before a sonant: *scuola, sperare, stella;* Ger. *snel* > *snello,* O. H. G. *slito* > *slitta.* This voicing is carried over into the Italian prefix *s*-, coming from Latin *ex*- and *dis*-: *sboccare, smettere, svenire.*

Sk', both in popular and in learned words, becomes *š*: *descendo* > *scendo, scœna* > *scena, scintilla* > *scintilla.* See § 88, 1.

FINAL

93. In Latin words that survived, the only single final consonants are: *d, k, l, m, n, r, s, t.* Of these, we have seen that *s* was weak and that *m* and *n* had maintained themselves only in monosyllables (§ 76): *donu', nome', non.* We have evidence, moreover, that *t* was already falling by the first century of our era in the vulgar speech of southern Italy.[1]

Of the final groups — *ks* (*x*), *nt, st* — it has been noted that *ks* was early reduced to *s* in polysyllables (§ 76).

For the addition of a vowel to a final consonant in foreign words borrowed by Italian, see § 54, 1. Cf. § 94, *L, r.*

94. *K* was assimilated to a following consonant in closely connected discourse; otherwise it disappeared: *dīc mī* > *dimmi, fac mī* > *fammi,*[2] *ecce hoc* > *ciò.*

D and *t* fell, except in monosyllabic proclitics: *apud* > *appo, amat* > *ama, amabat* > *amava, amavit* > *amaut* > *amó, sentiit* > *sentīt* > *senti.* Third person *audiui, posui* occur in Latin inscriptions.[3] At the end of a one-syllable proclitic, *d* and *t* were assimilated to a consonant, but before a vowel were preserved, the *t* in this case either keeping its surd quality or voicing to *d* (cf. § 104, *T*): *ad me* > *mme, quid nos* > *che nnoi, et pure* > *eppure,* *ot (= *aut*) *vero* > *ovvero; ad ipsam* > *ad essa, quid illa* > *ched ella, et illī* > *ed* or *et egli,* *ot (= *aut*) *ipsa* > *od essa. Ed, od* were preferred to *et, ot,* doubtless be-

---

[1] See C. H. Grandgent, *An Introduction to Vulgar Latin,* p. 120.

[2] For a possible example of *fa* for *fac* in Latin, see *Zs.,* XXV, 735.

[3] O. Densusianu, *Histoire de la langue roumaine,* 1901, I, 123.

cause of the analogy of *ad*, *ched*, and *ot* early disappeared; but, as far as we can ascertain, *et* was once freely used beside *ed* (Petrarch wrote *et* or *e*, never *ed* [1]). Then the forms without a final consonant, *a*, *che*, *e*, *o*, began to be used also before a vowel; *ched* has now gone entirely out of use. On the other hand, in the older language, on the model of *ed* and *ched*, we find *ned* for *nè*, *sed* for *se*, before a vowel. *Da*, which seems to be a fusion of *de* and *a* (= *ab*),[2] had from the start no final consonant, although it caused the doubling of an initial consonant in Italian (§ 88).

L, *r* fell in polysyllables: *bacchānal* (neuter) > *baccano*, *tribūnal* (neuter) > *tribuna; cĭcer* (neuter) > *cece, marmor* > *marmo, frater* > *frate, sŏror* > *suoro* then *suora*. Examples of the loss of *r* in Italy occur in Latin times.[3] *Sarto*, however, is probably from **sartus* rather than *sartor;* else the preservation of the nominative would be hard to account for. At the end of monosyllables, *l*, *r* remain with added *e*: *fĕl*, *mĕl*, *cŏr* (all neuter) > *fiele, miele, cuore*. In the case of *fiele, miele*, the single consonant and the diphthong preclude the possibility of derivation from the ablative or from a masculine **fellem*, **mellem;* hence *cuore* must be taken from *cor* rather than from a hypothetical masculine **corem* for **cordem*. The addition of the *e* is doubtless a very early manifestation of the tendency described in § 54, 1. It. *sale* may come from Lat. *sale* or from Lat. *sal* (masc. or neuter). As to *quattuor* and *semper*, it is likely that they had already suffered metathesis in popular Latin, becoming *quattro* and *sempre*.

S disappeared, like the other consonants, after an unaccented vowel: *habētis* > *avete, corpus* > *corpo, fuistis* > **fŭstis*

---

[1] See *Zs.*, Beiheft XIII, 23. In texts that use an abbreviation for the conjunction, one cannot be sure whether it stands for *e*, *ed*, or *et:* it simply means 'and,' as does our &. The sign used in the Middle Ages resembles a figure 7.

[2] E. Richter, Ab *im Romanischen*. Cf. *Zs.*, XXV, 602.

[3] See C. H. Grandgent, *An Introduction to Vulgar Latin*, p. 124; and *Zeitschrift für französische Sprache*, XLII, 2–4, 8.

>*foste, lampas* > *lampa, prægna* (*n*)*s* > *prẹgna*,[1] *tempus* > *tempo*.
When the preceding vowel was stressed, however, the *s* be-
came *i*, having doubtless passed through a stage of faint palatal *h*, such as one can still sometimes hear in Andalusian: *cras*
>*crai, das* > *dai, nos* > *noi, plus* > *piui, stas* > *stai, tres* > *trei,
vos* > *voi; credere* + **ás* > *crederai; magis* > **majis* > **mais* >
mai. *X* followed the same course: *sex* > *sei;* but **rei* from
rex is not found. When one of these monosyllables was used
proclitically (as some of them frequently were), the diphthong regularly lost its second element in Florentine (§ 42):
nos clamat > *noi chiama* > *no chiama* (later *ne chiama*); so
piui volte > *più volte, trei figli* > *tre figli, mai ditemi* > *ma ditemi,
rei Federigo > *re Federigo*. Hence arose several new forms.
Sei, however, prevailed over **se; trei* (used by Dante) is
still heard in the north.[2]

95. *M* and *n*, having become inaudible at the end of polysyllables, were in monosyllables assimilated to a following
consonant: *jam magis* > *giammai, jam factum* > *già ffatto,
jam partītus* > *già ppartito; cum me* > *co mme, cum tanto* > *con
tanto, cum suo* > *co ssuo; sum mortuus* > *so mmorto, sum
tornatus* > *son tornato, sum vetulus* > *so vvecchio; in tertio* > *in
terzo, in prīma* > *im prima, in fĭde* > *i ffede; non dat* > *non dà,
non placet* > *nom piace, non vĕnit* > *no vviene*. Similarly, no
doubt, one said *tam magnus* but *taŋ grandis, sum patrem* but
su ffilium (*sum* being a short form of *suum*).

Before a vowel, the form in *n* came to be regularly employed, that being presumably the commonest: *con amore,*

---

[1] *Prægna* is found in late Latin: I. Lhevinne, *The Language of the
Glossary Sangalensis 912 and its Relationship to the Language of Other
Latin Glossaries*, 1924, p. 58. From *pregna* is made a masculine *pregno*.

[2] See P. G. Goidánich, *L'origine e le forme della dittongazione romanza*,
1907, 211. S. Puşcariu, in *Studiĭ şi notiţe filologice*, Bucarest, 1901,
tries to show that the final *i* in Italian and Rumanian is in all these
cases analogical; his conjecture was favorably received by G. Paris in
Rom., XXXII, 476, but has not been generally accepted.

son io, in (or *inn*) *essa, non è;* but for *jam*, which was oftenest used independently, the form *già* prevailed (*è già uscito*). Like *jam*, so *non* and *sum*, when used not as particles but as independent words, discarded altogether the final consonant: *già! no! so* (occasionally in Old It. for *sono*); this *so*, however, being a term of infrequent occurrence, has given way to *son*, later *sono* (§ 95, 2).

All these words, indeed, have been standardized in spelling and to some extent in pronunciation. But the differentiation of *non* and *no* has persisted.

1. There are several examples of *no* for *non* in Latin inscriptions: *no pote, no esse bictu, no meriti, no dolui, no est*, etc. See P. Skok in *Rom.*, L, 227.

2. *Sono* borrowed its final *o* from the normal verb type: *amo*, hence *son-o*.

3. In Old Italian we find possessives, *mo, ma, so*, beside *mio, mia, suo*. These presumably go back to Vulgar Latin. If they represent forms in *-m*, the loss of that consonant is easily accounted for by the fact that they were generally used as enclitics, and therefore were treated like the ends of polysyllables: *padremo, madrema, signorso*. The *-mo* and *-ma* are extant in Roman dialect. *Ma* occurs, however, as a proclitic in *madonna*, a form prevailingly vocative or nominative.

4. *Collo* ('with the'), etc., go back either to *cu' illo* with absorption of the *i* (cf. § 40, 3) or to *cum 'llo* with assimilation of the *m*. *Nello* is of course *in illo*. In early Italian, and later in literary style, we find *nollo, nol* from *non lo*.

5. In archaic and poetic Italian we have *speme* and *spene*, equivalent to *speranza*. It is not likely that either of these comes directly from the Cl. L. 5th declension *spes*. *Speme* postulates a new Latin formation in *-men*: **spēmen*. *Spene* bears witness to a declension *spes spenis* etc.; the dative *Speni* (of the same type as the third century *mamani, tatani* from *mama, tata*) occurs on several tombs, being used as a proper name or epithet. See W. Heraeus in *Archiv für lateinische Lexicographie und Grammatik*, XIII, 152.

Final Consonant Groups

96. X or ks was discussed under S in § 94.

St occurs in *post* and *est.*

Post appears to have lost its t in Vulgar Latin; then *pos* became *poi* (§ 94, S). *De* + *poi*, used proclitically, is thought to have given *dopo*: *post prandium* > **poi pranzo* > **po pranzo* (§ 42), then **de po pranzo* > *dopo pranzo* (§ 45, 3).

Est, when accented, seems to have remained with an added e (cf. § 94, L, r): *este*, which occurs often enough in early Tuscan documents. Otherwise *est* is represented by *è* and, in the earlier language, by *sè* (printed *s'è*) and *èssi* (= *è* + *si*). We know that the anomalous *sum es est sumus estis sunt* was partially rectified in Italy by reconstructing *es*, *estis* into **ses*, **setis* (*sei*, *siete*). May not the third person have been similarly normalized into **set* and **et*, the latter being a cross between *est* and **set?* **Et* would then have given *è*, as *dat* gives *dà*, or as *vĭdet* gives *vede;* whereas **set* would have produced *sè*, which, mistakenly analyzed as *s'è*, would have given rise to *èssi* and a whole meaninglessly reflexive conjugation. An analogous explanation would apply to Provençal *ses* = *es*.

97. *Nt* occurs in the third person plural of verbs. It remained as n in oxytones (*dant* > *dan*), and also in paroxytones (*amant* > *aman*), but vanished entirely in proparoxytones (*dĕdĕrunt* > *diedero*), the breath or the attention weakening at such a distance from the accent. So we have, for example: *stan, son, sian; portan, portin, vendon, vendan, portavan, portaron, portasson* (< *portāssent*); *stettero, ebbero, seppero, tennero, vennero, corsero.* From the *diedero* type arose the practice of attaching an *-o*, at will, to any third person plural; these lengthened forms, *sono, amano, amarono*, etc., are now the commoner.

1. The mutual influence of the two preterit types, *diedero* and *amaron*, led to a multiplicity of forms. First came *amaro, furo*, etc.,

with the -*ro* ending, and, on the other hand, *dieder, stetter,* etc., with a consonant ending. Then, while the -*o* of *diedero, stettero* suggested *amarono, furono,* the vowelless *r* of *dieder, stetter* shortened *amaro, furo* to *amar, fur.*

2. The forms with *nn* seem to have a different origin, being modeled on the third person singular. Inasmuch as *ama* is distinguished from *amano* by the syllable -*no,* a new plural was made by adding -*no* to such singulars as *dàe, èe*—that is, *dà* and *è* with the echo vowel (§ 54): *dàe* + *no, èe* + *no* become, by assimilation (§ 88), *danno, enno; enno* is then sometimes shortened to *en* on the model of *dan, son. Enno* is still current in Lucca. Similarly we get in the preterit *dienno, fenno* from *dièe, fèe* (= *diè, fe'* for *diede, fece*: § 52). Next, the formation is extended to regular preterits, and *amǫnno* is made from *amòe,* etc. Contamination of *amonno* with *amarono, amaro, amar* (§ 97, 1) produces *amorono, amoro, amor;* and *amorono* + *amonno* results in *amorno* (still common in the south).

MEDIAL

98. Medial consonants, being always in close contact with sounds on either side, are particularly susceptible to the influence of *milieu.* The most effective principle in such influence is the principle of economy. In the labored utterance of primitive man, no doubt, there may have been abundant leisure for long shifts and slow transitions; but as speech becomes glib, it seeks short cuts: it tends to throw out altogether those sounds which are not necessary for comprehension, and to modify the remaining ones in such wise that movements shall be reduced to a minimum of effort and time.

For instance, in early Latin days it was discovered that the final *m* in such a word as *compŭtum* could be sufficiently indicated by slightly relaxing the soft palate while uttering the preceding vowel; so the last *u* became faintly nasal and the *m*- closure was no longer made. Next it was found that the word was intelligible enough without the medial *u;* and *computu* became *comptu.* But *p* between *m* and *t* served no real purpose: hence *comtu.* Now *m* and *t* are formed with stoppage in two different places, at the lips and at the upper teeth; if we articulate them both at the same spot, the first will still be sufficiently differentiated from the second by its voice and its nasality: the result is *contu*, or Italian *conto*.

When we say *rīpa*, the vocal cords are throbbing except while we produce the *p*, a seemingly needless interruption. Letting the pulsation go on through the whole word, we get *riba*, the Provençal form. Even in *riba*, however, the *b* makes a stoppage, checking the flow of breath which else would go on from the beginning of *r* to the end of *a*. Opening the lips and teeth just enough for an escape of air, we have *riva*, or French *rive*.

It is evident, then, that dissimilar adjacent consonants naturally tend to accommodate themselves to each other, and that a single consonant between vowels tends to make itself as vowellike as it can, becoming voiced if it is a surd, open or fricative if it is a stop. Such tendencies, for one reason or another, are stronger in one period, or in one place, than in another. Thus French *pipe*, a late borrowing from Low Latin **pipa*, retains its medial *p*. Thus Latin *ripa* became at about the same time *riba* in Provençal and *rive* in French. It may be noted that Italian has both *ripa* and *riva*.

The changes that a word suffers do not come all at once, but, for the most part, so gradually that its identity maintains itself in the consciousness of speakers and hearers. Moreover, both the older and the newer form are always current simultaneously; for some speakers change their fashions quicker than others. In fact, every community contains linguistic radicals and conservatives, the latter being, in the main, the possessors of vested interests due to superior acquisition — in other words, the more educated and authoritative people, who like to hold fast to the tradition of their elders. There is eternal strife between thrift and elegance; there is strife everlasting between ease of utterance and ease of comprehension. Members of both classes are

82　PHONOLOGY

quite irrational in their preferences; one and the same speaker will be a whig toward one class of words, a tory toward another. Hence we find, in the practice of every individual, examples of both proclivities. The one constant feature of linguistic change would seem to be inconsistency.

99. Standard Italian exemplifies in its treatment of medial consonants the opposing tendencies aforesaid. Attempts have been made to explain the contradictory results by means of accentuation or differences of vocalic environment, but such theories, plausible enough in the abstract, do not fit the concrete examples.[1] It is more likely that we have to do simply with diverse social or topographical strata, all of which have contributed to the vocabulary of Florence and to the standard tongue which emerged therefrom.

1. Concerning the usage of Bologna, Dante tells us in *De Vulgari Eloquentia*, I, ix and xv: "Et quod mirabilius est, sub eadem civitate morantes [discrepant in loquendo], ut Bononienses Burgi S. Felicis et Bononienses Stratæ Maioris " . . . "Si ergo Bononienses utrinque accipiunt, ut dictum est, rationabile videtur esse quod eorum locutio per commistionem oppositorum, ut dictum est, ad laudabilem suavitatem remaneat temperata."

Single Medial Consonants

100. Italians, except in the north, are very fond of prolonged medial consonants, and are ready to take advantage of any ground for doubling. The lengthening of initial and final consonants we have already discussed (§ 88; § 54, 1). We shall soon have occasion to consider a self-protective doubling of medial consonants before *l, r, w,* and *y* (§§ 113,

---

[1] W. Meyer-Lübke's judgments are set forth, not only in his *Italienische Grammatik*, but also in reviews in *Zs.*, XXVII, 368, XXX, 371, XXXI, 699. S. Pieri's opinions are expounded in the *Archivio glottologico italiano*, XV, 369, and XVI, 163, 175; also in *Studj romanzi*, IV, 167. See also E. G. Parodi in *Mélanges Chabaneau*, 1907, p. 774. An important contribution was made by J. T. Clark in *Rom.*, XXXII, 593, XXXIII, 246, XXXIV, 66.

116, 118, 121): e.g., *fabbro, tacque, rabbia, occhio* (and similarly *piǫppo* < **poppio* < **poplus* < *pōpŭlus*, 'poplar,' influenced, no doubt, by *ǫppio* < *ŏpŭlus*, 'maple'). We have
noted also the existence, in Latin times, of words with double
forms, one with long vowel + single consonant, the other
with short vowel + double consonant, and we have surmised
in some instances a third form combining both vowel and
consonant length (§ 14): to such a third form may perhaps
be attributed *brutto* < *brūtus*, *Lucca* < *Lūca*, *succo* < *sūcus*,
tutti totti < *tōti*.

Aside from such cases, we find not a few examples ot protraction by analogy: e.g., the *gg* of *figgo, fuggo, leggo, reggo,
struggo* (< V. L. **strugo*), *suggo, traggo* (< V. L. **trago*),
imitating in its quantity the *ddž* of *figgi, figge* etc. (§ 107);
so *cammino* for *camino* < *camīnus* ('hearth'), attracted by
cammino < *cammīnus* ('road'); *cattǫlico*, by *cattedra, cattedrale* (§ 101); *dramma* < *drama*, by *dramma* < *drachma, domma*
< *dogma; meccanica*, by *macchina* (§ 101); *rettorica*, by *rettore*.
There is no obvious explanation of *baccęllo* < *bacĭllum*, *bottęga*
< *apothēca, cappone* < *capōnem, reddire* (Dante) < *redire*, *vas-
soio* < *vas* + *-orium*, of the Semitic *caffè* and *caffo*, of the Greek
chitarra, graffito, tappeto, of the French *dettaglio*, nor of the
probably Germanic *botta, botte, botto, bottone*. There seems
to be a proclivity to double in unfamiliar words.

Very frequent, especially in borrowed words, is doubling
between the initial syllable and the tonic vowel, through the
analogy of compound words beginning with the prefixes *ad-,
com-, in-, sub-: accǫlito* < ἀκόλουθος (cf. *accorrere*), *allęgro* <
alacrem (cf. *allegare*), *allǫdola* < *alauda* (cf. *alludare*), *allǫro* <
laurus (cf. *allora*), *allume* < *alūmen* (cf. *alluminare*), *com-
mędia* < *comoedia* (cf. *commettere*), *immagine* < *imaginem* (cf.
immortale), *sollazzo* < *solatium* = *solacium* (cf. *sollevare*),
uccello < *avicellus* (cf. *uccidere*). Similarly *in* before a vowel
in Tuscan becomes *inn*, influenced by such words as *innocente,
innovare, innumerevole*, and by the example of doubling after

a, da, e, o (§ 88): *innalza, innamorare, innanzi, inn aria,* etc. The doubling in Old It. *etterno* is probably emotional.

101. In bookish or borrowed words there is a strong tendency to double a consonant (1) after the accented vowel of a proparoxytone and (2) after the vowel bearing the secondary accent in a long word. Here the protraction seems to have been due originally to an instant's hesitation before proceeding with an unfamiliar sequence of syllables. Examples: (1) *abbaco* < *abăcus, attimo* < ἄτομον, *azzimo* < ἄξιμος, *cattedra, cǫbbola* < Pr. *cobla, cǫllera* < *chǒlěra, cuccuma* < *cŭcŭma, fęmmina* < *fēmĭna, legittimo, Sǫddoma* < *Sǒdǒma, squallido, Zęffiro;*[1] (2) *abbandono, abborrire, accadęmia, appo té* < *apud tē, appostǫlico, Babbilǫnia, cattedrale, Catterina, coccodrillo* < *crocodĭlus, commestibile, diffinire, difformare, mattematica, pellegrino, pellicano, provvedere, Raffaele, scellerato, seppellire, strattagemma, tollerare, ubbidire* < *oboedīre, ubbriaco* < *ebriăcus.* In *diffinire, difformare* we have to consider also a substitution of prefix. *Strattagemma* seems to show in its *mm* the influence of *gęmma.*

Some doublings which appear to arise from a similar hesitancy do not fall into either of the above categories: *bellíco* < *umbilícus, mucillaggine.*

Some dialects carry the doubling tendency still further in proparoxytones. Lucca and several other towns use now *b,* now *bb,* in such words as *dębole.* In Pisa, Lucca, Siena, and Arezzo not only may *m* or *n* be prolonged, but the latter part of this consonant may be denasalized, with *mb, nd* as a result: *cambera* for *camera* (Pisa), *cendare* for *cenere* (Siena),[1] *nimbo* < *nemo* (Lucca).

1. The *mm* in such forms as *amammo, vedemmo, udimmo* was discussed in § 33, 3.

2. For a curious opposite phenomenon, the reduction of some consonants originally double, see § 109.

[1] See E. G. Parodi, *Sul raddoppiamento di consonanti postoniche negli sdruccioli italiani,* in *Mélanges Chabaneau,* 1907, p. 755.

102. This doubling tendency, however, affects after all only a small minority of the intervocalic consonants. Among those which remain single, the liquids and nasals nearly always resist change: *Fięsole, uomini, pure.* *D* and *f* also maintain themselves: *udire* < *audire, scrǫfa* < *scrōfa.* The rest in their development seem to give evidence of at least two different social or local habits.

103. Among the labials, *p* shows a dual history, remaining unchanged in one set of words, changing to *v* in another: *nipote, uopo, opera, sęnape* < σίναπι; *pruovo* < *prǫpe, pǫvero, vęscovo* < *epǐscǒpus.*[1] A few words have both forms: *rīpa* > *ripa riva, stīpare* > *stipare stivare.* Some of the *v* forms that occur are probably of Bolognese origin: *cavelli, coverto, savere, savore.* Dante, in his *Vita Nuova,* seems to use *sapere* in the prose, *savere* in the verse. *Lova* < *lǔpa* may be Lombard. *Travaglio* < **trepalium* is French or Provençal. In *befana* < *epiphania, bottęga* < *apothēca,* and a few others, we see the consonant checked, midway in its course from *p* to *v,* by the fall of the initial vowel (§ 40). Book-words keep *p: apologia, principe.* Why have we *padiglione* (Gallo-Italic?) for *paviglione* < *papilionem?* See § 103, 1.

M maintains itself: *avemo, prima, uomo.* *Nǫvero,* however, shows dissimilation of two nasals, *nǔmĕrus* becoming **nuberus,* then **nǫvero nǫvero.* Such forms as *andiàn* for *andiamo,* frequent in the Renaissance, probably arose from assimilation of *m* to an affixed particle with dental beginning: *andiamcene* > *andiancene,* so *andianne* (*Filostrato,* V, viii, 2, etc.), *facciànlo, lasciànla, moviànci,* hence *andiàn,* then *andiàno;* sometimes, before *l,* the *m* was completely assimilated, as in *impicchiallo* (*Novellino*), *meniallo* (Boccaccio). *Conenzare* for *comenzare cominciare* < **cominitiare* may be attributable to the substitution of the prefix *con-* (as in *contenere, continuare*) for *com-*.

[1] F. d'Ovidio, *Del sostantivo* stipa *in Dante,* 1917, pp. 97–98, expresses the opinion that all the *v* words come from non-Tuscan dialects, especially Venetian.

F stays: ἀφή>*afa*, *cŏphĭnus*>*cŏfano*, *epiphania*>*befanía
befána*, *raphănus*>*rafano*, *scrōfa*>*scrǫfa*, Στέφανος>*Stęfano*.
Such words as *cǫlpo*<κόλαφος, *pǫrpora*<πορφύρα date from
early Latin borrowing, when Greek φ became Latin *p* (§ 79).

B between vowels, and Latin *w* (written *u*) had both become β (§ 77), which in the great majority of words simply
turned to *v*: *avaro*, *avęre*, *bręve*, *chiave*<*clavem*, *lieve*, *nęvica*
<*nĭvĭcat*, *nuovo*, *ǫve*<*ŭbi*, *scrivere*, *vivere*; -*ęvole*<-*ĭbĭlis;*
-*ava*, -*ęva*, -*iva*<-*abam*, etc. *Habēbam*, however, being
sounded *aβęβa*, by dissimilation became *aβęa*, whence *avęa
avia* (§ 25, 3); from this came a second and third conjugation
ending -*ea* or -*ia* for -*eva*,[1] and by analogy in the fourth conjugation -*ia; vedea*, *credea*, *udia*. These forms were of the
third person as well as the first, and in the third person plural
we have -*ean*, -*ian*.

A contiguous back vowel often absorbed the β or *v*: so
Pistoiese *fao* for *favo;* so, at a very early stage, *bue*, *buoi* from
bos, *bo*(*v*)*is*, etc.; Benvenuto Cellini uses *aúto* for *avuto*,
Vitruio for *Vitruvio*. Before accented *u* or *o*, a β seems to
have disappeared regularly in some dialects, but not in others.
abŏrtat>*aǫrta*, *pavūra*>*paúra;* *devŏrat*>*divǫra*, *favōrem*>
favǫre, *labōrem*>*lavǫro*, *pavōrem*>*pavǫre;* *pavōnem*>*pavǫne
paǫne*, *bĭbĭtum* *bibūtum*>*bevuto beúto* (whence a whole inflection without *v*), *dēbĭtum* *debūtum*>*dovuto deúto* (whence
dee for *deve*, etc.), *habĭtum* *habūtum*>*avuto aúto*. From
-*avus* we seem to have in Italian only -*avo* (*cavo*, *ottavo*); but
-*avit* becomes -*aut*, then -*ǒ* and *ǎo* (*amǒ*, *amǎo*): see § 77.
From -*ivus*, on the other hand, we have both -*ivo* and -*io:
cattivo*, *ulivo*, *vivo; corsía*, *pendío*, *restío; divo dio*, *estivo estío*,
nativo natío, *rivo rio;* while -*ivit*>-*iut*>-*ío* (*salío*): see § 77.
Nævus apparently results in *nęo* (Neapolitan *niev*). Why
does *Faventia* become *Faenza?*

In book-words *b* is generally kept, but in an apparently

---

[1] Florentine usually kept -*ea* for the 2d and 3d, leaving -*ia* to the
4th. *Solei* for *solevi* in *Filostrato*, VII, lxxix, 7.

older stratum it becomes *v*: *cibo, debito, dubito, rabido, ribelle, sillaba, subito; favola, tavola.*

1. A curious and unexplained phenomenon is the substitution of *g* for *β* in certain words. These two consonants being separated from each other by the whole depth of the mouth, there would seem to be no possibility of a phonetic development. It must be observed that the sound in question is *β* and not *w*: *β* is only half of *w*, and precisely the half that has no affinity with *g*. We must look for some morphological cause, a confusion between two sets of endings, as a point of departure. Then there certainly developed in some dialects (especially in Siena) a preference for *g*, in others (notably in Lucca) a predilection for *v*. Dialect crossings subsequently mixed the two categories in the standard language.

Easily affected were the terminations *-golo* and *-volo. Spigolo < spīculum* may have given rise to *rigolo < rīvulus* and even to *strigolo < strīdulus; fragola < fragum* may be responsible for Sienese *diagolo = diavolo; mugola < *mūgulat mūgit* may have suggested *ugola < ūvula* and *nugolo = nuvolo; pegola < pīcula* may have attracted *stegola < stīpula* and *pigola < pīpīlat.* So *maghero = magro* may have led to *sughero = suvero < sūber.* Going further afield, we may find *luogora = luoghi* influencing *logoro <* Frankish *lōþr; pergola* turning *parvolo* to *pargolo. Paulus* regularly gives *Pǫlo*, but as a bookish word it remains *Paolo*, which, developing a transitional *v* (as in *caulis > cavolo:* § 33, 2), becomes *Pavolo;* this, attracted perhaps by such words as *pegola* and *ágora = aghi*, turns in Siena to *Pagolo.* Similarly we find from *taurus* an Apulian *tóvaru* and a Calabrian *táguru.*

Meanwhile, *sēbum > sevo sego*, on the example of *pegola, tegola; rōbur > ròvo rògo*, similar to *sugo < sūcus;* Arabic *diwan >* (Lucchese *dovana*) *dogana*, following *doga* of unknown parentage; *pavōrem > pavore paura pagura*, in imitation of *sciaúra sciagura* from **ex-augurare.* Then we have **re-ad-unare > radunare raunare* (§ 102) *ragunare; pavonem > pavone paone pagone; favorem > favore* and Sienese *fagore.* The exchange was made also in the other direction: Lucca has *tievolo* for *tegola, dova* for *doga, giovo* for *giogo;* similarly we find *fravola* for *fragola.*

Although Catalan does show a *pregon* for older *preon < profundum* and Provençal has *pagor* for *paor*, the phenomenon in question seems to be almost or quite confined to Italian and Rumanian. It may have begun before these two languages parted. Rumanian offers such examples as *fágur < *favulus < favus, négură < nĕbula, rug < rūbus.*

2. A few special irregularities are due to special causes: *bifolco* may come, not from *bubulcus*, but from some corresponding Oscan or Um-

brian form; *tafano* can be attributed to a *tafanus* which seems to have existed beside *tabānus; cánape*<*cannabis* shows the influence of *sẹnape* σίναπι; *gọmito* is *cŭbĭtus* + *cŭmbĕre; presbÿter*, attracted by *prœbĭtor*, became *prebiter*, which gave *previte* (Abruzzese), and this, in pretonic position and influenced by *frate*, was reduced to *prete*, which in turn proclitically dwindled to *pre'*, just as *frate*>*fra*. Is *episcopus* responsible for the *p* in *Jacopo*<*'Ιάκωβος 'Ιακώβ?* *Giacomo* comes from **Jácomus* (cf. the Fr., Pr., and Sp. forms), which is doubtless to be connected with the *'Ιάκουμβος* occurring as the name of an Alexandrian Jew early in the second century; this development of a nasal before the stop seems to be a Semitic phenomenon, which may be accountable also for the *m* of Fr. *samedi:* see D. S. Blondheim, *Les parlers judéo-romans et la Vetus Latina*, 1925, p. xxxi.

3. *Ha* (also *hae*) for *ave* follows *da* and *sta*, favored perhaps by *aúto* for *avuto:* § 103, *B. Dee* for *deve* probably starts with *déuto* for *dovuto* and is strengthened by *èe* = *è, hae* = *ha. Bee* for *beve* comes apparently from *beúto* for *bevuto. Debbe* for *deve* follows *dovrebbe;* hence *debbo* and *debba.*

4. In Vulgar Florentine *v* between vowels is often suppressed: *aéa* for *aveva.*

104. Of the dentals, *d* regularly remains intact: *cade, udite, vedere.* For such apocopated forms as *fè, piè, mercè, sie', mo', como,* see § 52. For *perdei,* etc., see § 140. *Aocchiare, aorare, raunare,* etc., beside *adocchiare,* etc., are probably imitations of Old French *aoillier, aorer, reunir,* etc.; other forms without *d,* such as *aempiere, ausare,* were made on that plan. *Avọltero* for *adúltero* is doubtless from Old French *avoutre,* whose *v* is explained by P. Marchot (*Petite phonétique du français prélittéraire,* 5) as a transition sound developed between *a* and *o.* In *ẹllera* from *hĕdĕra* the *ẹ* and the *ll* are unexplained. For *strigolo* see § 103, 1. Why did *cicāda* become *cicala? Palafrẹno* from *paraverēdus* shows the influence of *frẹno.* For *disto, disiare* (Lat. *desiderium*) there is no good explanation. *Rasente* represents *radente* + *raso.*

N remains: *cane, cẹnere, frássino, tuono.* In *calọnaco* for *canọnico* and in *Girọlamo*<*Hieronÿmus* we seem to have dissimilation of two nasals; in *anẹmolo* for *anẹmone* the nasals were originally three, and we have also the substitution of a familiar suffix. What is the relation of *Palermo* to *Panormus?* *Tie', vie'* for *tiene, viene* probably follow *sie'* for *siede* (§ 52). *L* is stable: *catálogo, cielo, male, Milano, sale, stęlo, vuole.* *Tali, vuoli* before a vowel (as in *tali anni, vuoli andare*) become *tagli, vuogli;* and these forms, used before a consonant (as in **tagli giorni, *vuogli venire*), became *tai, vuoi* (§ 42; § 59, 1). By imitation of *tai, quai,* we have such plural forms as *animai.* In *ámido* < ἄμυλος, *dattero* < δάκτυλος, *sędano* < σέλινον the peculiarities may go back to the Greek. *Melancǫnico* seems to have suffered dissimilation under the influence of *canǫnico,* etc. Why *Cágliari* < *Calăris, mǫdano* < *mŏdulus, muggine* < *mūgĭlis?*

R remains: *mare, morire, misero, sera.* In some vulgar Tuscan (and non-Tuscan) dialects, *r* and *l* are much confused: *scilinga, scilocco, sciloppo* for *sciringa,* etc. A consequence, doubtless, of such confusion is *ciliegio* < *cereseus.* Dissimilation accounts for *mercoledì, palafreno, pellegrino; chiedere, fiedere, rado:* from *Mercuri die, paraverēdus, peregrinus; quærere, ferire, rarus.* *Muoi* follows *muoiamo* (§ 129) and *vuoi.* *Cinghiale* < *singularis* follows *maiale* < *majalis.* *Mandragola* < *mandragŏrem* takes the common suffix *-ola.* Why *tempia* < *tempora* ('temples')?

T in some words remains, in others is voiced to *d* [1]: *fatica, lieto, lievito* < **lĕvĭtum, prato, sęte* < *sĭtis; Adige* < Ἀταγις, *gridare* < *quirītare, scudo, strada.* Some words have both forms, either with or without a differentiation of sense: *contrada contrata, mutare mudare, lido lito, potere podere.* All second person plural forms have *t,* and so have all perfect participles in *-tus; -ate, -ete, -ite; -ato, -uto, -ito.* All abstract nouns in *-tas* and *-tus* have both: *bontade bontate, virtude virtute.* For the apocopated forms see § 52: *bontà, virtù.* Book-words keep *t: erętico.*

---

[1] See S. Pieri in *Archivio glottologico italiano,* XV, 369.

1. Some of the words with *d* are probably not Tuscan: *amadore*, *armadura* may be Provençal; *ladino* is perhaps taken from the north; *masnada, rugiada*, have a foreign look.

2. *Et* before a vowel seems to give *ed* and *et;* *ot* ($=$ *aut*) gives only *od.* See § 94.

3. *Può* (for *puote* < *pŏtet* = *pŏtest*) seems to come from proclitic use; *puot' fare* > *puo ffare;* see § 51. *Puoi* (for *puoti*) followed *può* and *vuoi.* *Obbliare* and *vallea* are French.

4. The ending *-aticum*, which might have been expected to give *-acco*, was early supplanted by *-aggio*, borrowed (like Spanish *-aje*) from French or Provençal: *coraggio, viaggio.* In bookish words we find *-atico: simpatico.*

5. In vulgar Tuscan speech, *t* in endings has a tendency to become *h* or *þ: birbonahe* for *birbonate.*

105. *S*, like *t*, is voiced in some words but not in others: *asino, casa, cǫsa, naso, pisello* < πίσος, *riso*, with the surd; *caẓo, Fieẓole, miẓe, oẓa, uẓare, viẓo*, with the sonant. Some words have both pronunciations: *susina* Fl., *suẓina* Lucca; *Tereẓa* Fl., *Terẹsa* Lucca. All adjectives in *-oso* and all verb forms from *-ens-* have surd *s: golǫso, strepitǫso; accẹse, pẹso, scẹsi, spẹsero.* So have nearly all nouns and adjectives in *-ese: inglẹse, milanẹse, senẹse*, etc.; but *cortẹẓe, francẹẓe, marchẹẓe, paẹẓe, palẹẓe* have the sonant, also *lucchẹẓe* in Lucca and Pisa. Bookish words all have voiced *ẓ: applauẓo, cauẓa, teẓǫro.*

The stage usage has *ẓ* in all words. Outside of Tuscany, we find *ẓ* in all cases in the north, *s* in all in the Marches, Rome, and the south. The other Romance languages have generalized either *ẓ* (as in French) or *s* (as in Spanish). The two types of *s* have rimed together in Italian verse from the earliest times.

All the theories proposed to explain the Tuscan inconsistency — influence of accent, dialect borrowing, difference of prehistoric Latin prototypes [1] — are unsatisfactory. Can it

---

[1] W. Meyer-Lübke, *Grammatica storico-comparata della lingua italiana e dei dialetti Toscani*, §§ 111, 113; S. Pieri, *Archivio glottologico italiano*, XVI, 163; G. I. Ascoli, *Archivio gl. it.*, XVI, 175.

be that Tuscan intervocalic *s* was once always voiced and is now in process of transition from ʂ to *s?* Such a change seems to have occurred in Spain.

1. Just how *co (n)suere* developed into *cucire* or *cuscire* has not been made clear; Neapolitan has *cósere; cosere* and *cusire* existed in late Vulgar Latin.[1] *Cugino* is supposed to come from Fr. *cousin* < *co (n)so-brīnus.* Why do we find *vagello* for *vasello?*

106. The palatals we have to consider are *k′* and *y.* Latin *g′* had already opened into *y* in the common speech of the Empire: § 78.

K′ becomes *tš: croce, sedici, suocero, vicino.* But in colloquial usage, in Tuscany, Umbria, and Rome, the *t* is suppressed, and only the *š* remains: *višino,* etc. Cf. § 85, 1. Bookish and popular terms are treated alike. For words like *dire, dite, fare, fate, piato, vuoto,* see § 71, 1, 2. The dialects of Siena and Lucca (and perhaps some others) have a certain tendency to voice *tš* into *dž:* Sien. *cortigela, dige, Piagensa, piagere;* Luc. *arbugello, magello, ugello.* Such practice may be responsible for *dugento* and *ugello* in the literary language; also for *vagellare* if it comes from *vacillare,* and for *tregenda* if it is connected with *trecento* (see *Rom.,* XXXVI, 250). But *augello, damigella, plagere* must come from outside of Tuscany.

1. In words like *cæcus cæci, cæca cæcæ,* where the singular has *k* and the plural *k′,* there was a long struggle between phonetic principle and the tendency to level. In feminine plural forms the analogy of the singular triumphed: *cieca cieche.* In masculine plurals, usage is divided: the *k* of the singular has prevailed, with very few exceptions, in paroxytones; whereas the phonetic *tš* has been retained, with somewhat more numerous exceptions, in proparoxytones: *cieco ciechi, mendico mendichi;* but *medico medici.* In Dante's time there was still much hesitation: *biece, bieci, bobolce, caduci, fisice, force, mendici, vinci.* Cf. § 107, 3.

[1] See F. G. Mohl, *Etudes sur le lexique du latin vulgaire;* I. Lhevinne, *The Language of the Glossary Sangalensis 912 and its Relationship to the Language of other Latin Glossaries,* 62; F. d'Ovidio, *Note etimologiche,* 52.

In verb-forms the phonetic principle has prevailed, except in the first conjugation: *dico, dica, dici, dice;* but *reco, rechi, recherà.*

2. *Mancia* probably comes not directly from the singular *manĭca,* but by way of a plural *mance* <*manicæ:* see F. d'Ovidio, *Note etimologiche,* 81.

3. *Fa* beside *face* follows *da, sta;* and on the pattern of *fa* for *face* we have *fe'* for *fece. Di* or *die* for *dici* is apparently taken from the imperative. *Dui* for *duci* perhaps follows *fai,* which is modeled on *dai, stai.*

4. For an old spelling *pacie* = *pace,* etc., see § 85.

107. *Y* is the late Vulgar Latin representative of earlier *j,* g', $d\rho$, di, $g\rho$, gi, z (§ 78). In really popular speech it gives two results, *ddž* and *y,* probably the outcome of two conflicting tendencies in different localities or different social strata. For the influence of accentuation on the development, a better argument can be made, to be sure, in the case of *y* than in the case of other intervocalic consonants; but even here it is far from satisfactory. Examples of *ddž:* *pejórem* > *peggiọre,* **fugíre* > *fuggire, legénda* > *leggenda, mugíre* > *muggire, sagína* > *saggina, sigíllum* > *suggello* (§ 38, 4), *Ludiánum* > *Luggiano, Magiánum* > *Maggiano; péjus* > *pẹggio, légit* > *lẹgge, rūgit* > *rugge, invídia* > *inveggia, pódium* > *pọggio, vídeo* > *vẹggio, exágium* > *saggio, fágeum* > *faggio, régia* > *rẹggia, cōrtem + -iʒω* (§ 78) > *cortẹggio; múgilis* > *muggine, régere* > *rẹggere.* Examples of *y:* *majális* > *maiale, adjútat* > *aiuta, medietátem* > *meitade metà* (§ 42); *bója* > *bọia; cógitat* > **coita cota* (§ 35), *lógicus* > *loico, mágida* > **maida madia* (§ 35, 1), **pagina* > **paina pania* (§ 35, 1), *rúgidus* (from *rūga*) > **ruido ruvido* (cf. §143). Some words have both forms: *majôrem* > *maggiore maiore, meridiáre* > *meriggiare meriare, radiáre* > *raggiare raiare regiónem* > *Montereggione rione* (Rome), *domina + -iʒειν* > *donneggiare donneiare* (also *donneare*); *május* > *maggio maio, hódie* > *ọggi ancoi, vídeo* > *veggio veio; bájulus bájula* > *baggiolo balia* (§ 42, 1).

If this Italian *y* is followed by accented *i* or *e*, it is absorbed by that vowel: *fagina*>*faina, magistrum*>*maestro, nigéllum* >*niẹllo, pagénsis*>*paẹse, regina*>*reina* (*regina* is learned), *vagina*>*guaina* (§ 80, *W*); cf. *fuggire, leggenda*, etc., in the other stratum. In Arezzo the *y* seems to be retained before *e*: *maiestro, paiese;* cf. *Zs.*, Beiheft XV, 90. In *vẹnti, trẹnta* from *vīgĭntī, trīgĭnta*, not only the *y* but the preceding *i* seems to have been absorbed in Italy (as in France). The tens between *decem* and *centum* show peculiar developments everywhere.

As was stated in § 78, there was certainly a school pronunciation that retained *dy*, reinforced it, and then turned it to *ddz;* and in a few words this style has maintained itself, sometimes displacing the more popular form: *mĕdius*>*mezzo* (cf. *mei', me'* in Dante and Boccaccio), *radius*>*raggio razzo*. Late formations were apparently pronounced in this fashion: *ŏleo*>*ŏlĭdus*>*olidius*>*olẹzzo, rŭdis*>*rŭdius*>*rọzzo, prūrīre* >*prūdĕre*>*prūdia*>*pruzza* (first with *ddz*, later with *tts*); so perhaps *schĕdium*>*schizzo*.

1. Bookish words keep as close as possible to the original spellings: *Caio, immagine, pagina, Pompeio, sagẹna, strage, invidia, regione, ozọno*.

2. Verb forms ending in *-eo* and *-io* (*video, audio*, etc.) tend to drop the *y*, in conformity with the second and third persons, which have no such element (*vides, audit*, etc.). Hence **vĭdo*>*vẹdo* (while *vĭdeo*> *vẹggio), *audo*>*ọdo;* similarly, in the third person plural and in the present subjunctive, **audunt*>*ọdon, *audam*>*ọda*. *Vẹggo* is due to the example of *leggo, reggo, figgo, fuggo*, etc. (for the doubling, see § 100).

3. In the plural of words in *-ga* and *-go* there was the same conflict between phonetic and analogical principles that was described for the *-ca* and *-co* words in § 106, 1. Dante, for instance, wrote *plage* and *piage*. Usage has chosen *ghe* and, with few exceptions (all learned), *ghi*. Cf. § 106, 1.

In verb-forms, the phonetic principle has prevailed, except in the first conjugation: *figgo, figga, figgi, figge; piango, pianga, piangi, piange;* but *piago, piaghi, piagherà*.

108. There remain the velar stops, *k* and *g*.

K is usually kept, but in a considerable number of words is voiced to *g*: *amico, dico, fico, pęcora, piędica, sicuro, vacanza, vocale; ago < acus, annegare < necare, fǫlaga < fŭlĭca, fregare < frĭcare, lago, pręgo, spigolo < spīcŭlum, sugo.* Some words have both *k* and *g*: *acuto aguto, festuca festuga, mica miga.* Pisa and Lucca are more inclined to *g* than Florence: *pogo, segondo, siguro.* — In popular Tuscan, except in Arezzo, *k* was long ago opened to χ, which now in Florence, Siena, and Pistoia is generally no more than a strong *h*, and in Lucca and Leghorn is no longer audible (cf. §87, 1): *dico = diho, poco = poho.* This habit, though regarded as a vulgarism, creeps occasionally into the speech of the cultivated. — For the ending *-aticum*, see § 104, 4. — For *mancia*, see § 106, 2. — *Fiaccola* may owe its double *c* to the *y* which once followed (§§ 113, 141): *facula *facla > facchia *fiacca fiaccola.* A similar metathesis of *y* is found in some other words, such as *fiaba < fabula, pioppo < pōpulus*, and probably *chioma < *comula.* — *Poco* is often reduced, doubtless through proclitic use, to *po'*: *un poc' meno*, for instance, would become *um po mmeno.*

G regularly remains unchanged: *agosto, figura, fragola, gastigare, negare, pagano, piaga, ruga.* In a few words, however, it seems to have disappeared in Vulgar Latin (perhaps becoming first a fricative) either in the whole Empire or in a part of it: *ego* everywhere became *eo*, whence It. *io;* beside *a(u)gurium* was *aúrium* (cf. B. Cellini's *aúrio*), whence a verb **ex-a(g)urare*, whence *sciagura sciaúra; regalis *realis > regale reale.* Siena has *aosto* for *agosto*, *fiura* for *figura.* To a similar local fall, perhaps, we owe *striazzo*, ' witchcraft,' beside *stregaccia*, 'old witch,' from *strĭga.* From the French, apparently, are *alleare, reame, leale* (Arezzo *leiale*).

For the conflict between analogy and phonetic principle, see §§ 106, 1, and 107, 3.

1. In *faticare* and several other verbs *-igare* has yielded to the common ending *-icare.* Hence the noun *fatica.*

2. *Sparagio* for *sparago < asparagus* probably arose through a plural *sparagi.*

3. *Fravola* for *fragola* was discussed in § 103, 1; likewise *giovo* for *giogo*, etc.

4. In early texts intervocalic *k* is often spelled *ch*, before back as well as before front vowels: *uno paio di chalçari, de la chasa*. As in the cases described in § 85, we cannot tell whether we have to do merely with an accident of spelling (e.g. *rachonciatura* on the analogy of such forms as *maniche*), or with an early manifestation of the popular Tuscan pronunciation. The former is perhaps the safer hypothesis, although Florentine *f. Arrihi* (i.e., *figlio di Arrigo*) in 1211 (Monaci, p. 22, l. 110) tempts one to the latter.

Double Consonants

109. By a double consonant is meant one whose closure or stricture is held about twice as long as that of a single consonant. Compare English *coat-tail* with *hotel, misspent* with *whisper, steam-mill* with *steamer, unknown* with *funny, foully* with *folly, meanness* with *meaning;* Italian *fatto* with *fato, stẹssa* with *stẹsa, sọmma* with *sọma, sẹnno* with *sẹno, palla* with *palo, innocente* with *inornato.*

Latin double consonants regularly remained unaltered in Italian: *abbattere, sẹcco, addurre, affatto, aggravare, villa, fiamma, anno, cappa, cọrro, spẹsso, mẹttere.* Northern dialects reduce them to simple consonants.

Perhaps as a reaction against the habits described in §§ 100, 101, we find occasionally in Florence a tendency to shorten a double consonant before the accent: *abate; ufizio* for *uffizio; Alighieri* from *Allaghieri, balẹstra* < *ballista, bulicare* < *bullire, Calimala* < *calle mala, canọcchia* < *canna, colazione* or *colezione, colisẹo, coloro* < *eccu'illorum, colui* < *eccu'illui; comando, comune, consumare* < *summa; corẹggia* < *corrĭgia; batista* for *battista;* so *me lo, te lo, se lo, ce lo, ve lo* from *m'ẹllo,* etc. Petrarch generally wrote *dela* or *de la* for *della,* etc.; and his practice has been imitated by many poets since the middle of the nineteenth century. See *Zs.,* Beiheft XIII, 22.

1. It is likely that in *comando, comune,* and also in *cọmodo,* the compound was analyzed as prefix *co-* plus a word beginning with *m.* Or

comunis may have been understood as *com-* + *unus.* See *Mélanges Chabaneau,* 770; and F. G. Mohl, *Etudes sur le lexique du latin vulgaire,* 8.

2. *Canape* < *cannăbis* was apparently influenced by *sęnape* < σίναπι. *Cica,* 'nothing at all,' from *cĭccum,* 'trifle,' has evidently felt the attraction of *mica* < *mīca.* So *coręggia* < *corrĭgia,* 'belt,' may have been associated with *cŏrium,* 'leather.'

3. Dante uses in the rime *galeoto, scimia, perdési* for *perdéssi* = *si perdè, fuci* for *fucci* = *ci fu,* and several similar forms. Do these represent real spoken Tuscan usage, or did the poet in these cases affect a northern pronunciation, or did he simply take advantage of prevalent inconsistency in spelling?

4. **Carricare* > *carcare* then *caricare* (§ 62). *Collocare* > **colcare corcare* (influence of *carcare*) then *coricare.*

5. *Ille* in V. L. generally became *ĭllī* on the model of *quī.* Then *ĭllī,* singular or plural, before a vowel became *egl' egli: ĭllī amat, ĭllī amant* > *egli ama, egli aman.* This *ęgli,* used before a consonant, developed into *ei* and, in Florence, into *e'* (§ 42): *egli tace* > *ei tace* > *e' tace.* From *quello* similarly came *quegli, quei, que'.* Hence, by analogy, such plurals as *capęgli, capęi.*

6. From *vessīca* we have *vescica;* beside *dissipare, discipare;* beside *Assisi, Ascesi.* Cf. § 84, *S* and § 84, 2.

Medial Groups

110. Learned words generally keep consonant groups as far as the habits of Italian will allow: *negligere* (compare *negghiente* < *negligentem*), *tecnico* (usually pronounced *tennico*), *concilio* (cf. *consiglio*).

111. The prefixes *ad-, sub-* regularly assimilate their *d-, b-* to a following consonant: *arrivare, sollevare;* so *soggetto, oggetto,* as compared with *obbietto, abbietto* or *abietto,* without assimilation. *Con-, in-* assimilate to the extent of changing *n* to *m* before a labial, to *l* before *l,* to *r* before *r: compiacere, illaidire* < *laido, corrędo* < *redo.*

112. For the sake of convenience, we may divide medial groups into three great classes: (1) those ending in *l, r, w,* or *y;* (2) those beginning with *l, m, n, r,* or *s,* and not ending in *l, r, w,* or *y;* (3) all others.

Groups ending in L

113. Latin *l*, which must have had from the beginning a somewhat palatal character, intensified that quality when preceded by a velar or palatal stop, which carried the arched tongue up into the middle part of the mouth; then the palatalization spread imitatively to *l* after other consonants. Finally, perhaps no earlier than the twelfth century, the *l'* relaxed into *y*. At this point the foregoing consonant, being in danger of absorption in the *y*, fortified itself by doubling, unless another consonant stood before it. For instance, *ŏcŭlus* > *ǫklus* > *ǫk'l'o* > *ǫk'yo* > *ǫk'k'yo* = *occhio*.[1] Cf. § 89.

Early *tl* > *kl*, the latter being very much commoner than the former, and the two groups being nearly identical to the ear (English *climb*, *clock*, for instance, are very often pronounced with *t*): *vĕtŭlus* > *veclus* > *vęcchio*, *capĭtŭlum* > *capęcchio*.

Ml prematurely denasalized the end of its *m* into a transitional *b*, becoming *mbl*. *Rl* usually remained. For *dl*, *nl*, and late *tl*, see § 115.

Examples: PL, *capulum* > *cappio*, *cōpula* > *cǫppia*, *dŭplex* *dŭplus > *dǫppio*, *ŏpulus* > *ǫppio*, *stĭpula* *stŭpula > *stǫppia*, *exemplum* > *scęmpio*, *tĕmplum* > *tęmpio*; BL, *ĕbulum* > *ębbio*, *fībula* > *fibbia*, *nĕbula* > *nębbia*, *sabulum* > *sabbia*; ML, *sĭmĭlare* > *sembiare* (also *sembrare*); FL, *conflat* > *gǫnfia*; FFL, *sŭfflat* > *sǫffia*; GL, *tēgula* > *tęgghia*, *vĭg(ĭ)lat* > *vęgghia*, *cĭngula* > *cinghia*, *ŭngula* > *unghia*; KL, *genĭculum genŭculum* > *ginǫcchio*, *ŏculus* > *ǫcchio*, *spĕculum* > *spęcchio*, *cĭrculus* > *cęrchio*, *exclarire > *schiarire*, *inclūdere* > *inchiudere*, *sarculum* > *sarchio*; TL, *capĭtulum* > *capęcchio*, *fistula* > *fischio*, *rŏtulus* > *rǫcchio*, *sĭtula* > *sęcchia*, *vĕtulus* > *vęcchio*, *testula* > *tęschio*; RL, *Carolus* > *Carlo*, *ōrulum* > *ǫrlo*.

1. *Rl* in early Italian sometimes assimilated the *r* to the *l*: *amarlo* > *amallo*, *vederlo* > *vedello*, *per lo* > *pello*. Much oftener it remained unchanged: *burræ* *burrula > *burla*, *mĕrula* > *męrla*. The only remaining trace is *pello*, etc., still used beside *per lo*, etc.

[1] See *Archivio glottologico italiano*, XIII, 361 and 452; *Romania*, XXX, 453.

2. *Ad-vinculat>avvinghia, perhaps under influence of cinghia. Ob(b)liare ubbliare (from oblītare) is French. Giullare may have been borrowed from Provençal joglar<jocularem. Sirocchia<sororcula seems to have lost an r by dissimilation. Why should scŏpulus have given scǫglio?

3. In vulgar Tuscan, sk'y is often replaced by sty: fistiare, mistio, rastiare for fischiare, etc. Such forms are common in texts of the sixteenth century. Cf. § 89, 1.

4. Learned words generally keep the l: replęto, ręplica, amplesso, recluso, sęmplice; but bibbia, esempio.

114. Beside the regular Tuscan forms with k'k'y and g'g'y there are some forms with l', nearly all belonging to poetic diction: lenticchia lentiglia, orecchia oreglia, parecchio pariglio, specchio speglio, vecchio veglio; mugghia muglia<*mugulat mūgit, stregghia striglia<*strigula strĭgĭlis, tegghia teglia, vegghia veglia. So artiglio, coniglio, miraglio (miracolo), periglio (pericolo), spiraglio (spiracolo), triglia<τρίγλα. These l' forms are probably all borrowed from Provençal or from central or southern dialects. See F. d'Ovidio in Archivio glottologico italiano, XIII, 361.

Similarly for ngl we find double forms, with ng'y and with n', the latter being probably always borrowed from outside of Tuscany: cinghia cigna <cĭngula, cinghiale cignale<singularis, ringhiare rignare<*ringulare ringi, unghia ugna< ŭngula.

115. In a subsequent linguistic stratum occur the groups dl, nl, tl (formed too late to become kl: § 113), which simply assimilate the first element to the second: ad lo>allo, ad latus>allato; ben lo>colloquial bello, con lei>colloquial collei, con lo>collo, ĭnula>ella, lūnula>lulla, man levare>mallevare, non lo>nollo nol, *planula>pialla, spīnula>spilla; *corrotulare>crollare, spathula>spalla. Cf. Latin corolla< corōnula, ullus<ūnulus, villum<vīnulum. Modern usage has generally restored non lo and to some extent con lo.

Groups ending in R

116. *Kr, pr, tr* have a double development parallel to that
of intervocalic *k, p, t* (§§ 103, 104, 108); that is, they remain
unchanged in some words, while in others they become
respectively *gr, vr, dr: sacro, magro; capra, sovrano; pietra,
madre.* *Dr* (like intervocalic *d*) persists: *quadro.* Pisa and
Lucca have *quara.* *Gr*, too, is similar to *-g-* in that the first
element remains in some words, while in others it disappears:
ęgro < *ægrum, nęro* < *nĭgrum. Lr, llr, nr* become simply *rr: varrò,
tǫrre* < *tŏllĕre, pǫrre* < *pōnĕre.* *Br, fr*, in a reaction against
assimilation, double their first element: *fabbro, Affrica* (now
oftener *fr* in Tuscany). *Mr (mmr)* and *sr* develop a transitional consonant, *b* or *d: membrare* < *memorare, sdraiare* from
isdraiare < **ex-radiare.* Then *mbr* and also *mpr* tend to ease
the accumulation of consonants by forming an *e* before the *r*:
gambero < *gammărus; comperare comprare* < *comparare.* Other
groups of three consonants remain unaltered: *altro, mandra,
aspro.*

Examples: KR, *lavacro, lucro* < *lŭcrum, sacra sagra; agro, allęgro* <
**alĭcrem alacrem, lagrima lacrima, magro macro, segretario, segreto
secreto, vinagro: gr* seems to be the really popular form. PR, *aprile,
aprire avrire, capra, capriola cavriola, coprire covrire, ginępro* < *juneperus
juniperus, lępre* < *lĕpŏrem; sopra sovra; ovra, ricov (e)rare* < *recŭperare,
scev (e)rare* < *separare, sovra- sopra-, sovrano soprano sobrano* (Cellini):
the genuine Tuscan is *pr*, the *vr* forms being in the main Bolognese. TR,
Chiatri, dietro < *de rĕtro, pietra, Pietro, vętro; adro* < *atrum, ladro, madre,
padre:* here both forms seem native, *tr* being originally the more elegant.
DR, *cattedra, quadro.* GR, *agręsto* (' green grape '), *ęgro* < *ægrum, fra-
granza, pellegrino, pigro* < *pĭgrum; gnaręsta* (' sour grapes ') < *vinea
agrestis, intęro* < *intĕgrum, nęro* < *nĭgrum, pęrito* < *pĭgrĭtor:* in some
words the loss of the *g* goes back to Vulgar Latin, in others it belongs
probably to rustic Italian. LR, LLR, *varrò, vorrò, tǫrre.* NR, *Arrigo,
orrato = onorato, pǫrre, terrò, verrò.* BR, *fabbro, febbraio, fębbre, labbro,
lĭbbra, ubbriaco* < *ebriācus.* FR, *Affrica Africa.* MR, MMR, MPR, *membrare, gambero, comp (e)rare.* SR, *(i)sdraiare, (i)sdrucciolare* < **ex-
roteolare.* OTHER GROUPS OF THREE, *altro, andrò, destro, ęmbrice* <
ĭmbrĭcem, finestra, mandra, offre, oltre < *ŭltra, ombra, Sandro, settembre,
soffre, vespro.*

1. *Lẹbbra* < *lĕpra* seems to imitate *fẹbbre*. *Sor-*, as in *sorprendere*, is probably not from *sŭper*, but from the first syllable of *sorrẹggere* < *surrĭgere* (i.e., *sub* + *regere*), *sorrídere* < *subrĭdēre*, which was understood as meaning *sŭper*.

2. *Burro* < βούτυρον is perhaps borrowed. *Porò* = *potrò* follows *sarò* and *arò* = *avrò*. *Piero* is not of Tuscan origin.

3. *Quadragēsima*, It. *quarẹsima*, is irregular in various languages. The fall of the *d* may have started in Gaul.

4. *Ottọbre* is perhaps learned. *Lira* seems to have been imported into Tuscany. *Avrò*, from *aver'ò*, is not an example of *br; arò* follows *darò, farò, starò*. *Opprobrium* > *brobbio* shows both assimilation and dissimilation.

Groups ending in W

117. We must make a distinction between Classic Latin *w* (as in *lingua, sequi*) and Classic Latin *u* in hiatus (as in *placuit, voluit*) which became *w* in Vulgar Latin.

As to the first, which occurs only after *g* and *k*, we have to note that during the Empire, if not before, it fused with a following *u* or *o*: *distinguo* > **distingo; antĩquus* > *anticus* > *antico, cŏquus* > *cocus* > *cuoco, torqueo* > **torquo* > **torco* > *tọrco*. Hence, by analogy, we get It. *antica, cuocere, tọrcere*. On the other hand, we find *sẹguo* < *sĕquor* in imitation of *sẹgui, sẹgue*.

Otherwise *gw* remains in Italian; and so does *kw*, except that between vowels it voices the *k*: *lingua, sangue; cinque; adæquare* > *adeguare, æqualis* > *uguale, *de-lĩquare* > *dileguare, sĕquit (ur)* > *sẹgue*.

1. *Aqua* for some reason doubled its *k* in Vulgar Latin: *acqua*, so It. *acqua*. Perhaps it fell under the influence of such words as *placuit, tacuit* (see § 118).

2. In book-words, *gu* and *qu* are kept throughout: *aquila, estinguo, iniquo*.

118. Secondary *w* (i.e., *ŭ* preceded by a consonant and followed by a vowel) caused a prolongation of the foregoing consonant, which was apparently in danger of absorption:

jacui > *giacqui*. If the consonant was a labial or a dental, the *w* then fell: *habuit* > *abbe ebbe*, *pŏtuit* > old *pǫtte*. If it was a liquid, the *w* either fell or became *v*: *vŏluit* > *vǫlle*, *paruit* > *parve*.
Perfects in which the ending *-vi* immediately follows the root vowel (*cognōvi, crēvi*) appear to have prolonged their *w* (*krẹwwi*). At any rate, the outcome of such a *-vi* is identical with the result of *-bui: crevi* > *crebbi, habui* > *abbi ebbi*.

Examples: PW, *sapui* > *seppi*; BW, *bĭbī* *bĭbuī > *bẹbbi* (Siena), *habuit* > *abbe ebbe*; WW, *co*(*g*)*nōvit* > *conǫbbe, crēvit* > *crẹbbe*; TW, *pŏtuit* > *potte*; DW, *cĕcĭdit* *caduit > *cadde, vīdit* *vĭduit > *vidde*; NW, *Januarius Jenuarius* > *gennaio, manuaria* > *mannaia*, *mĭnuus > *menno, tĕnuit* > *tẹnne, vēnit* *vēnuit > *vẹnne*; LW, *bēlua* > *bẹlva, dŏluit* > old *dolve, vŏluit* > *vǫlle*; RW, *paruit* > *parve*; KW, *jacui* > *giacqui, nŏcuit* > *nǫcque, placuit* > *piacque, tacui* > *tacqui*.

1. Sometimes the analogy of the present stem invades the perfect: *bẹvvi* (cf. Sienese *bẹbbi*) < **bĭbui, mǫvve* < *mōvit, piǫvve* (Sienese *piǫbbe*) < *plovit pluit, with *vv* instead of *bb*, and old *ricevve* < *recĭpuit recēpit, with *vv* instead of *pp*, follow the lead of *bẹvere, mǫvere, piǫvere, ricẹvere*. *Febbraio, morto* seemingly come from *Febrarius, mortus*, with *w* already lost.

2. In early book-words, *ua* > *ova*, whence masculine *ovo: continuus* > *continovo, Genova, manuale* > *manovale, Mantova, vĭdua* > *vẹdova, victualia* > *vettovaglia*. Cf. § 74.

3. In later book-words, *ua, ue, ui, uo* were kept, and *uu* > *uo: persuado, tẹnue, mutui, infatuo, strẹnuo,*

Groups ending in Y

119. Two strong tendencies are here in conflict: the tendency to absorb or assimilate and the tendency to resist absorption. Their extremes may be illustrated by *area* > *aia* and *trĭvium* > *trẹbbio*.
Already in Vulgar Latin times, as we have seen (§§ 78, 107), *d* and *g* had in popular speech been swallowed up in *y*; hence the groups *dy* and *gy*, having become *y*, need not come under consideration in this place. The combination *ndy*,

however, calls for a word of mention. We have noted that
beside the regular development of *dy* into *y* there was a school
pronunciation *ddy* which became *ddz: radius* gave both *raggio*
and *razzo.* Thus *ndy* might produce colloquially *ny* > *n'*, and
scholastically *ndy* > *ndz:* on the one hand *verecŭndia* > *ver-*
gǫgna; on the other, *prandium* > *pranzo,* *mandium (cf.
mandra) > *manzo.*

120. Of the groups that remained at the close of the Vulgar
Latin period, *ly* and *ny* and *sy* lent themselves easily to complete, *k'y* and *ty* to partial assimilation. Hardest to fuse were
ry and labial + *y:* in the case of *ry* the upshot was the entire
loss of the first element; in the case of labial + *y,* a reinforcement of it.

121. Let us consider first the labials, which offered such
vigorous and successful resistance.

My > *mmy: sīmia* > *scimmia, vindēmia* > *vendęmmia.* Such
forms as *temiamo* are of course due to the analogy of *temete,*
etc. Latin *mmy* remains: *commeātus* > *commiato; congedo*
is French.

By and *βy* both give *bby;* after a consonant, *by: habeāmus*
> *abbiamo,* Ger. *laubja* + *-onem* > *lubbione, objectum* > *obbietto,*
habeat > *abbia, dēbeo* > *debbio, labium labia* > *labbia, rabies*
rabia > *rabbia, rŭbeus* > *rǫbbio, scabies scabia* > *scabbia, cam-*
biat > *cambia; gavia* + *-ānus* > *gabbiano, cavea* > *gabbia, Igū-*
vium > *Gubbio, trĭvium* > *trębbio.* There are, however, some
cases of *ddž,* borrowed from Sicilian, French, and Provençal:
dēbeo > *deggio, habeat* > *aggia, laubja* > *lǫggia, rŭbeus* > *roggio;*
fǒvea > *fǫggia, allěviat* > *allęggia,* *leviarius > *leggęro.* The verb-
forms are doubtless Sicilian, the others mostly French. From
the French surely comes *saggio,* ' sage,' whatever be its ulti-
mate source. *Piǫggia* seems imported from the south, its
parent being *plǒvia for *plŭvia,* from *plǒvěre* = *plŭěre* (§ 29,
5); in early Tuscan the commoner word is *piova,* a postverbal
formation from *piǫvere. Soggetto* < *subjectum* is an example

of the assimilation of *sub-* (§ 111); hence, by imitation, *oggetto* and *aggetto*.

Py > *ppy;* after a consonant, *py: pipiōnem* > *pippione*, *sapiamus* > *sappiamo, apium* > *appio, ŏpium* > *ǫppio, sēpia* > *sęppia; ĭmpius* > *ęmpio, scorpiōnem* > *scorpione*. Corresponding to the cases of *ddž* from *by* and *βy*, we have a few instances of *ttš* from *py*, all borrowed. French contributed *approcciare* from **ad-propeare*. Southern are probably *piccione* < *pipionem, saccente* < *sapientem, saccia* < *sapiam*. From *pŭppa *pŭppia* we have *pǫccia,* ' nipple,' which is either southern or influenced by its synonym *ciǫccia* < *ciocciare*, an onomatopoetic variant of *succiare* < *sūctiare*.

1. In a few proper names *vy* become *y: Bovianum* (Gr. Βοïανον) > *Boiano, Danŭvius* > *Danoia, Octavianus* > *Ottaiano, Vitrŭvius* > *Vitruio*.

2. By imitation of *dovrębbe,* a *dębbe* develops beside *dęve *dęve* < *dēbet*. Hence *debbo,* and then subjunctive *debba,* which supplant *debbio, debbia*. Modeled on *debbo, debba* are *abbo, abba; abbo* got the better of *abbio,* but *abbia* maintained itself against *abba*.

3. How did *grĕmium* become *grębmo?* Perhaps **gremmio *grembio* (cf. *grembiale*) *grembo* (influenced by *lembo* < *limbus*). See *Zs.,* XXX, 300.

122. *K'y* and *ty,* in Tuscany, became respectively *t't'š* and *tts;* after a consonant, *t'š* and *ts: placeo* > *piaccio, ŭrceus* > *ǫrcio; pŭteum* > *pǫzzo, Martius* > *marzo*. That is, the attraction of the *y* drew *k* forward, and lifted the blade and middle of the tongue for *t,* giving to both stops a palatal formation: *k'y, t'y*. The stop was then reinforced, to resist the *y: k'k'y, t't'y;* later both were shifted forward to *t't'y, tty*. Finally, the *y* itself, dominated by the strong explosive hiss of the double consonant, became a sibilant, *š* after *t'* and *s* after *t: t't'š, tts*. An original *k'k'y* gives the same result as *k'y: bracchium* > *braccio*.

If *k'* and *t'* are carried to the extreme of palatalization, they meet on common ground, and become indistinguishable. It was natural, then, that endings containing these elements

should be confused, as they sometimes were in Vulgar Latin: [1]
solacium solatium > sollazzo. So *Alētium > Lecce,* *com-initiare
>comenzare cominciare, **ex-cŭrtiare>scorzare,* *ex-quartiare
>squarciare; cf. the bookish *offĭcium>ufficio uffizio, pronun-*
tiare>pronunziare pronunciare. Even *tt* was affected: *gŭtta,*
hence **gutteare>gocciare,* hence *goccia.* Some localities and
some individuals reduce *tts* to *ss; bellessa, nassione* in Arezzo
and Genua.

There was also abundant confusion of *ty* and *sy,*[2] which
resulted in frequent *ž* (written *g:* see § 127) for *tts: indūciæ*
indūtiæ **indūsiæ>indugia, pretium>prezzo pregio, rationem*
>ragione (Siena *razzone*), *stationem>stagione* (old *stazzone*),
traditionem>tradigione, palatium>palazzo palagio, servitium
>servigio (learned *servizio*). There are some seventeen such
words, five of which have also *zz* or *z.* Aside from these,
there are about twenty-five words in *-ĭties -ĭtia* which show an
ending *-igia* instead of the regular *-ęzza;* five of them have
both: **alteritia > alterigia alterezza, cupiditia > cupidigia*
covidigia.

1. There is a considerable number of forms with *zz* or *z* from *k'y,*
borrowed from other dialects or languages: *calza* from *calcea is northern; *brazzo* for *braccio, Franza* for *Francia* are southern, so *lonza* if it

[1] H. Schuchardt, *Der Vokalismus des Vulgärlateins,* 1866–68, I, 150 ff.;
E. Seelmann, *Die Aussprache des Latein nach physiologisch-historischen
Grundsätzen,* 1885, 320 ff.; A. J. Carnoy, *Some Obscurities in the Assi-
bilation ti and di before a vowel in Vulgar Latin,* in *Transactions of the
American Philological Association,* XLVII (1916), 145 ff.; F. d'Ovidio,
Ancora dello zeta in rima, in *Raccolta di studii critici dedicata ad A.
D'Ancona,* 617 ff. For a different view, see S. Puşcariu, *Lateinisches ti̥
und ki̥ im Rumänischen, Italienischen, und Sardischen,* 1904 (reviewed
by A. Zauner in *Literaturblatt für germanische und romanische Philologie,* XXVII, 64).

[2] Schuchardt (above), I, 153 (*nunsius, osiosus, marsius,* etc.);
Seelmann (above), 322–323 (*consiensia, observasione, sepsies,* etc.); A.
Horning, *Zur Ti-Frage im Französischen,* in *Zs.,* XXXI, 200. Cf.
Literaturblatt (above), XXVII, 65.

comes from *lyncea<lynx¹; paonazzo, popolazzo seem Roman; romanzo probably is from Old French romans romanz<Romanĭce (with z voiced by influence of manzo, pranzo).

123. Examples: K'Y, facienda>faccenda, jaceamus>giacciamo, cortĭcea>cortęccia, placeo>piaccio, -aceus>-accio, lanceare>lanciare, Francia>Francia, ŭrceus>ǫrcio; K'K'Y, bisaccium>bisaccia; KWY, laqueus>laccio.

TY, Capitianum>Capezzano, *minūtiare>minuzzare, Puteóli>Pozzuoli, vitiosus>vezzoso, palatium>palazzo, platea> piazza, prĕtium>pręzzo, pŭteus>pǫzzo, spatium>spazzo, -atius>-azzo, -ĭtia>-ęzza, *altiare>alzare, cantionem>canzone, linteóla>lenzuola, martius>marzo, -antia>-anza, -entia >-enza; TTY, mattea>mazzo, *pettia>pezzo.

Kty, pty, tk'y seem to have been utterly mixed, giving at random t't'š or tts: *dīrēctiare>dirizzare, *dŭctiare>docciare, factionem>fazzone, *impactiare>impacciare, *extractiare> stracciare, *sūctiare>succiare, suspectionem>sospeccione sospezzone; captiare>cacciare, (comere) comptus *comptiare> conciare; nuptiœ + *nŏvius (<nŏvus)>nǫzze; *ex-corticiare? >scorzare (now pronounced with voiced z in Tuscany).

For SK'Y, STY, see § 128.

1. Book-words have tsy from ty, tsy or t'šy from k'y: stazione; uffizio or ufficio. This ts is pronounced long (tts) between vowels in central Italy west and north of the Tiber. In southern dialects (except Sicilian) book-words have tsy from ty or k'y, ttsy from kty or pty: orazione, giudizio; azzione, concezzione. So it seems to have been in Florence in the sixteenth century. Southern forms with t't'š, though numerous, are all borrowed, the only regular local development being tts or ts.²

124. Ly>l', ny>n', sy>ž, ssy>š, but ry>y: mĕlius> męglio, vĕnio >vęgno, phasiana>fagiana, bāsium *bŭssium> bascio, paria>paia.

---

¹ See A. Levi in Giornale storico della letteratura italiana, XLIV, 190.

² See F. d'Ovidio in Studi letterari e linguistici dedicati a Pio Rajna, 40–41; J. Jordan, Lateinisches cį und tį im Süditalienischen, in Zs., XLII, 516.

1. In the thirteenth and fourteenth centuries there was a fashion of dropping *i̧* or *ȩ* after *l, n, s,* and *r* in clerical Latin, and Italian Latinisms coined at that time show this peculiarity: *evangel(i)um > vangę̄lo; Babilona, domino, extran(e)us > strano, Lavina, letane = litanie, Macedona, pane = panie, pecuna, scrutinium > squittino, Tarquino; eccles(i)a > chiesa, fisonomia, tons(i)onem > tosone; contraro, desidę̄ro, impę̄ro, ingiura, matę̄ra, memǭra, varo,* etc. Some of these forms have persisted: *vangę̄lo, strano, chię̄sa, impę̄ro.*

2. Another stratum of bookish forms, not clearly accounted for, is illustrated by *palio < pallium, ǫlio = ǫglio < ǒleum, sǫlio = sǫglio < sǒlium; cǫnio = cǫgno < cǒngius, farnia < farnea, miniare < miniare (< minium), smánia* from *smaniare < *ex-maniare (< mania); ariuǫlo < hartǒlus, oriuǫlo < ?*hōriǒlum = horologium.* Words in *-aria -o, -eria -o, -oria -o* are all learned, as are nouns in *-sione:* e. g., *criterio, pensione.*

3. Such forms as *celiamo, teniamo, posiamo, bussiamo, moriamo* owe the preservation of the *l, n, s, ss,* or *r* to the analogy of *celate, tenete,* etc.

125. Examples of *ly* and *lly:* LY, *saliamus > sagliamo, valeamus > vagliamo, figlio, mę̄glio, mŭlier > mǫglie, talea > taglia, *ex-ēlĭgit *exę̄l'jit > scę̄glie;* LLY, **tolliamus > togliamo, cǒllĭgit > cǫglie.* This *l',* between vowels, is long.

Before a vowel, *belli, delli, elli, quelli, tali, vuoli* change their *lli* or *li,* through *lly* or *ly,* to *l'* (§ 78): *begli occhi, degli anni, egli esce, quegli uomini, tali* or *tagli animali, vuogli andare.* Then, these forms with *l'* being used (for the Italians are fond of palatals) before a consonant, the *l'* regularly develops into *i* (cf. § 59, 1): *bei capelli, dei secoli, ei parte, quei giovani, tai cavalli, vuoi venire.* For the subsequent fate of *bei,* etc., in Florence, see § 42.

1. Some dialects have *g'g'y* instead of *l',* an intensification of the long palatal fricative having brought about a complete closure of its beginning, with a subsequent relaxation of its end: *fīlius > figlio > figghio.* Such forms are usual in the south, but they are found also in spots even in Tuscany — for instance, in Certaldo.

2. *Dolgo, salgo, tolgo, valgo* beside *doglio < dǒleo, saglio < salio,* etc., are sometimes explained as a phonetic development; but the situation here is very different from the one just described. It is much more likely that we have to do with imitation of the type *colgo < collĭgo,*

scelgo < **ex-ēligo*. Sicilian regularly has *doglio*, etc. Following *dolgo*, etc., vulgar Tuscan has *dolghiamo*, etc.; hence *volghiamo* for *vogliamo*. Cf. § 126, 1.

126. Examples of *ny, lny, mny, ng'y, nny:* NY, *vinearius* > *vignaio, castanea* > *castagna, těneo* > *tęgno, věnio* > *vęgno;* LNY, *balneum* > *bagno;* MNY, *omnia* > *ogna, omne* > *onne* > before vow. *ogni, somnium* > *sǫgno;* NG'Y, *cǒngius* > *cǫgno, spǒngia* > *spugna;* NNY, *pinna* > **pinnionem* > *pignone.*

1. *Tengo, vengo,* beside *tegno, vegno,* have apparently copied the pattern set by *giungo* < *jungo, piango* < *plango,* etc., which have also the forms *giugno, piagno,* etc., on the model of *giugne* < *jungit, piagne* < *plangit,* etc. (§ 130). Dante's *punga* for *pugna* seems to be a postverbal from *pugnare *pungare* modeled on *giugnere giungere.* Following *tengo, vengo,* vulgar Tuscan has *tenghiamo, venghiamo.* Cf. § 125, 2.

2. B. Cellini frequently uses *gnene* for *gliene,* a partial assimilation of *l'* to following *n.*

127. *Sy* developed into a voiced sibilant first written *sg*(*i*) or *sc*(*i*), later spelled *g*(*i*): *occasionem* > *casgione cagione.* It is likely that the sound has in central Italy always been *ž.* But the spelling *g*(*i*) has led to a pronunciation *dž* outside of Tuscany and Umbria — that is, outside the region that reduces *dž* to *ž* between vowels (§ 86, 1). For instance, a Roman, pronouncing *la gente* as *la džente,* naturally interpreted *cagione,* not as *cažone,* but as *cadžone.*[1]

Examples: *Ambrogio, Anastagio, Apusiana* > *Pugiana, *cěrěsea* > *ciliegia, occasionem* > *cagione, pe*(*n*)*sionem* > *pigione, Perusia* > *Perugia, phasiana* > *fagiana.*

1. In several words the *sy* appears to have developed like *ssy* (§ 128): *Perůsia* > *Peroscia* beside *Perugia* and Sienese *Perogia, Petrusiana* > *Petrosciana, Cœsianum* > *Cisciana.* Here we may have to do merely with an original spelling *sci* for *sgi,* which led to a pronunciation *š.* Likewise in the case of *camicia* or *camiscia* from *camisia,* we may perhaps assume that the *sci,* primitively intended for *ž,* was interpreted *š* and thus gave rise, in Tuscany, Umbria, and Rome, to a spelling *ci,* which there meant the same as *sci.* *Cucio* or *cuscio* for *consuo consio* is

[1] For different theories, see N. Caix, *Origini della lingua poetica italiana,* 161; F. d'Ovidio, *Note etimologiche,* 52, 56, 70.

obscure, even after F. d'Ovidio's penetrating discussion in the *Note Etimologiche*, 52 ff. (§ 105, 1, with footnote). Somewhat different seems to be the history of *caseus > cascio cacio* and *basium > bagio bascio bacio*. It is not unlikely that *caseus* and *basium* belong to the class of words with double forms described in § 14 — i.e., that beside *cāseus, bāsium* there existed **căsseus *băssium*. The latter forms would then give *cascio, bascio*, while *bāsium* would give *bagio*. *Cacio* and *bacio* would be central Italian spellings equivalent to *cascio* and *bascio;* used outside the central region, they would have there led to a pronunciation *catšo, batšo* instead of *cašo, bačo*.

2. *Nksy* becomes *nsy* in *anxia > ansia*.

128. *Ssy* gave a long *š*, and so did *sk'y, sty*, and *ksy:* SSY, *Bassiana > Basciana, Messianum > Misciano, *reversius *revessius* (§ 76, *R*) *>rovescio, *subversius *subvessius > sovescio;* SK'Y, *fascia > fascia;* STY, *angŭstia > angǫscia, pŏstea > pǫscia;* KSY, *Brĭxia > Bręscia*.

1. If *bru(s)ciare* comes from *combūstum*, with or without the influence of German *brunst*, the spelling without *s* has doubtless the same origin as *bacio, cacio* (§ 127, 1): **com-brustiare > brusciare bruciare.*

2. *Esco* probably comes from **exo* for *exeo*, on the analogy of *cresco, conosco, finisco. *Exo* itself lost its *y* as did so many other verbs: *aud(i)o > ǫdo, sent(i)o > sento, vid(e)o > vedo*, the *y* falling because the other persons had none (*vidyo vides videt vidēmus vidētis vident*).

129. *Ry > y:* *moriamur > muoiamo, variolus > vaiǫlo, area > aia, -arius > -aio, glarea > ghiaia, paria > paia, Pistorium > Pistǫia, -torius > -tǫio, varius > vaio.*

1. The plural of *-arius* being *-ari*, we have, in Tuscan, sing. *-aio*, pl. *-ari;* hence, by analogy, sing. *-aro* and pl. *-ai:* *marinaio* or *marinaro*, pl. *marinari* or *marinai*. Cf. *crederei* for **crederiei*. By the analogy of *marinaio marinari* we have from *Giudeo* an old plural *Giuderi;* we find also *batistèo* as a singular of *batisteri*.

Groups beginning with L, M, N, R, S

130. Groups beginning with *l, m, n, r,* or *s,* and not ending in *l, r, w,* or *y,* regularly remain unchanged: *alba, tempo, vento, corpo, posta.* Some combinations, however, show special developments.

L before a consonant tends to become popularly u in Lucca and Pisa, i in the dialects of Florence and Pistoia: *autro, fauce, vause; aitro, moito.* The change to u is found also in Venice and in parts of the south. Dante, *De Vulg. El.*, I, xv, cites *munto* for *multo* in Parma. The words *mǫta* < *maltha* and *tǫpo* < *talpa* show the vocalization of l to u; but, inasmuch as the resulting *au* has become $ǫ$, these forms must have been imported from outside of Tuscany. The Tuscan retains *talpa* in its original sense of 'mole.' *Sŏlĭdus* gives not only the noun *sǫldo* but also the adjective *sǫdo*. L is lost also in Florentine *comígnolo* < **culmineum* and in *mugnaio* < **molinarius.*

Lg' > *ly* > *l'*: **exēlĭgit* > *sceglie.* See § 125. Such words as *álgere, fúlgido* are learned; *fulvido* < *fulvus* + *fulgidus.* Why did *mulgēre* become *múngere?*

Lg: *bolgia* apparently comes from *bulga* through the French.

Lk': *dolze* (for *dǫlce* < *dŭlcem*) is doubtless Provençal.

Llk: *collocare* > *corcare,* perhaps under the influence of *carcare* < **carricare.*

Lv: for *Elba* < *Ilva,* cf. *Rv* below. Why have we *vǫlgere* from *volvĕre?* *Sciǫgliere* from *ex-solvĕre* follows *cǫgliere.*

M is assimilated to a following dental, becoming n; *conte* < *cŏmĭtem, danno, Sansone, sentiero* < *semitarius.*

Mb: beside *ambedue* (also *ambeduo, ambedui*) from *ambœ duœ,* feminine of *ambo duo,* we find the strange form *amendue,* which has not been satisfactorily explained:[1] see J. T. Clark in *Romania,* XXX, 593; W. Meyer-Lübke in *Zs.,* XXIX, 246, N. Maccarrone in *Arch. glott. ital.,* XVIII, 504, note. Rumanian, also, has *amîndoĭ.* In Old French and Provençal we find *amdui, andui;* in Provençal and Catalan, *abdos.* Other Italian words with *mb* are regular: *cambio, colomba, piombo.*

Nd, usually preserved (*dando, mandare, onda, onde*), suffers a curious reduction in *ne* from *inde:* see J. T. Clark in

---

[1] *Filostrato,* V, I, 2, has *intramendue.*

Romania, XXX, 593; W. Meyer-Lübke in *Zs.*, XXIX, 246; S. Pieri in *Studj romanzi*, I, 34. Southern dialects regularly change *nd* to *nn* (*quanno*, *tannu* for *quando*), but Tuscan *ne* can hardly be an imported form. Provençal has *ent*, *en*, *n*, and a *ne* which developed out of *n*. Early Italian texts have *inde, nde, de*. Furthermore, *inde* was often used for the preposition *in;* there seems to have been in the latest stage of Latin in Italy a confusion of *in* and *inde*, the latter having been sometimes taken, apparently, for a compound of *in* and *de*. *In illa via*, for instance, might become *inn ella via* (see § 100, third paragraph) or *in d'ella via*, in which phrases -*ne*- and -*nde*- are employed interchangeably. This, possibly, was a starting-point for the use of *ne* instead of '*nde* as an adverb and then as a pronoun. — Cf. § 42, § 45, 5. *Manducare* probably became *manicare* through **mancare:* see § 62. *Mangiare*, like *giuggiare* and *vengiare*, must come from French or Provençal. — *Sovente* comes from *sub inde* not directly, but through Old French *sovent*.

Ng', which one might have expected to develop always like *ny* (§§ 78, 126), gives a double result, *n'* or *ndž*, the former prevailing in Pistoia, the latter alone being used in Pisa and Lucca, while both are current in Siena. Florence, while admitting both, inclines to *ndž*. Ex.: *angĕlus* > *ágnolo ángiolo, cignere cingere, fignere fingere, giugnere giungere, piagnere piangere*, etc. *Gingiva* is probably learned.

Ng: piagno for *piango, pigno* for *pingo*, etc., come from the alternation of *piagnere* and *piangere*, etc. See *Ng'*.

Nm > *mm: conviemmi, tiemmi. Anima*, however, by an early differentiation became *alma*.

Nt shifts to *nd* in *polenta* > *polenda*, under the influence of *molenda*, ' miller's tithe.'

Nv: imbolare, beside *involare*, is probably of southern origin. Cf. § 83, 1.

Rg' never becomes simple *y* (see §§ 78, 129); it seems to give regularly *rdž: *ex-cŏrrĭgit* > *scǫrge, pŏrrĭgit* > *pǫrge*. From *argentum,* however, we have not only the usual *argento,* but also *ariento:* see S. Pieri in *Studj romanzi,* I, 33.

Rm: syrma > sirima. See § 62.

Rv alternates with *rb* in Latin, where we find, for instance, *cerbus, corbi, curbati, ferbui* from *ferveo, serbat, verbex* and *berbex* for *vervex;* hence Italian *corbo, nerbo,* etc.: see E. G. Parodi, *Del passaggio di* v *in* b, in *Romania,* XXVII, 177. Cf. § 83, 1.

S before a sonant is generally voiced in modern Italian: *exmovēre > ismuǫvere smuǫvere.* Cf. § 40, 1.

Sk' > long *š: piscem > pęsce, florescit > fiorisce.* From *lusciniola* we have *lusignuǫlo usignǫlo,* probably influenced by *rosignuolo < Pr. rosinhol; usignolo* has lost its *l-* by confusion with the article (cf. § 84).

Sm in the interior of a word develops an *i* between the two consonants: φάντασμα *> fantásima,* σπασμός *> spasimo.* Cf. §§ 58, 62, 72.

Miscellaneous Groups

131. Of the groups not included in the foregoing classes, some consist of three consonants, some of two. Among the latter, twenty or twenty-one groups simply assimilate the first consonant to the second: BD, *suddito;* BS, *osservare;* BT, *dēbita > dętta, dŭbitat > dǫtta;* DS, *ad satis > assai;* DT, *cauda trĕpida? > *cuttretta cutrętta;* GD, *frīg(ĭ)dus > freddo;* GG', *aggere;* GK, **figicare? > ficcare;* GM, *flemma, frammento* (but *aumento*); ꞣꞣ', *accendere;* ꞣM, *nec minus > nemmęno;* KN, *tecnico* pronounced *tęnnico;* KT, *atto, dętto, fatto, nǫtte, ǫtto, strĭctus > strętto* (but *autore, ętico, pratico, trǫta < τρώκτης*); PF, *sapphīrum > zaffiro;* PS, *capsa > cassa, ipsum > ęsso* (but learned *capsula cassula, Hypsipȳle > Isifile,* and popular *ant'ist'ipsum? > testeso,*[1] *met-ipsimum > medęsimo*); PT, *atto, cattano, crĕpitum > crętto, scritto* (but learned *stitico < stypti-*

---

[1] More likely *teso teso:* Meyer-Lübke in *Archiv für das Studium der Neueren Sprachen,* CLIII, 245.

cus); TM, *marĭtĭma*>*marẹmma* (but learned *ritmo*); TP, *et* *pūre*>*eppure;* TS, *aut sĭt*>*ossía;* TV, *aut vēro*>*ovvẹro;* VT, *cīvitātem*>*cittá.* The commonest of these are evidently *kt* and *pt.*

1. In early texts, *tt* is often spelled indiscriminately *ct* or *pt: fapto, scricto.*

132. The remaining two-consonant groups show something more than simple assimilation. The most important are *gn* and *ks.*

Dk' seems to give *ddz* in *duodecīna>*dozzina,* but the word is probably borrowed from French; North Italian says *dozena,* Neapolitan *dozzana. Sozzo,* which in Florence now has *ddz,* is of doubtful origin. See F. d'Ovidio, *Ancora dello zeta in rima* (in *Raccolta di studii critici dedicati ad A. D'Ancona,* 617) and *Versificazione italiana e Arte poetica medioevale,* 127.

Gn>*n':* degno, legno, pugno, regno, segno. Latin *gnosco* having become *nosco, cognosco* also lost its *g* in common speech. *Punga,* used by Dante and Villani for *pugna,* has to do with the analogy of such double forms as *pugno* and *pungo, pugnere* and *pungere,* etc.: § 130, *Ng', Ng.*

Kn: cycnus *cĭcĭnus*>*cẹcino cẹcero* beside *cigno.*

Ks has a double result, a long *š* and a long *s* (written *ss*): *cŏxa*>*cǫscia, saxum*>*sasso; ĕxit*>*ẹsce, dīxit*>*disse; maxilla* >*mascella, taxillus*>*tassello; exāmen*>*sciame, exagium*> *saggio,* with loss of the initial vowel (§ 40, 1). An examination of over 50 examples seems to indicate that the differentiation is not primarily due to stress, but is originally local or social. Directly after the accented vowel, however, *ss* is much commoner than *š,* being used in all perfects (*dussi, trassi,* etc.); while before the accent *ss* and *š* are about equally frequent (*sessanta, uscire*). *Laxare* gives both *lassare* and *lasciare.* Learned words all have *ss,* except that *ex-* before a vowel gives *es-* (with voiced *s*): *massimo, tossico tosco; esempio, esilio, esordio,* etc. *Fixus*>*fiso,* following *riso, viso,* etc.

Pd retains the glottis position of its first element with the tongue position of its second: *rapidus* > *ratto, cauda trepida?* > *cutretta.*

Td also keeps the voicelessness of its first member: *pūtidus* > *putto, nĭtidus* > *nẹtto.*

133. Groups of three consonants, not hitherto accounted for, all drop one member, some losing the first, others the second. *Llg* simply omits one *l* in the spelling: *cŏllĭgo* > *cọlgo. Llg'*, as we have seen (§§ 124, 125), becomes *l'*: *cŏllĭgit* > *cọglie.*

Those whose middle consonant was *s* lost their first element, which was evidently assimilated to the sibilant: BSK', *oscẹno;* BSK, *oscuro;* BST, *substare* > *sostare;* KSD, πύξιδα > *busta.* It will be noted that *bsk'* develops as if it had always been *sk'* (§ 130, *Sk'*), and that the *d* of *ksd* is unvoiced by the *s* (cf. § 132, *Pd, Td*). Here belong compounds with *ex-* + cons.: *scuotere, slanciare, smuovere, esprimere, estrarre.*

All the others eliminate the middle element, which in every case is a stop:

Lk'p: calce pistare > *calpestare.*
Lk't: cŭlcĭta *cŭlcĭtra* > *cọltre* (also *cọltrice*).
Lpt: scŭlptus > *scọlto.*
Mps: κάμπτειν > *ex-campsare* > *scansare, sampsa* > *sansa, sumpsi* > *sunsi.*
Mpt: compŭtus > *cọnto, assunto, exemptus* > *esente, redentore.*
Ndk: mándūcáre > **mancare manicare; manucare* is a cross between *mandúca* and *manicare;* see §§ 62 and 130, *Nd. Mangiare* is French or Provençal, as are also *giuggiare* and *vengiare.*
Nks: anxius > *ansio.*
Nkt: cinto, pianto, santo, tintura, unto.
Ntk': *infanticellus > *fancello fanciullo, pantĭcem* > *pancia.*
Rkt: with a shift of accent, *ērectus* > *ẹrto, pŏrrectus* > *pọrto, sŭrrectus* > *sọrto.*
Rps: excerptus *excarpsus > *scarso* (also *scarzo*).

Rpt: assorto.

Sk't: *fascitellum > fastello.

Spm: βλάσφημος *bláshphēmus > bias (i)mo.*

Stm: asthma > as (i)ma; ansima shows contamination with *ansia < anxia.*

It is to be observed that in *mps* and *mpt* the *m*, after the fall of the *p*, is assimilated to the dental (*assumptus > assunto*); and that the *sm* resulting from *spm* and *stm* inserts an *i* as does original *sm* (*asthma > asma asima*, cf. *spasmus > spasmo spasimo:* cf. § 130, *Sm*).

IRREGULAR CHANGES

134. The developments considered hitherto have shown so high a degree of coincidence that deviations from the commonest type have assumed the aspect of a challenge; and, in fact, for most of these departures from the norm a plausible apology can be found — in bookish influence, in the attraction of analogy, in differences of local or class dialect, in the migration of vocables. There are, however, certain kinds of eccentricity which, though capable of classification, affect only a small minority of the vocabulary and elude the usual forms of explanation. Generally they have emanated from some one social centre, often from one person, whose linguistic *faux pas* have been imitated either in admiration or in derision. Sometimes they have started with blunders so easy to make that many members of a generation have made them concurrently. A good proportion of the latter originate in childhood (when speech-growth follows, at a disconcerting rate, its own uncharted ways), and have not been corrected in adolescence. Others reflect the childish reaction of the adult to a foreign or literary or technical word. Often the cause is to be found in vague memories and associations. Tongues are continually slipping, all about us, but nearly all the lapses vanish as soon as made, because they are not repeated often enough to impress themselves. Those which

recur with sufficient frequency to win a place in the dictionary, but, sticking to particular words instead of spreading
through whole categories, are not comprehensive enough to
set themselves up as "phonetic laws," may be called "irregular" or "sporadic" alterations. With regard to a sporadic
change the question always asked and hardly ever answered
is why, under conditions seemingly identical, the innovation
appears in one word and not in others.[1]

135. The more or less erratic doubling of consonants has
been described in §§ 100, 101. In § 103, 1 has been set forth
the occasional interchange of *v* and *g*. The rest of the phenomena in question may be classified under these heads: imitation, diversification (dissimilation), transfer (metathesis),
insertion (epenthesis), abbreviation. To this last process
are due a lot of nicknames, which really constitute a group
by themselves. It will be seen that the consonants most
affected are the liquids; next, the nasals.

Imitation

136. That is, assimilation of a consonant to another that
is not contiguous — a rare phenomenon. In all authentic
cases the influence is exerted by a consonant yet to come on
one now being spoken; the concept of a sound still in the
future is clearer than the consciousness of one immediately
impending.

Examples: *opprŏbrium* > *obbrŏbbio brŏbrio brŏb (b)io, Sicilia* > *Cicilia*
(used by Boccaccio and still occasionally heard), *gladiolus* > *giaggiŏlo,
Jūlius* > *luglio, similare* > *sembrare; sūctiare* > *succiare ciucciare ciocciare*
and *vespertilio* > *pipistrello* are partly onomatopoetic; *caligarius* >
galigaio, caligare > *galigare, castigare* > *gastigare* may belong here (see
§ 87). *Maninconia* for *melancolia* seems to show both diversification
and imitation, as well as the influence of *mania*.

[1] See M. Grammont, *La dissimilation consonantique dans les langues
indo-européennes et dans les langues romanes*, 1895; E. Schopf, *Die
konsonantischen Fernwirkungen*, 1919 (reviewed by W. Meyer-Lübke
in *Zs.*, XLI, 597). E. Hermann, *Assimilation, Dissimilation, Metathesis
und Haplogie*, in *Neophilologus*, VIII, 128.

Diversification

137. Human speech, in a reaction against the primitive tendency to repeat syllables or sounds, has, in more sophisticated times, a stronger impulse to avoid repetition. Sometimes the recurrence is prevented merely by omission, as in *de retro > dietro* or *drieto;* sometimes by the substitution of, a different sound for one member of the pair, as in *ululare > urlare, prora > proda.* The two commonest nasals, *m* and *n,* may be so similar in effect as to call for differentiation. The usual substitutes for *l* are *n* and *r;* for *r, l* and *d;* for *m,* a denasalized *m* (i.e., *b*) which between vowels becomes *v*: *numerum > novero.* Some of the dissimilations go back to the Vulgar Latin stock, others are peculiar to Italian.

138. For liquids, L-L may be illustrated by *filomela filomena, remulcare*remulculare > rimorchiare, ululare > urlare.* Unusual and more or less incomprehensible are *līlium > giglio, lŏlium > giŏglio.*

R-R is commoner: *arbŏrem > albero, arbitro albitro,* Frankish *heribĕrga > albergo, Malgherita, paraverēdus > palafreno, peregrinus > pellegrino,* Celt. *vertrăga > veltro; corsaro corsale, mercoledì, mortarium > mortaletto, remorari > remolare; quœrĕre > chiedere, ferīre *fĕrĕre > fiedere; armadio, contradio, porfido, proda, rado; opprobrium > brobbio, *de-retranus > deretano, de retro > drieto, proprius > propio; de retro > dietro, Frederīcus > Federigo.*

139. For nasals, M-M: *moventaneo;* M-N, *thўmĭnus > tĕmolo;* N-N, *Bononia > Bologna, venēnum > velĕno;* N-M, *numerare > noverare, Hieronymus > Girŏlamo, Panormus > Palermo.*

140. The most notable case of all is the early dissimilation of β-β in *habēbat > aβeβa > aβea,* whence *avẹa avia* and a general imperfect ending *-ẹa* or *-ia,* with a plural *-eano* or *-iano,* for the 2d and 3d conjugations; whence also the conditional in

-ia. Nearly as momentous is the suppression of the second *d* in the perfect ending *-dĕdi* for *-dĭdi* (§ 9, 3), as in *perdĕdi* > *perdẹi* (later *perdẹi*); this phenomenon, combined with the influence of *credĭdĭsti* *creddesti > *credẹsti* and *credĭdĭmus* *credĭd'mus* > *credẹmmo*, etc., and with the analogy of the 1st and 4th conjugations, gave rise to a new type of perfect for the 3d conjugation: *-ei, -esti, -é, -emmo, -este, -érono*, to match *-ai, -asti, -ò*, etc., *-ii, -isti, -i*, etc. See § 201.

Transfer

141. We may distinguish two kinds of transfer: the shift of one consonant and the exchange of two consonants. Of the former type, *r* furnishes a large share of the examples: *capestro capresto, coccodrillo, dentro drento, frenetico farnetico, frumento formento, Agrigentum* > *Girgenti, cancer* + *-ulus* > *granchio, calce pistare* > *calpestare scalpitare, storpiare stroppiare* < *stŭprare, strumento stormento, stupro strupo*. Frequent also is the transfer of *l* or of the *y* which comes from it: *abbattulare > *abbacchiare abbiaccare, nŭcleus* > *nọcchio gnọcco, publĭcus* > *piuvico, stloppus* > *schiọppo scọppio;* from the suffix *-ulus, bŭda* *budula > *biọdo, cŏma* *cŏmula > *chiọma, fabula* > *fiaba, pōpulus* > *piọppo*.

1. In *singhiottare* < *singulare* + *gluttire* we have an instance of contamination.

2. The south Tuscan transfer of a *y* preceded by a vowel has been mentioned in § 35, 1; cf. § 71, 1: *bajula* > *baila balia, cognĭtus* > **cointo contio, magida* > *maida madia.

142. The exchange of two consonants may be illustrated by: *anhelare* > *alenare, blaterare* > *battolare, filọsdfo* > *fisọlafo, fracĭdus* > *fracido fradicio, ghiottoneria ghiottornia, palude padule, rumigare* > *rumigare rugumare, sūcĭdus* > *sucido sudicio*. In *culcĭta* *culcĭtra > *coltrice, tš* and *tr* swap places.

1. For *gnocchi* see § 84, 5; for *rovistico*, § 84, 6.

Insertion

143. The intrusion of *g* in such words as *Pagolo, pagura, ragunare* has been discussed in § 103, 1.

Between two vowels one of which is *u* or *o*, a *v* often develops, especially in bookish or borrowed words (§§ 33, 2; 74): *caulis>cavolo, continovo, fluidus>fluido fluvido, Gẹnova, Johannes>Gioanni Giovanni, manovale, Mantova, mĭnŭĕre *minuare > menovare, naulum > nọlo návolo, Patavium *Padua>Padova, Paulus>Pọlo Paolo Pavolo, ruīna>rovina, rūgidus>*ruido ruvido, vĭdua>vẹdova, victualia>vettovaglia, viọla vivọla* (Boccaccio).

1. *Parvenza* is probably Provençal.

144. Some dialects have a tendency to denasalize the close of an *m*, especially before two unstressed syllables: *gammarus >gambero, vŏmĕrem>vọmere bọmbero, rŭmĭcem>rọmice rọmbice; commeatus > commiato combiato, grĕmium > grẹmio grẹmbo.* Cf. § 101. In this last case we may see the influence of *lẹmbo.*

145. There is a tendency, which began in Vulgar Latin times, to insert an *r* in the endings *-ta, -te, -to.* Perhaps the original suggestion is to be found in such words as *arbĭtrum, canĭstrum, fenĕstra, palœstra, vĕntrem.* Furthermore, the word ἔγκαυστον *encaustum,* 'ink,' being associated with *claustrum,* gave *inchiọstro.* One would like to trace some connection between this word and *registro<regesta,* but the latter has *r* in several languages.

Examples: *arbŭtus>albatro, anătem anĭtem>anatra anitra, ballĭsta >balẹstra, bis sextus>bissestro, cœlestis>celeste cilestro, cŭlcĭta>cọltre, jaspis>diaspro, genesta>ginestra, *jŭxtat>*Pr. jọsta>It. giọstra, scĕlĕtus *schĕlĕtus>schẹletro, valente valentre.*

146. In some words an apparently intrusive consonant is there by rights. *Ciascheduno* and *qualcheduno* contain *quid.*

Dicidotto for *diciotto* contains *et*, just as *diciassette* contains *ac*. *Struggere, traggere* go back to Vulgar Latin **strugere = struere, *tragere = trahere*, with the same stop that is found in the perfect and the participle (*-struxi -structus, traxi tractus*) and in the noun *tragula;* the example of *agere* and *regere* may have played some part.

In others, the insertion is due to the suggestion of an associated term: *adĭtus>andito*, cf. *ambĭtus; agonia angonia*, cf. *angoscia; asima ansima*, cf. *ansio ansare<anxius; capitolium >campidoglio*, cf. *campo; reddere>rendere*, cf. *prendere; saturēia>santoreggia*, cf. *santo; occĭdere + avis *aus?> aucĭdere>*It. *uccidere*, also *aucidere* whence *alcidere* (but why *ancidere?*). What suggested the *w* of *uguanno<hoc anno, hoque? unguanno<hunc annum* (cf. *ancora<hanc horam*)?

Occasionally we have a real fusing of two words: στραβός *strabus* + **bambus* (cf. βαμβαλίζειν, Bambalio, It. *bambo bambino bambolo*)*>strambo; lampas + vapor>vampa* (also *vampo vampore*); *rastellus + rastrum>rastrello*.

1. Sometimes the disturbing influence cannot be identified: *laicus >laico ladico, lābrūsca>lambrusca* (cf. Fr.), *lūtra>lontra, papilionem >parpiglione, vītĭcem>vetrice*.

Abbreviation

147. From childish language, no doubt, come such expressions as *gua* or *guar* for *guarda* (emphatic abbreviation?), *va dormì* for *va a dormire*. To the slovenliness permissible in words that cannot be misunderstood we owe *ser* for *messer* <Pr. *messer*, *pre'* (proclitic) for *prete<prévite* (Abruzzi)< **præbĭter* for *presbÿter*.

148. Nicknames are cut down in accordance with puerile tendencies.[1] Hard consonant groups are likely to be smoothed out, and *r* is liable to neglect. Most of them fall into these three groups:

[1] P. Fanfani, *Le accorciature dei nomi propri italiani*, 1878.

1. All that precedes the accented syllable is omitted, the rest is kept (cf. *Bert, Lizzie, Beth, Bess, Betty*): *Aldobrandino, Dino; Alessandro, Sandro; Ambrǫgio, Bǫgio; Andręa, Dręa Dęa; Bartolomęo, Męo; Contęssa, Tęssa; Francęsco, Cęcco; Giacobino, Bino; Guidǫtto, Dǫtto; Michęle, Chęle; Nicǫla, Cǫla.*

2. All before the stressed syllable falls, and the consonant that precedes the accented vowel is assimilated to the consonant that follows it (cf. *Bob*): *Angelǫtto, Tǫtto; Giovanni, Nanni; Girǫlamo Girǫmo, Mǫmo; Giusęppe, Pęppe* (why *Bęppo?*); *Guglielmo, Męmmo; Luigi, Gigi.*

3. Everything drops out except the initial consonant, the accented vowel, and the last syllable: *Beatrice, Bice; Benedętto, Bętto; Benvenuto, Buto; Durante, Dante*[1]; *Francęsco, Fręsco; Gherardo, Gaddo; Giovanni, Gianni; Lodovigo, Ligo; Loręnzo, Lęnzo; madǫnna, mǫnna; signǫr, sǫr; signǫra, sǫra.*

---

[1] M. Scherillo, *Alcuni capitoli della biografia di Dante,* 44–51.

MORPHOLOGY

149. The phonetic evolution of a language inevitably disturbs its inflectional system, which from time to time needs readjustment. For instance, *filiam* and *filias, filium* and *filios* having early become identical in Italy, the language of that country (and also the Rumanian) resorted to the *nominative* plural to express plurality, whereas the other Romance languages used the accusative of both numbers: It. *figlia figlie, figlio figli;* Sp. *hija hijas, hijo hijos.* In the third conjugation, the fall of -*s* and -*t* reduced to identity the descendants of *credis* and *credit,* which both became *crede;* a new sign of the second person was needed, and was borrowed from the fourth conjugation, which had in that form a long *i:* *audis* > *odi;* hence *credi.* The fall of unaccented vowels so differentiated from one another the parts of *adjutare* (*adjūtat* > *aiúta, adjutātis* > *aitate*) that the verb split into two, *aiutare* and *aitare* (Florentine *atare*), each with a complete inflection.

150. A strong influence is the desire to level, to remove apparent inconsistencies, to standardize. For example, inasmuch as *pes* and *pedem* seem to have different stems although they indicate the same member, speakers reconstructed a nominative *pedis,* on the model of *canis canem,* which was felt to be the regular type. In Italian, the plural of *bianco* would by natural phonetic process be *bianci;* but to avoid incongruity of stem it was replaced by *bianchi.* The eccentric *posse* and *velle* were reshaped according to the second conjugation pattern: *posso* or *poteo, potere; voleo, volere.* Similarly *esse* became *essere.* Vulgar Latin **páraulâre* (from **paraula* < *parabola*) gives *parlare,* while **paraúlo* would naturally give **parólo;* but this form has been made to harmonize with the other type, and we have *parlo.* Latin *ĕrat* became *iera* when stressed, *era* when unaccented; but the latter was generalized and the former abandoned. Thus *sei* in the singular and *siete* in the plural have been preferred to *siei* and *sete* — the two pairs coming from **sĕs* = *es* and **sĕtis* = *estis*. We have seen (§ 129, 1) how a singular in *-aio* leads to a plural in *-ai*, while a plural in *-ari* leads to a singular in *-aro;* words in *-orius* always have sg. *-oio*, pl. *-oi*.

151. Analogy often extends a phenomenon from an isolated form to a whole category. Examples on a small scale are **tī* and **sī*, for *tibi* and *sibi*, on the model of *mī* for *mihi;* also *illujus illui* and **istujus *istui* (and *altrui* from *alter*), patterned on *cujus cui*. From the monosyllabic *dic* and *fac*, assisted by the influence of *audire* and *dare*, came the verbs **dire* and **fare*. The dissimilated **aβea* from **aβeβa* = *habebam* (§ 103, *B*) gave rise to a whole imperfect inflection in *-ea* beside *-eva*. Similarly the entire weak perfect inflection in *-ei*, etc., sprang from the abridged **-dei* for *-dedi* in such words as *perdere* (see § 140).

1. Sometimes the whole public developed an unexplained liking for some termination, and passed it on to many words to which it did not originally belong. So *-ora*, inherited in *corpora, pecora, tempora*, was in Old Italian bestowed on more than thirty nouns of the second declension: *campora, luogora, pratora*, etc. Thus *-ggo*, arising in *figgo, leggo, reggo*, etc., invaded *andare, cadere, chiudere, credere, fiedere, vedere*, creating *vaggo, caggo, chiuggo, creggo, fieggo, veggo; -ggio*, starting with *seggio* < *sedeo* and *veggio* < *vĭdeo*, produces *chieggio, creggio, fieggio; -ngo*, from *giungo, piango*, etc., begets *pongo, rimango, tengo, vengo; -lgo*, from *colgo* < *collĭgo* and *scelgo* < **ex-ēlĭgo*, is responsible for *dolgo, salgo, sciolgo, valgo, velgo*. Final *-o* in the third person plural, which belonged properly to such perfects as *diedero* < *dedĕrunt*, was extended to all tenses of all verbs.

2. Some forms seem chronically unstable; for instance, the first person plural. *Vidēmus* became *vedémo*, which, however, in late medieval times already began to yield to *vediamo*, the subjunctive ending *-iamo* crowding out all the present indicative terminations *-amo, -emo, -imo*; then, in modern colloquial style, *vediamo* itself has had to give way to *noi si vede*.

3. We sometimes find a persistent reciprocal influence in two sets of forms: for instance, the past subjunctive (*dicessero*) got its *-ero* from the perfect (*dissero*); while the fourteenth century *dissono* received its *-ono* from the past subjunctive (*dicessono, udissono*), which in turn derived it from the weak perfect (*udirono*).

152. Furthermore, human speech is inclined to discard (though very slowly) inflectional forms representing distinctions which are no longer felt to be necessary or which have found a new mode of expression. Hence the disappearance of symbols for the dual number, the middle voice, and many cases and tenses. Hence the Romance abandonment of the meaningless neuter gender, all nouns becoming masculine or feminine; hence the Vulgar Latin reduction of the declensions from five to three. In both these latter instances, of course, the simplification might without loss of clearness have been carried still further.

Oftenest, perhaps, the rejection of old fashions ensues upon the creation of new ones, more in accord with the contemporary way of looking at things. From early times, Latin speakers appear to have felt a certain inadequacy in their passive, originally a deponent inflection and never, it would seem, completely attuned to its theoretical classic use; ultimately Romance substituted for it a periphrasis which unequivocally emphasized passivity; while the reflexive idea received an analytical expression of its own: *amatur > amatus est, dicitur > se dicit.* For some reason, too, the Latins became discontented with their future, for which they substituted various circumlocutions, the most popular of which primarily indicated necessity, duty, or desire: *dabo > dare habeo* or *volo dare.* Nearly all the Romance tongues finally agreed in the use of the compound with *habeo.*

It will be seen that many of the changes we shall have to consider are due to a fundamental inclination to analyze a concept and to express each member of it by a separate word. This tendency has, in general, been at work in European languages from prehistoric times down to the present day; it may have to do with an increasing need of rapidity and exactness in communication. A striking example is the introduction of prepositions to specify the particular functions of the ambiguous Latin cases; then, the prepositions once established, the case-endings themselves became needless and could without detriment be confused or lost.

1. Words, as well as inflections, are discarded, and new words are created, the reason in many cases being quite obscure. Why, for instance, should Latin *nihil* or *nil* have given way to the inexplicable Italian *niente?* *Parecchio* < *particulus, alcuno* < **aliqu' unus* are easier to understand; *qualcuno* evidently followed *alcuno; qualcheduno* has in it a *quid,* perhaps borrowed from *aliquid.* Several pronouns contain the Greek distributive preposition κατά, carried around the Mediterranean by Greek merchants: *ciascuno, ciascheduno* (cf. Old It. *cescheduno*), which contain *quisque* and *unus* blended with κατά; *catauno, cadauno, caduno* are now obsolete.

153. We shall now consider briefly the Italian inflections from the point of view of the principles just formulated. Changes ensuing inevitably from well-known phonetic development need not be considered.

DECLENSION

TYPES

154. When the Latin neuter gender, which was only an inflectional category, died out, early in the Romance period, the old neuter nouns became masculine: *il corpo, il dono, il fiume, il mare, il nome.* But some neuter plurals in *-a,* used collectively, had already passed into the feminine singular class: *arma, foglia, pecora.* Also Greek neuters in *-ma,* if really popular, generally became feminine: κῦμα > *cima,* σάγμα > *soma.*

1. Other parts of speech, phrases, etc., used as nouns, are regularly masculine: *il bello, il perchè, il viaggiare, il portavoce,* etc. But in many

idiomatic phrases we find *la* representing an indefinite idea, as in *battersela, pagarla cara, scapparla bella;* in these — or at least in some of them which served as models for the others — a specific feminine noun was doubtless originally meant.

2. A real neuter remains among demonstrative, interrogative, and indefinite pronouns: *ciò, che, nulla.* So *maggio, meglio, meno, peggio.*

155. Between masculine and feminine there was little confusion. Second and fourth declension feminines, however, nearly all eventually became masculine: *fraxinus, ficus; manus* retained its gender. Names of trees, and *albero* itself, took or kept the masculine gender, perhaps following *melo* < μῆλον (*mālum* is from Doric μᾶλον), *pero* < *pĭrum*, as well as *frassino, fico,* etc.; *il noce, il ciliegio, il susino.* But names of fruits are mostly feminine: *ciliegia, pera, susina, la noce.* Some masculine designations of persons were made feminine by changing *-e* to *-a*: *marchesa, signora.*

1. There are a few cases of differentiation of gender on the ground of bigness, concreteness, or association: *fossa, fosso* = 'big ditch'; *la podestà, il podestà* = 'the mayor'; *il carcere, la carcere* after *la prigione.*

156. Of the five Latin declensions, the three big ones absorbed the two little ones. The first declension remained the specifically feminine type, the second the specifically masculine, while the third continued to be a jumble of the genders. Nouns of the fifth which survived in popular Tuscan passed into the first: *faccia, ghiaccia, rabbia, scabbia; dì,* however, remaining masculine, is invariable (cf. Sicilian *dia*). Nouns of the fourth which had not already in Classic times moved into the second (as did *domus, ficus*) made the shift in Vulgar Latin: *fructus, manus.* This last word, retaining its feminine gender, shows an occasional inclination to become *mana,* as we find it in Cellini.

1. *Meridies* > *meriggio; merigge* is poetic, as are *speme* and *spene* (from **spemen* and from *spes spenis*). Such words as *serie, spezie,* etc., are bookish.

157. Among the three remaining declensions there were some exchanges. From the first there sometimes passed a masculine noun, as πειρατής > pīrāta > pirata pirato; also a feminine or two whose plural form in -e was mistaken for a singular of the third declension, as ala, pl. le ale = l'ale, taken to be la ale, hence le ali (on the model of animale, -i, etc.); likewise a few feminines whose singular in -a was for some reason understood as a plural of the neuter type, as auricula oricula > orecchia f. sg., then le orecchia (on the model of le labbra, etc.) and a singular orecchio (like labbro).

From the second dropped of course those neuter plural forms which came to be used as feminine singular (§ 154): fata, foglia, etc. Also some names of fruits (§ 155): mela, pera, poma, etc. Patrōnus became padrone evidently on the model of ladrone < latrōnem; but why have we il pome beside pomo and poma? Nouns in -iero, -iere are doubtless borrowed from French or Provençal: cavaliero, -e.

From the third, as from the second, fell such neuter plurals as had become feminine singular: e.g., pęcora, which had strangely come to mean 'a sheep.' Latin frondem, frondes became la fronde, le fronde; then for le fronde was devised a new singular, la fronda (similarly la ghiande > la ghianda). Final a turned certain words into the first, final o turned others into the second declension: soma (§ 154); marmo < marmor, rovo < rōbur, zolfo < sūlfur, corpo < cŏrpus, tempo < tĕmpus. Such forms as fŏlgore < fŭlgur, rŏvere < rōbur (beside folgo, rovo) seem to indicate the early development of a masculine declension, beside the neuter, for these words. Animale, gĕnere, on the other hand, are probably learned. Distinctively feminine significance changed suoro < sŏror into suora, while a masculine association seems to be responsible for glīs glīrem > ghiro, passer passĕrem > passero, sōrex sŏrĭcem > sorcio.

158. Among the adjectives, the two great types, represented by bonus-a-um and grandis -is -e, were preserved:

buono buona, grande. From the *bonus* to the *grandis* type there were very few shifts: *somnolentus>sonnolento -e* modeled itself on words in *-ente; malěficus>malęfice* followed *carnęfice<carnǐfǐcem.* Such a word as *leggiere* is either French or Provençal.

Change from the *grandis* to the *bonus* class is much commoner: *tristo* goes back to Vulgar Latin; *magro<macrum* attracts *agro < acrem* (and possibly *allęgro < alacrem?*); *agresto, alpestro* may have felt the influence of *onesto,* etc.; *rebellis>rubelle -o,* conforming to *-ello; comune -o* shapes itself on *uno, rude -o* on *crudo, sublime -o* perhaps on *imo.* *Pauper* has already in Latin times a feminine *paupera:* It. *pǫvero pǫvera.* *Prægna(n)s>*apparently *pregna,* whence a masculine *pregno.* *Urbs Vetus>Orvieto Orbivieto;* but *vetus* eventually developed forms on the *bonus* model — *vieto vieta.*

1. For the loss of the final vowel in *bel, buon, gran, qual, san, tal,* in the intertonic position, see § 51. By analogy with *tal,* the adjective *sol* was sometimes used as an invariable form between the indefinite article and a noun: *una sol volta* (Berni). *Maggio* and a few other originally neuter forms were, in the older language, not infrequently employed as masculine or feminine: *maggio cura, la peggio son io;* so, in modern speech, *lui è peggio.*

159. Of the old comparative forms we find surviving in Italian: *maggiore, migliore, minore, peggiore,* and learned borrowings such as *inferiore, superiore;* also the neuters (used also as adverbs) *maggio, meglio, meno, peggio.* *Vivacius>* *vaccio,* which lost its comparative significance and served as an adverb and adjective meaning 'quick.' Cf. § 158, 1. Of the old superlatives, *massimo, męnomo, primo,* and *sǫmmo* are left, and the more bookish *ǫttimo, pęssimo, prǫssimo, ultimo; -issimo,* used in Italian simply as an intensive suffix, is presumably of learned origin.

The Romance languages adopted an analytic method of indicating comparison. Italian attaches *più<plus* to the positive to make the comparative, and prefixes the definite article to the comparative to form the superlative.

1. The successor of Latin *quam* is *che*, a derivative of *quid* which eventually crowded out *co* from *quod* and *ca* from *qu(i)a* and *quam*. The expression of comparison by an ablative is represented in Italian by the use of *di*, which now occurs when the second member is a noun, a pronoun, or a numeral.

2. Ordinal numerals after *quarto*, with the possible exception of *dęcimo*, seem to be of bookish origin: *quinto, decimo primo* or *undęcimo* or *undicęsimo, decimo sesto* or *sedicęsimo, ventęsimo*, etc.

CASE AND NUMBER

Case

160. Phonetic development — the confusion of quantities, the change of *-u* to *-o*, and the loss of final *m, n, r, s* — quite wrecked the Latin declension in Italy; but the analytic impulse above mentioned (§ 152) had already provided adequate substitutes. In many instances, indeed, it is impossible to tell whether the habitual use of a preposition undermined the inflection or the loss of the inflection necessitated the use of the preposition. The two causes worked together, the result being a reduction of the six cases to one in the singular of Italian nouns; then the plural likewise cut down its cases to one.

161. The genitive and dative early began to succumb to prepositional constructions — the genitive, to *de* (or *ex*) with the ablative; the dative, to *ad* with the accusative. When the collapse of the inflectional system came, these cases were too feeble to resist. Only in Rumanian do we find, in the first declension, a slight trace of the Latin dative.

The vocative was in Latin identical with the nominative, except in the second declension; the identity was ultimately extended to that type also. Even the Italian *Iddío*, from bookish *domineddío*, presupposes a Latin *Domine Deus*. Dante's *figliole* is simply Latin *filiole* pronounced in Italian fashion.

The locative, which had almost vanished from Classic Latin, remains even to-day, however, as an invariable form in certain place-names: *Clūsium Clūsī>Chiusi, Florentia Florentiæ>Firenze, Aquæ Aquīs>Acqui, Tībur Tībŭrī> Tivoli.* Cf. § 55, 3.

1. Genitive forms remain (aside from pronouns) in several petrified phrases: *lūnæ die>lunedì*, etc., *est ministerī>è mestieri, (de) noctis tempore>di notte tempore* (later *tempo*); in a great many family names, such as *Paoli, Pieri;* probably in *Monte Vergine, Porto Venere;* certainly in the learned *acquavite, terremoto, lingua angeloro, regno feminoro* (note the *-o-*). A genitive disguised as an accusative appears in *araneæ tēla>ragnatelo, (illa) Dei mercēde>la Dio merzè, die judicii>al die giudicio.*

162. There are left the nominative, accusative, and ablative. These, in Italy, became identical in the singular of the first and second declensions: *lūna lūnam lūnā>luna, mūrus mūrum mūrō>muro;* the type *faber* fell in with the more usual one, its nominative yielding to its accusative-ablative (*fabbro*). In the third declension there is more variety: the *canis* type has the same form throughout (*canis canem cane >cane*), and to this the *turris* type conforms (*tŭrris tŭrrim tŭrri>tŭrris tŭrrem tŭrre>tọrre*); a word on the pattern of *frater* may get two forms (*frater>frate, fratrem fratre>fratre*), of which either the first or the second is destined to be discarded (*frate; padre*); in a neuter like *cŏrpus* or *flūmen* the nominative-accusative prevails over the ablative (*corpo, fiume*).

Words like *comes* and *ratio* usually show in Italian no trace of their nominative: (*comes*) *cŏmĭtem cŏmĭte>conte,* (*ratio*) *ratiōnem ratiōne>ragione.* However, a few of them, designating persons, prefer the nominative form: *mọglie<mŭlier* (cf. Old It. *mogliera<mŭlĭĕrem*), *prete<*præbĭter* for *presbyter* (§ 147), *re<rex, uomo<hŏmo, suora suoro<sŏror* (cf. *frate* above); *nievo<nĕpos,* on the other hand, gave way to *nipote. Ghiotto, ladro* are probably not nominatives, but are

derived from *ghiottone* < *gluttōnem*, *ladrone* < *latrōnem*, the *-one* being understood as a pejorative suffix (as in *birbo, birbone*). Why have we *ǫrafo* < *aurifex*, *sarto* < *sartor*, *lampa* < *lampas?* For *vieto* see § 158.

1. Inasmuch as most Italian nouns look like Latin ablatives (*luna, vento, fiore, parte*), it became customary, when borrowing new terms, to borrow them in their ablative form: *caligine, culmine, fulmine, genere, germine* (so, by mistake, *termine* for *termino*). Of much rarer type are such Latinisms as *giovęntu, maięsta, onęsta, pięta, podęsta*, taken from the nominative; likewise nominative are *bronchite, lapis, sermo;* thus, with a change of gender, are made *dazio, ęco, passio, prefazio*. *Tempęsta* probably goes back to Vulgar Latin. Some writers make *eco* feminine.

2. Petrified ablatives survive in such adverbs as *freddamente, parimente* and in a few set phrases: *quest'anno, questa volta, vendere cento soldi,* and probably the ablative absolute *ciò fatto*, etc.

Number

163. The outcome is a single form for the singular of each noun. It was natural, then, that the plural should reduce its forms to one. For the first and second declensions the form preserved was that of the nominative, since the accusative would not have been distinguishable from the singular (§ 149): *ūvæ* > *uve; mūrī* > *muri*. Masculines of the first declension, after hesitating a long time between *-e* and *-i*, finally chose the latter: *omicida -e -i, poeta -e -i*. *Mano*, the only feminine of the second declension, has *mani*, but the old language offers occasional examples of *le mano*. Some original neuters — and, following them, some masculines — have a plural in *-a*, which has become feminine: *miglia, uova; dita, mura*. Most neuters, however, follow the masculine pattern: *agli, doni, poggi*.

When the final vowel was preceded by *c* or *g*, there was a conflict between phonetic principle and analogy: *piaga, piage* or *piaghe; greco, greci* or *grechi; mago, magi* or *maghi*. There was some hesitation in the older language, but analogy

before long gained a complete victory in the first declension:
comiche, spighe, rughe; duchi, colleghi. In the second, analogy
won as far as *g* was concerned; for *c*, analogy was the stronger
in paroxytones, while phonetic tendency prevailed in proparoxytones: *lunghi,* so *aghi, laghi, luoghi; ciechi, fuochi;
mędici, mǫnaci.* Book-words usually follow the same rule:
catáloghi, opáchi, cántici. See §§ 106, 1 and 107, 3.

1. There are still some irregularities in the *-co, -go* words: scientists'
names in *-logo,* such as *fisiǫlogo,* have *-gi; greco, porco, amico* and its
derivatives have *-ci; cárico, stǫmaco* and some others have *-chi,* while
lástrico and *párroco* are changing and *síndaco* has recently changed from
-chi to *-ci.*

2. In the early centuries certain feminines of the first declension
occasionally show a plural in *-i: calendi, cimi, erbi, festi, pagini, porti,
spalli, veni, le mali femine.* These probably are reflexes of the feminine
third declension conflict between *-e* and *-i*: see §§ 55 and 164. Some
scholars, however, regard them as descendants of the ablative, and point
out that in the second declension also the ablative may be regarded as
one of the factors in the ending *i.*

3. The inherited plurals in *-a* (about twenty) generally have a col-
lective sense: *le braccia, le labbra, le miglia, le uova.* They have attracted
some new formations, such as *le grida* from *grido* < *gridare* < *quirītare,*
and some masculines of similar character, such as *le dita, le gǫmita*
(also *-i*), *le mura, le sacca* (generally *-chi*). *Le castella, le prata* are
poetic Latinisms. A few of the *-a* forms developed a new plural in *-e*:
il frutto, i frutti, le frutta, le frutte; il legno, i legni, le legna, le legne.
By the analogy of such words as *braccia, labbra, dita, gomita,* certain
feminine singular words denoting parts of the body (*guancia, mascella,
nocca, unghia*) came sometimes to be used as plurals (*le unghia,* etc.);
we have seen that *orecchia,* so used, developed a masculine singular
orecchio.

4. The ending *-ora,* starting in the third declension with such neuter
nouns as *cǫrpora,* was extended, without distinction of gender, to more
than thirty nouns of the second declension: *campora, lagora, luogora,
pratora,* etc. These plurals are now obsolete.

5. For *-ariu' -ari, -oriu' -ori,* see §§ 129, 1 and 150. Of *-ĕriu'* there
is probably no popular example; *impęro, mistęro* are old book-words.

6. For the development of *belli, mali*, etc., into *begli, magli*, then *bei, mai*, then *be', ma'*, see §§ 42 and 109, 5. Such substantive plurals as *augei, capei, cavai, figliuoi*, common in Tuscan poets but not in Tuscan speech, seem to be imitations of *bei, mai*, etc.

7. When the plural ending *-i* follows an *-i-* in the stem, the two combine: *studio, studi* (which may, however, be spelled with *-i, -ii, -î,* or *j*).

164. In the third declension, Latin *-ēs* phonetically gave *-e*. For the gradual supplanting of this vowel by the distinctively plural *-i*, see § 55. On the whole, it is unlikely that the Latin accusative *-īs* had any important share in the modern forms. Very early, masculine words began to borrow the second declension *-i;* a similar thing occurred in French, Provençal, and Rumanian, and there may be a few traces of it in Vulgar Latin. There is still some confusion among masculines, though not much, in the thirteenth century, at which time, apparently, feminine adjectives and nouns began to follow the masculine example. First *i padre, le madre;* next *i padri, le madre;* then *i padri, le madri*. The change was not complete in literary Italian before the eighteenth century, and in the dialects is not yet complete. *Padre* is still a regular plural in the Abruzzi; *chiave, gente, parte, torre* may still be heard as plurals in Tuscany.

Neuters, except those in *-s*, conformed to the masculine pattern: *lume lumi, capo, capi, cuore cuori, marmo marmi, zolfo zolfi*. Those in *-s* long kept their old plural in *-ora*, although they eventually formed a new one in *-i: corpora corpi, latora lati, lidora lidi, pegnora pegni*. This *-ora* plural (extended, as we have seen, to the second declension) was very frequent in old Tuscan, Umbrian, and Roman, and is still current in the Abruzzi and the south, though unknown in the north and in Sardinia. It has disappeared from literary Italian and nearly or wholly from Tuscan dialects.

1. For the development of *quali, tali* into *quagli, tagli*, then *quai, tai*, see §§ 42 and 104, *L*. Hence a poetic plural *animai*, etc.

2. Truncated words (§ 52) became invariable: *città, dì, fè, piè, re* (§ 42), *virtù*. So are foreign words ending in an accented vowel or diphthong: *bambù, caffè, tranvai*. Words ending in -*i*, -*ie*, or a consonant, all borrowed, are invariable also: *crisi, spezie, lapis*.

165. Other parts of speech used occasionally as nouns in a peculiar way have no plural form: *i quando*. Compound words consisting of two substantives or of substantive + adjective, if entirely grown together, generally inflect the latter part: *capolavori, capofitti*. If they are not wholly amalgamated, the principal substantive is inflected, and the adjective, if there is one, agrees: *capi d'opera, teste dure*. Compounds containing a noun and a verb are regularly invariable: *portavoce, cavatappi*.

166. Words ending in *lo, le, no, ne, ro*, or *re* may lose their final vowel in the interior of a phrase (§ 51), and in poetry even before a pause: *animal grazioso, buon giorno, amor mio; in mezzo a lor*. Such words drop the plural -*i* freely in poetry, and occasionally in popular speech: *picciol sassi, quei fior; i can barboni*.

Numerals

167. Of the numerals, *uno*, preceding a noun, drops its -*o* except before *s* + cons. or *ts* or *dz;* the feminine, *una*, loses its -*a* only before a vowel. When used as a pronoun, *uno* has a full inflection: *gli uni e gli altri*.

For ' two ' we have: *duo* < Lat. *duo, dui* < V. L. *dui* (which substituted plural -*i* for dual -*o*), *due* < Lat. fem. *duœ, dua* < Lat. neuter *dua* for *duo*. These words were in Old Italian generally used indiscriminately, although some authors (*e.g.*, Ariosto) reserved *due* for the feminine. The final preference for *due* as a sole form is probably due to the influence of *tre*. *Duo* survives in the south.

Mille has in Old Italian, beside *mila*, a plural *miglia milia millia* < Lat. *mīl(l)ia*. At present *miglia* means only ' miles.' *Mila* is a learned formation from *milia* on the same model as *vangelo, strano, impero, chiesa*: § 124, 1. *Milione* (once also *millione*), a late word meaning 'big thousand,' made up from *mil(l)ia*, has a plural *milioni*.

The other cardinal numerals are invariable.

1. *Uno* came to be employed in Italian as the indefinite article. This use, which began sporadically in Classic Latin times, grew to be rather frequent in Vulgar Latin.

2. *Děcem < diece*, which subsequently, attracted perhaps by *venti*, took the plural ending *-i*. For the first *i* of *diciassette, diciannove*, see § 36, 1. The tens, between 10 and 100, are irregular in Italian, as they are in the other Romance languages: see J. Jud, *Die Zehnerzahlen in den romanischen Sprachen*, 1905; cf. *Archiv für das Studium der neueren Sprachen und Literaturen*, XXIV, 400.

Pronominal Inflections

168. Pronouns are usually more conservative than nouns and adjectives. Several of the Latin pronouns, to be sure, went out of use, but those which remained kept remnants of their old inflection.

Is, idem, and *hic* disappeared almost entirely; a relic of the first is *desso < id ipsum;* traces of *hic* linger in *ancora, uguanno, unguanno; ciò < ecce hoc.* As personal pronoun of the third person we find *ille*, sometimes *ipse*. The adverb *inde* (It. *ne*) acquired the function of a genitive neuter pronoun, ' of it,' ' of them.'

169. Among inflectional innovations, the most striking is the imitation of *quī* by *ille*, a process which results in a masculine singular declension *illī, illūjus, illūi, illu, illō.* On this model, starting with a feminine dative *illœ* (for the literary *illī*), we have corresponding feminine singular cases *illa, illœjus, illœi, illa.* In the plural, on the other hand, *illarum* gave way entirely to *illorum. Illīus* left no trace, but dative *illī* remained in common use.

Another phenomenon is the substitution of *quī* for feminine *quœ* and the complete confusion of the interrogative and relative inflections; the form *quis* disappears, while *quĭd* is frequently used for *quŏd*.

1. Italian *ched che* from *quĭd* assumes not only the pronominal but also the conjunctional functions of *quod*. In early Italian three words were in competition as pronoun-conjunctions: *co* < *quod*, *che* < *quid*, *ca* < *qu(i)a* + *quam*.

170. A word naturally develops differently according as it is stressed or unstressed, and some of the pronouns and pronominal adjectives had such a dual development. Adjectival *ille*, when unaccented, became the definite article.

To a stressed form ending in a vowel, in the older language, was often added a particle *ne: mene = me, cione = ciò*, etc.[1] The origin of this enclitic is unknown, but it may have started with such double verb-forms as *tiè tiene, viè viene* (cf. §§ 52 and 204, 1). It is particularly common with verbs (*ene = è, fane = fa, saline = salì*), occasionally with doubling of the *n* (*honne = ho*). Sometimes it is attached to adverbs: *ine = i* ('there'), *quine = qui*. As far as Tuscany is concerned, this *-ne* appears to be most at home in Arezzo.

Personal Pronouns

171. In the development of personal pronouns [2] of the first and second persons, it is to be noted that *ĕgo* in Vulgar Latin everywhere lost its *g;* that *mĭhi* early contracted into *mī*, which led to **tī, *sī* beside *tĭbi, sĭbi;* that *mī, *tī, *sī* and *mē, tē, sē* before the accent would all in Italian naturally have *i*, while in the enclitic position the *ē* and the *ī* would phonetically be differentiated; that *nōs, vōs* regularly became *nọi, vọi* (§ 94, *S*).

In point of fact, Vulgar Latin *eo*, — which became *io* in nearly all of Tuscany, — remained *eo* in Arezzo and in most

---

[1] See S. Pieri in *Zs.*, XXX, 339.

[2] See Aline Furtmüller, *Zur Syntax der italienischen Personalpronomina*, in *Zs.*, XXXIII, 148.

non-Tuscan dialects, *eu* being still a usual form in Sicily. Pretonic *io* was reduced to *i'* in Tuscan (§ 43). Between the originally dative and accusative forms there is no trace of distinction in Italian; *mi*, etc., came to be used in the unstressed, *me*, etc., in the stressed position. With the addition of the *-ne* mentioned in § 170, we have *mene, tene, sene*. From *tĭbi, sĭbi*, came Old Italian *teve, seve*, and by analogy *meve;* from *nobis, vobis* the south got *nobe, bobe*. *Mecum*, etc., give *mę̇co*, etc.; hence Vulgar Latin *noscum, voscum* for *nobiscum, vobiscum*: It. *nosco, vosco*.

Noi, voi, used proclitically, as in *noi vede =* 'he sees us,' *voi dico =* 'I tell you,' regularly become *no, vo* (§ 42), which we find in the thirteenth century in Florence, Arezzo, and Siena. Beside them occur in Arezzo and Siena *ne* and *ve*, in Florence (as in Sicily) *ni* and *vi*, modeled on the singular forms *me, mi, te, ti*. In Florence, however, the Aretine *ne*, reinforced by *ne<inde*, supplanted the native *ni* (Calabrian has *ndi* for *ci*); but *vi* was kept. *No* and *vo* were crowded out. Inasmuch as the word for 'you' had now come to be identical with the word for 'there' (*vi<ibi*), the word for 'here' came to be used for 'us.' This word is *ci<ecc' ĭc* (i.e., *ecce hīc*), which gradually took the place of *ne*, the latter being at present confined (in the sense of 'us') to archaic and poetic diction. In Calabrian *nci = gli, le, loro*.[1]

1. In Old Italian the order of words was freer than it is now. A conjunctive pronoun used with an infinitive did not invariably follow; nor did the pronoun always precede a declarative verb. Indeed, it regularly came after a verb that started a sentence: e.g., *Pregoti*, as compared with *Io ti prego*. When a verb had both a direct and an indirect object, both of them conjunctive pronouns, the indirect did not necessarily precede: one might say *lo gli dico* as well as *glie lo dico*. *Ne* did not always follow other pronouns; such a phrase as *ne mi parla* was

[1] *Me lo, te lo, se lo*, etc. are probably not originally Florentine, but a Bolognese or Aretine substitution for *lo mi*, etc., after *me ne, te ne* had supplanted *mi ne, ti ne*: see J. Melander in *Studia Neophilologica*, II, 3, 169.

quite possible.[1] In old Florentine *lo mi, lo ti.* etc., are regular; see *Filostrato,* V, v, 5: *follami* (= *me lo fa) lasciare.*

2. The use of *me, te, se, ve* rather than *mi, ti, si, vi* before *lo, la, li, le* probably goes back to a stressed form of the demonstrative: *mī ĭllu' dat > m'ęllo dà = me llo dà,* which in Tuscany becomes *me lo dà* as *eccu' illui > *collui colui* (§ 109, end).[2] In the south the double *l* is kept. The forms with *e* were brought into use also before *ne,* either by imitation or through a similar process, such as *mī ĭnde dat > m' ęnde dat > *m' ęnne dà = me nne dà > me ne dà.* By analogy, the words *ci* and *gli* (masculine or feminine) substituted an *e* for their *i* whenever they stood before *lo, la, li, le,* or *ne*: as *ce lo dice, glie ne parlo.* In the early language we often find a curious invariable *gliele,* wherein the second element may represent *lo, la, li,* or *le.*

172. In the third person, the form *ĭllī* (representing *ĭlle, ĭllī,* and perhaps *ĭllīs:* § 169) became *ęlli,* then *ęgli* before a vowel; and *ęgli* used before a consonant was reduced to *ęi,* later in Florence to *e':* § 42. *Illa* and *ĭlle* (representing *ĭlla ĭllam ĭllā,* and *ĭllœ*) became *ęlla* and *ęlle.* *Illūjus* and *illœjus* (§§ 151, 169) left no trace in Italian; but *illūī* and *illœī* gave *lui* and *lęi,* the initial vowel being lost, presumably by elision, as in such a phrase as *a 'llui, e 'llei.* Similarly *illōrum,* which was used for both masculine and feminine, become *lǫro,* which served as a dative plural, corresponding to *lui* and *lei;* its genitive meaning was retained only in its function as a possessive. *Lui, lei, loro* are now employed as stressed objective forms, after a verb or a preposition. Inasmuch as *egli* was of both numbers (*egli ama, egli amano*), the plural *egli* came to be distinguished from the singular by the addition of the verbal ending -*no* (*egli ama, eglino amano*). On this model was built a feminine *elleno.* *Eglino, elleno,* and plural *egli* are now obsolete, being supplanted by *loro, essi, esse.* In modern colloquial Italian, *lui* and *lei,* also, are employed as nominatives, taking the place of *egli* and *ella.*

[1] See H. Henz, *Die Stellung der Objectspronomina in Verhältnis zum Verbum wie auch unter sich im Altitalienischen,* 1908.

[2] See *Zs.,* XXX, 17.

Ello and *elli* were lost in Tuscan, but survived in Sicilian.

1. From *ĭpse* we have *esso, essa, essi, esse,* used as alternates for the derivatives of *ĭlle.*

173. In the unstressed, or conjunctive, use of the pronoun, its first syllable is lost; and the long forms *illui, illæi, illorum* do not appear, the dative singular being m. *ĭllī*, f. *ĭllī* or *ĭllæ,* the dative plural *ĭllīs. Illī* (representing, therefore, *ĭlle,* dat. sing. *ĭllī,* nom. pl. *ĭllī,* dat. pl. *ĭllīs*) became *li,* then *gli* before a vowel; and *gli* used before a consonant was reduced to *i* (§ 42): *gli è difficile,* 'it is hard'; *li dico* or *gli dico* or *i dico,* 'I say to him' or 'to her'; *li vede* or *gli vede* or *i vede,* 'he sees them'; *li* or *gli* or *i parliamo,* 'we speak to them.' *Illo* (= *ĭllum* and *ĭllō*)>*lo. Illa* (= *ĭlla, ĭllam, ĭllā*)>*la: la non viene,* 'she does n't come'; *vedetela,* 'see her.' *Ille* (= *ĭllæ*)>*le.*

It is noteworthy that pronouns, as well as nouns, use the originally nominative plural forms as accusatives.

Ne from *inde* is used as an unstressed pronoun meaning 'of it,' 'of him,' 'of her,' 'of them.' Furthermore, the adverbs *ci* and *vi* take the place of an unaccented neuter dative singular or plural: *ci si conforma,* 'he adapts himself to it'; *vi sono assuefatto,* 'I am used to them.'

The modern literary language discards *i* altogether, distinguishes dative singular *gli* from accusative plural *li,* restricts dative singular *gli* to the masculine, and replaces the original dative plural by *ci, vi,* or the stressed form *loro.*

1. In early Italian, and later in archaic or poetic diction, we very often find for *lo* a form *il,* which seems to have developed out of *l* in such constructions as *lo odo*>*l'odo, non lo vedo*>*nollo vedo*>*nol vedo, te lo dico*>*tel dico;* whence *io l dico, tu l dici, egli l dice* written *io il dico,* etc., until finally we have *il dice* = *lo dice,* etc. *Filostrato* often has *el* for masc. or neut. subject or object.

2. For the position of conjunctive pronouns, see § 171, 1.

3. For the development of *glie,* see § 171, 2.

Definite Article

174. As Latin progressed, the demonstrative adjectives came to be used more and more for the purpose of simple specification; and thus grew up the Romance definite article. In most of the territory the word so employed stood regularly before its noun, but in Rumanian it came after. Some small districts (among them Sardinia) preferred *ipse* for this function; *ille*, however, was the commonest favorite, and from adjectival *ille* comes the Italian article.

1. The Sardinian forms are *su, sa, sos, sas*.

175. From accented (or half-accented) *ĭllum, ĭllam, ĭllī, ĭllæ* come *ęllo, ęlla, ęlli, ęlle*. *Ello* before a word not beginning with *s* + cons. (or *ts* or *dz*) loses its then intertonic *o* and shrinks to *el* (§§ 57, 58); becoming wholly unstressed, before the accent, it develops further into *il* (§ 38). *El*, with a plural *ei, e'*, is found in Arezzo. *Ella, elle*, as long as they preserved a stress, apparently remained unchanged (see § 176). *Elli* before a vowel became *egli*, which before a consonant other than *s* + cons. (or *ts* or *dz*), losing its accent, was reduced to *ei*, then to *e'* (§ 42), then to *i* (§ 38, 2).

Now the preposition *de*, combining with *ello*, etc., produces *dello, del, della, delli degli dei de'* (§ 59, 1), *delle*. Similarly *in* + *ello*, etc., makes *nello*, etc. On the model of these are constructed *allo, collo, dallo*, with *a, con, da* and the article. *Pello, sullo*, probably coming later still, seem to be patterned on *collo*.

1. Beside *nello*, etc., in the older language, we find *indello*, etc., due apparently to a confusion of *in* and *inde:* § 130, Nd.

2. For the principles of elision, see § 53; for the development and the loss of a vowel before *s* + cons., see §§ 39 and 40, 1. The use of *lo* before ' *s* impure ' is originally due to the absorption of the *i*- by the preceding -*o*. Then, by association of *st* with *ts*, the form *lo* comes to be used also before *ts* and even *dz* (both written *z*): *lo istilo* > *lo stilo*, then *lo zio*, then *lo zigolo*.

176. When *ello*, etc., are used quite proclitically, they lose their first syllable. *Ello, ella, elle*, then become *lo, la, le*. We have already seen (§ 175) how *elli* is reduced to *i;* the same result may come by way of an earlier loss of the first syllable — viz., *illī*, *'li*, then *gli* before vowels, and *gli* before consonants becomes *i*, remaining *gli* before vowels. So, beside the *il* which evolves from accented *ello*, we have an *l* from unaccented *illu'*, *'lu'* before a vowel: *illu' ŏleu' >lu' oleu' >l'olio*.

177. The prevailing Tuscan forms are originally *lo l il, li gli i; la, le*. Through Guittone and his school, however, the Aretine *el* and *ei* came more or less into poetic use in the rest of Tuscany. In early prose, before consonants other than *s* + cons. (or *ts, dz*), *lo, li* and *il, i* seem to have been used indiscriminately; but in the verse of Dante's time *il* and *i* are not syllabic, being employed only after a vowel (e.g., *sì che il piè fermo . . ., le vene e i polsi*). A poetic preference for *lo* persisted through several centuries. Moreover, in the phrases *per lo più* and *per lo meno* the *lo* has maintained itself, even in colloquial usage, to the present day.

1. In current prose *lo* and *gli* are restricted to the position before a vowel or before *s* + cons. (or *ts, dz*). *Lo* and *la* regularly elide their *o, a* before any vowel; *gli* and *le* usually drop their *i* or *e* only before an identical vowel.

2. The Sicilian poets seem to have used *lo l u, li gli; la a, le* (doubtless pronounced *li*).

Possessives [1]

178. The Vulgar Latin words were probably *mẹus*, **tọus*, *sọus*, the last two showing a dissimilation of *uu:* see § 29, 5; *nọstru'*, and by analogy *vọstru'*. *Mẹus mẹu' > *mieo mio, mẹa > *miea mia, mẹe > *miee mie*, but *mẹi>miei:* see § 27, end. So **tọus *tọu> *tuoo tuo, *tọa> *tuoa tua, *tọe> *tuoe tue*, but **tọi>tuoi* and *tui:* see § 31. *Sọus* followed the same course as **tọus*. From *nọstru', vọstru'* we get *nostro-i-a-e, vostro-i-a-e*.

[1] See L. E. Menger, *The Development of Possessive Pronouns in Italian*, 1893.

In Old Italian we find a masc. and fem. pl. *mia*, perhaps originally a neuter: *le mia sorelle, li fatti mia*. A singular *mie* (*la mie porta*) is probably a shortening of **miea*. So an occasional fem. *tuo* (*la tuo bontade*) seems to be an apocopated **tuoa;* it leads to a rare fem. pl. *tuoi, suoi* (*delle suoi genti, le suoi castella*). The rather indiscriminate use of forms was no doubt encouraged by the diversity of words for ' two ': *dua, due, dui, duo, duoi.*

Very frequent in early poetry is *meo*, which is generally a Latinism, although in Arezzo and in Sicily it may have been in spoken use. *Sui* and *tui*, common in the old language, are surely in many cases pure Latinisms, but they seem nevertheless to have really existed in current speech, beside *suoi* and *tuoi*, which ultimately crowded them out.

1. The thirteenth century *Fiore* has *seo* for *suo* — evidently an imitation of *meo*.

179. ' Their ' is expressed by the invariable *loro* < *illōrum*. *Suo* in this sense occurs very often in poetry, where, in all probability, it is for the most part a Latinism; occasionally it stands in prose, where it doubtless represents a popular survival.

180. Beside the longer forms, Vulgar Latin certainly had monosyllabic *sus*, presumably **tus*, and possibly **mes*. These appear occasionally in Italian poetry as *me mi, tu, su;* in Bolognese speech as *mi, to, so*. We have also the old-fashioned enclitic *mo, ma, so:* e.g., *padremo, madrema* (still heard in the south), and Dante's *signorso*. Sometimes we find *ma* attached to masculine nouns: *cognatoma, fratelma*. So regularly in Calabrian.

181. The possessives in modern Italian are preceded by the definite article or some other determining word, except when used adjectively in the predicate, or with a vocative, or with a singular noun of relationship otherwise unmodified.

142   MORPHOLOGY

In the old language, the practice was much the same, although there was more freedom. The very common poetic use of the possessive without the article is a Latinism. Certain set phrases, however, have come down, with no article, from a time before the article was fully evolved: e.g., *da parte mia, in casa sua.*

Demonstratives

182. Latin possessed a demonstrative interjection *eccum* (made up originally of *ecce* + a pronoun), which, after *ille* had come to be used as an article and as a personal pronoun, was regularly prefixed to that word when a real demonstrative sense was to be expressed: *illu' amicu' > l'amico, eccu' illu' amicu' > quell' amico; *illī exit > egli esce, eccu' illī exit > quegli esce.* To *iste*, as well, this *eccum* is generally prefixed; but the pronoun continued in existence also without the particle — in *stanotte, stasera, stavolta,* and, by analogy, *stamane,* beside *questa notte,* etc.; in *stęsso < istu' ipsu';* and, in Old Italian, in detached *ęsto-a-i-e.*

1. *Ipse* gives us *ęsso-a-i-e,* generally used as a personal pronoun. It came to be employed also, after some prepositions, as an invariable intensive particle: *con esso lui,* then *con esso lei* = 'together with her.'

2. Another demonstrative adjective and pronoun, associated with the second person, is *cotęsto* or *codęsto-a-i-e,* apparently from *eccu' *tĭ ĭstu'.* It has a masc. sing. substantive form *cotesti.*

183. The derivatives of the different forms of *eccu' illu'* and *eccu' istu'* are similar to those which come from the pronoun *ille: quelli quegli quei que'* (§ 172), *colui colei, quello-a-i-e, coloro; questi, costui costei, questo-a-i-e, costoro* (for the contraction of *u + ĭ,* see § 37, 4). These are used as pronouns, *quegli quei* and *questi* being reserved for the nom. sing. masc., 'that man,' 'this man,' 'the former,' 'the latter.'

In adjectival function we have only *quello-a-i-e* and *questo-a-i-e.* Furthermore, *quello* and *quelli* used proclitically develop forms similar to those of *di* + the definite article: *quel quell', quei quegli.* *Questo, questa* used proclitically, may elide their final *o* or *a* before a vowel.

The Sicilian poets, both in pronominal and in adjectival use, write *quello-a-i-e, questo-a-i-e,* without reduction.

Relatives and Interrogatives

184. In Vulgar Latin, *quī* was used for *quis* and for the fem. sing. *quæ;* and *quid* encroached upon the domain of *quod.* We have, then, as an outcome of the combined declension of *qui* and *quis*: *chi<quī, cui<cui, che<quid* (and perhaps *quem, quæ), co<quod.* In Old Italian, before a vowel, we often find *ched<quid. Co* seems not to be native in Tuscany. Non-Tuscan, too, is *ca<qua quia* (and perhaps *quam*), which is common in the dialects. These three words, *che-d, co, ca,* were for some time in competition, both as pronouns and as conjunctions, but *che-d* was at last preferred in both uses.

1. *Chi* is used only of persons, and only as an interrogative or as an indefinite relative (' he who ' or ' one who '). *Che* as an interrogative is neuter; as a relative it may stand for either number or any gender. *Cui,* representing both persons and things, may be used objectively with a verb or a preposition; in the phrase *il cui,* 'whose,' it has a genitive function.

2. Modern Italian keeps the *d* of *ched* only in *ciascheduno* and *qualcheduno.*

3. *Qualis>quale,* pl. *quali,* masc. and fem. alike. It is used as an interrogative adjective and pronoun; and, with the definite article prefixed, as a relative. For *quai,* see § 42; 59, 1; 104, *L.*

4. For *chiunque,* as for *qualunque* and *qualche,* see § 56.

CONJUGATION

185. Among the four great types of Latin verb-inflection there were some shifts in Vulgar Latin and more in Romance. There were also, of course, new formations: these, in Italian, are all made in the first conjugation (*biondeggiare*) or in the fourth (*ingelosire*); some belong to both (*arrossire -are*).

The first conjugation maintained itself well in Italian, gaining a quantity of new formations and losing only *arrogere* (whose shift started apparently with a perf. part. *ad-rŏgĭtus* > *arroto*).

The second was on the whole a loser. It early gained from the third *cadere, potere, sapere, volere*, but lost to it some fifteen verbs, of which the most important are *mescere, muovere, nuocere, ridere, rispondere, torcere;* to the fourth it lost *compire* and *empire* (cf. *cómpiere, émpiere*), *fiorire, pentire, putire, sparire* with *comparire* and *apparire* (retaining, however, *parere*). In most of these cases, one can see no adequate reason for the change. *Potere* and *volere* are examples of standardization; *sapere* early came under the sway of *habere*, presumably on account of similarity of sound; but what attracted *cadere?*

The third gained much but lost more. In addition to the shifts mentioned, it sacrificed to the fourth some verbs in *-io* (*capire, fuggire, morire*), many bookish words (*applaudire*), and sundry others (*offrire, seguire,* etc.). It lost to the first a small part of *facere fare*, to the fourth a small part of *dicere dire*. On the other hand, it won from the fourth *fiedere* < *ferire, riedere* < *redire*, and a couple more.

The fourth, as we have seen, suffered few losses and received a good many deserters, not to speak of numerous fresh conscripts.

Fare, dire, and rare Old Italian *dure* (beside *facere, dicere, ducere,* which were current in the early centuries) call for some special explanation. Monosyllabic *fac, dic* led to a plural imperative *fate, *dite, whence indicative *fatis, *ditis and infinitive *fare, *dire (strongly influenced by *dare, stare* and perhaps by *audire*). *Dure* may have followed a similar course; *durre* follows *torre* < *toll're*. Dante's *die = dici* and *ridui = riduci* are not satisfactorily explained.

186. Far more important, however, were the fundamental innovations caused by the analytical tendency described in § 152. The entire passive and the entire formation of perfect tenses were made over. Here and there, from the beginnings of Latin literature, we can detect sporadic evidences of an inclination to the analytic constructions, but this inclination, if we are to judge from written documents, was held in check by tradition. It is only in the several Romance languages that the tendency comes to obvious fulfilment; but the likeness of the outcome in the various tongues would seem to indicate a considerable alteration, before the disruption of the Empire, in the usage of the populace.

187. The new passive was built by combining the perfect participle of the verb in question with the appropriate forms of the verb ' to be '; *sono amato, eran amati, fu amato, sarete amati*, etc. The auxiliary is *ęssere* < *esse*, except in northern Italy, where it is *fìr* < *fieri*. The whole apparatus of the old passive inflexion disappears; only the gerundive seems to have lingered in a few combinations. Deponent verbs become active: *mori* > *morire, sequi* > *seguire*.

One result of the disuse of the older passive is an extension of the distinctly reflexive construction: *ponitur* > *se ponit* > *si pone*. Cf. *Zs.*, XXXIII, 135.

1. It is noteworthy that the Germanic languages created for themselves a new passive in the same fashion.

2. The Italians sometimes use as auxiliary, to distinguish more clearly an act from a state, the verb *venire:* as *viene punito* for *è punito*. The use of *andare* with the participle indicates obligation: *va fatto così* = ' it must be done thus.'

3. *Fiat* > *fia*, which, with the plural *fian*, is used in poetic diction as a future of *essere*.

188. The perfect tenses were made by combining the perfect participle with the proper forms of *habere* — or, eventually, in the case of passive, reflexive, and most neuter verbs, the corresponding forms of *esse* > **ĕssĕre:* e.g., *feci* > *ho fatto*, *fecerat>aveva fatto, fecerint>avranno fatto; factus erat>era stato fatto* or *si era fatto; venerunt>sono venuti.*

1. Here again the Germanic and the Romance languages followed parallel lines.

2. The occasional literary use of the simple preterit in a perfect sense, as *dissi* = ' I have spoken,' seems to be a Latinism.

189. The Latin perfect indicative was kept in its aorist sense. The pluperfect indicative was lost in the greater part of Italy, but in the Napoletano, in Apulia, in the Abruzzi, and in Umbria (as in Provençal) it was retained as a conditional; one form, *fora<fuerat,* found and kept a place in general poetic usage; cf. *Zs.,* XXXIII, 129. The future perfect indicative and the perfect subjunctive have left but few (and doubtful) traces even in the earliest Italian: cf. *Zs.,* XXXI, 24. Except in Sardinia, the imperfect subjunctive vanished, having been supplanted by the *pluperfect: veniret>venisset>venisse.* Both in the perfect and pluperfect indicative and in the pluperfect subjunctive only the contracted forms were used: *amāsti, amāstis, amārunt; audieram (>audīram),* etc.; *audīssem,* etc.

Of the imperative, only the second person singular and plural remained; when other persons were needed, they were supplied from the present subjunctive; some verbs, indeed, which do not readily lend themselves to command, took from that source their entire imperative. The future participle went out of use, as did the supine and, almost entirely, the gerundive. The ablative gerund was kept and assumed gradually most of the functions of the present participle. This latter form was retained mainly as a verbal adjective. The perfect participle stayed, and, as we have seen, its use was so extended that all verbs had to have one, whether Classic Latin afforded a model or not. The infinitive maintained itself and grew in importance.

1. The first person plural of the subjunctive, when used imperatively, was felt to be a real imperative, as is shown by the position of the conjunctive pronoun or adverb: *diciamolo, andiamovi.*

190. The Latin future had ceased to be satisfactory, perhaps because in some types it suggested the imperfect indicative, in others the present subjunctive. At any rate, it was used with less and less frequency, being replaced now by the present indicative, now by various periphrases: instead of *dicet*, people said *dicit, dicturus est, debet dicere, volet* (= *vult*) *dicere, dicere habet.* This last expression won the preference in Italy, as in most of the Empire; thus the future tense came to be a compound of the infinitive with the present indicative of *habere:* e.g., *crederà, sentiranno.*

When the new future was well established, it led to another fresh formation — a past future or conditional. To match *si venit audire habet* people said *si venibat* (or *venisset*) *audire habebat.* The Tuscans, however, in such cases, said *habuit* instead of *habebat:* thus *verrebbe*, rather than *verria*, came to be the standard Italian form; *verria*, however, which comes from *venire habebat*, prevailed in the south, and has been extensively used in Italian poetry.

1. It is evident that the forms of *habere* were considerably reduced when employed as future endings. Notably the *av-* was left out of infin. + *avemo avete*, infin. + *avea* (§ 140) etc., and infin. + *avesti avemmo aveste.* Probably the persons having the shortest forms were used first, and the longer ones, when brought into the scheme, were cut down to match them. Furthermore, inasmuch as the present indicative of *habere* had several different inflections, the future endings varied correspondingly. Beside *habeo habes habet*>*aggio* (or *aio*) *avi ave*, we have (on the model of *dare* and *stare*) **ho *has *hat*>*ò ai à.* These last were chosen in Tuscany, *aggio* etc. in the south. There was also an *abbo;* see § 197, 2. For *anno* see § 97, 2.

2. The Tuscan conditional, in its first and third person singular and its third person plural, had originally *-abbi* etc.: e. g., *crederabbi, crederabbe, crederabbero.* Soon we find an *-ei*, seemingly taken from the early perfect *credęi*<*credędi*<*credĭdi* (§ 140), supplementing the *-abbi*, and occasionally an *-è* for *-abbe.* A contamination of *-abbi* and *-ei* is the probable source of *-ębbi*, used first as a conditional ending, next as an independent form for *abbi*<*habui;* then the *ę* spreads to the third person, giving *-ebbe* or *-è, -ebbero.* The language has inconsistently chosen

-ẹi, -ẹbbe, -ẹbbero. In Old Italian one occasionally meets *ei* and *è* employed independently as rivals to *ebbi* and *ebbe.*

    3. Old Sardinian has traces of the conditional made with *habui.*

191. In standard Italian we have left, of the original Latin active inflection, the infinitive, the present and perfect participles, the ablative gerund, the present, imperfect, and perfect indicative, the second person of the imperative, the present and pluperfect subjunctive. As a new creation, we have the passive system, the formation of the perfect tenses, the future and past future.

It is to be noted that the great innovations are syntactic rather than phonetic and that they are common to all or most members of the Romance group.

    1. The rôle of the subjunctive in conditions and in indirect discourse is somewhat curtailed from Latin usage.

INCEPTIVE VERBS

192. Latin had an inchoative suffix *-sco: irascor, floresco, sentisco, cognosco.* For some reason, the Italian (while keeping the word *cognosco*) utilized of these four types of formation only the *-isco,* which it vastly extended, making it a regular element in the inflection of most verbs of the fourth conjugation: *finio > finisco.* At the same time, it deprived the suffix of all its original meaning, and restricted it to the singular and the third person plural of the present indicative and subjunctive: *finisco, finisci, finisce,* finiamo, finite, *finiscono; finisca,* etc. In the vulgar dialects, however, the *sc* is generally carried through all the persons of the present, as it is in French.

ACCENTUATION

193. We find certain cases of deviation from the Latin stress, some common to the Romance group, some peculiar to Italian.

On the model of *mandāmus mandātis, sedēmus sedētis,
audīmus audītis,* the verbs of the third conjugation stressed
their penult in the first and second persons plural of the present indicative and in the plural imperative: *credīmus credītis
credīte > credęmo credęte credęte. Dite* and *fate* keep the accent
on the root syllable, but these forms are derived from monosyllabic *dīc > di', fac > fa'.*
In the strong perfect, the 1st pers. pl. stresses its penult,
imitating the 2d pers.: *facęmmo facęste,* as compared with
fēcĭmus fecĭstis. Here the weak perfects may have been
taken as a model, inasmuch as *mandāvimus, audīvimus* presumably became, at one stage, *mandámus, audímus.* The
doubling of the *m* probably started with such forms as *dĕdĭmus
ded'mus > demmo, fēcĭmus fec'mus > femmo, stĕtĭmus stet'mus
> stemmo, credĭdĭmus credid'mus > credemmo;* it then spread
to other perfects (*volemmo,* etc.), being readily adopted by
the weak types because in them it served to distinguish the
perfect from the present (*mandammo, mandamo*). The only
remnants of the original accentuation are Old Italian *dĭssimo
vĕddimo* and Sienese *lĕssimo, stiĕdimo;* to which we may add
ĕbbimo < habuimus (§ 9, 2).
In the pluperfect subjunctive the 1st and 2d pers. pl. shift
the accent to the antepenult, thus keeping it on the same
vowel throughout the tense: *mandāssēmus mandāssētis >
mandássimo mandáste, audīssēmus audissētis > udíssimo udíste,
credidissēmus credidissētis > credéssimo credéste,* to match
mandāssem mandāsses mandāsset mandāssent, etc.

1. Popular speech often levels the stress in the imperf. ind., using,
for instance, *-ávamo -ávate* in the 1st and 2d pers. pl. On the other
hand, we find *aveàno* for *avéano,* to match *avevámo avevàte.* An ending
-ieno, wherever and however it arises, tends to become *-ièno: avièno,
dièno, sièno, stièno,* all influenced, no doubt, by the example of the common diphthong *ie.*

2. In the early poets we occasionally find such forms as *nasciène =
ne nasce, vatténe = vàttene. Vattenne* is still current in Naples.

194. Some verbs, for phonetic or analogical reasons, develop in different parts different forms of the root syllable.
The root vowel may act diversely according to the stress: *dolēre>dolẹre, dŏlet>duole; audire>udire, audit>ọde.* Hence double stems. In many such cases one type crowds out the other: in *parlare* we see the victory of the atonic stem, if we may so designate the one in which the vowel in question is unstressed (**páraulátis>parlate,* hence *parla* instead of **parọla*); in *vietate,* the triumph of the tonic (*vĕtat>vieta,* so *vietate* instead of *vetate* or **vitate*). In a few instances the two types separate, forming two different words: *adjūtare> a(i)tare* and *aiutare,* from *a(i)táte* and *aiúta.* Generally, however, both types remain in one and the same verb, although there is still some tendency to level: *uscire esce, venire viene, volere vuole; negare, niego* or *nẹgo.*

195. Verbs in which *k* or *g* immediately precedes the ending develop differently according to the vowel with which the ending begins, the consonant being palatalized before a front, but not before a back, vowel: *duco duce, piacqui piaci, fugga fugge.* In most such verbs the two stems are kept: *cresco, cresce; dico, dice; sorgo, sorge;* etc. In some, however, the palatal stem infects the other: *coglie, colgo* and *coglio; piagne, piango* and *piagno;* etc. *Figgo, fuggo, leggo, reggo, struggo, traggo* probably owe their long *g* to the long *dž* of *figgi figge, fuggi fugge,* etc. (§§ 100, 107).

196. Words with a *y* stem have a somewhat more complicated history. If the verb assumed the originally inceptive *-isco* (§ 192), the *y* was of course lost in the *i: finio, finisco; capio, capisco.* It must be remembered, furthermore, that the group *yé,* after a consonant, regularly became *e* (§ 37, 2): *paríetem pariétem>parẹte, quiĕtus quĕtus>chẹto.* So *faciebam>facẹva, faciendo>facendo* (though *faccenda* and early *faccendo* have *ttš*, following *faccio* < *facio* and *faccia* < *faciam*).

Now, when the last consonant of a root has after it a *y* in the 1st pers. sing. (or the 1st pers. sing. and the 3d pers. pl.) of the present indicative and throughout the present subjunctive (as in *sentio sentiunt, sentiam sentias sentiat sentiāmus sentiātis sentiant*), we have a group of cons. + *y* in these forms but in no other part of the verb: *vĭdeo = vĭdyo*, but *vĭdes vĭdet vĭdēmus vĭdētis vĭdent; audyo* and *audyunt*, but *audis audit audīmus audītis*. By a leveling process the *y*, in many of these verbs, was eliminated very early: *fuggo, odo, parto, persuado, sento*, etc. In others the *y* was kept and each stem developed in its own way: *habeo habet* > *abbio ave, facio facit* > *faccio face, sapio sapit* > *sappio sape, voleo volet (= volo vult)* > *voglio vuole*, etc. In others still, the *y* has been gradually displaced, wholly or partially, by the stem without the *y*: *debbio deve*, then *devo; muoio muore*, then *muoro* (but conversely *muoi* from *muoio*, which remained the more usual form); *seggio siede*, then *siedo; veggio vede*, then *vedo*. In *cadere*, which passed from the third conjugation to the second, we get apparently *cado* > *cado* and **cadeo* > *caggio*.

1. From a hortative *eāmus* comes *giamo*, whence a new verb *gire*, which became very popular.

197. Many verbs get a new stem by imitation of other verbs. For some instances in the 1st pers. sing. of the present indicative, see § 151, 1.

Influenced by *dare* and *stare*, the new verb *andare* for *vadere* gets *vo* (beside *vado*) *vai va vanno, facere fare* gets *fo fai fa fanno* (beside *faccio face*), *avere* gets *ho hai ha hanno* (beside *abbio avi ave*); and *sapere*, conforming to *avere*, gets *so sai sa sanno* (beside *sappio sape*). Old Italian *arò* for *avrò* follows *darò, starò;* so *sarò* for earlier rare *serò*, and Old Italian *porò* for *potrò*. For the forms with *nn*, see § 97, 2.

1. Beside *do, sto* there must have existed in Vulgar Latin **dao, *stao*, keeping the root vowel; also **daunt, *staunt*. Descendants of these

exist in some dialects, with corresponding forms of *andare, fare, avere,* and *sapere.*

2. *Abbo* is probably due both to *abbi* < *habui* and to *debbo.* And *debbo* copies *debbe,* which in turn imitates *dovrebbe* (§ 190, 2). *Abbio* is the regular Tuscan descendant of *habeo;* so *debeo* regularly gives *debbio. Aggio, deggio* are southern developments of *habeo, debeo;* but they may come also, in Tuscany as well as in the south, from Vulgar Latin **ayo, *deyo,* which seem to have existed, perhaps following the lead of **veyo* from *vĭdeo. Aio* is found in some southern dialects.

3. *Esco escono esca escano,* corresponding to *exeo exeunt exeam* etc., seems to have fashioned itself on *conosco, cresco, finisco,* etc.

4. *Bevere* and *dovere* develop perfect participles *bevúto beúto, dovúto deúto* (§ 103, *B*), whence *bere, beo bei bee,* etc., and *dei dee denno* (also *die, diè,* a subjunctive *dea dia,* and a strange *dino* = *devono*). These account for an occasional *vei vee* for *vedi vede.*

5. *Pōnere pŏn're* > *pǫrre, tŏllĕre tŏll're* > *tǫrre;* hence, by analogy, *cǫrre* for *cǫgliere* (then *sciǫrre* and *scęrre*), *durre* for *ducere, trarre* for *traggere* (§ 146). Latin *trahere* can hardly be responsible for *trarre,* for it should have given *trare* (cf. *aerem* > *aire are*); but *traho trahis trahit* etc. are represented by *trao trai trae* etc., *traeva* etc., *traessi* etc., beside *traggo traggi tragge* etc.

6. *Velle* reconstructed itself (starting with *volui*) according to the standard of the second conjugation: *volēre, voleo voles volet,* etc., It. *volere, voglio vuoli vuole,* etc.; for *vuoi,* see § 125. Similarly *posse* made itself over into *potēre,* but in Italy kept *possum* > *posso,* whence *possono, possa,* etc. (also, in Sienese and many non-Tuscan dialects, *posseva, possei, possessi* for *poteva,* etc.); *puoti* > *puoi* by imitation of *vuoi, puote* > *può* by fall of intervocalic *e* (*puote fare* > *puot'fare* > *puŏ ffare*), *ponno* is made like *hanno* (§ 97, 2); old *porò poria* follow *darò daria.*

7. *Esse,* a very composite verb, was harder still to regularize. The infinitive, conforming to the third conjugation type, became *essere;* hence *essendo, essuto, *esserò,* and by elision *sendo, suto, serò sarò* (following *starò*), but *essuto issuto suto* was replaced by *stato* from *stare.* For the pres. ind., see §§ 95, 96, 97; *enno* is similar to *ponno, hanno* (§ 97, 2). Imperfect *eravamo eravate,* with their intrusive *-va-,* follow *avevamo avevate.* The pres. subj., in Vulgar Latin, adopted a typical third conjugation inflection, **siam *sias *siat* etc. > *sia* etc.; hence *dia* for *dem, stia* for *stem,* and even *dia* for *debeam.*

8. Popular Latin, having two verbs meaning ' to go,' *vadere* and *ire*, utilized the former for the sing. and 3d pers. pl. of the pres. ind., and all the pres. subj.; the latter for the rest of the inflection. Now when the new word *andare* (of mysterious origin) was introduced, it assumed the place of *ire*, leaving to *vado* its function in the pres. ind. and subj. *Vo vai va vanno* are of course on the model of *dare* and *stare*. *Ire* did not, however, go out of use altogether. We have seen how *eāmus* > *giamo* gave rise to another new verb *gire* (§ 196, 1).

9. The alternative forms *face* and *fa* led to *fe'* beside *fece;* a contributing factor may have been *fēc'mus* > *femmo*. We find also *feo* and *fee;* then *fenno* for *fecero* and *fei* for *feci*. Next we sometimes have *faea* and *fea* for *faceva*, *faessi* and *fessi* for *facessi*, *faesti faemmo faeste* and *festi femmo feste* for *facesti* etc. The *e* was close. These forms induced similar inflections in the preterit and imperf. subj. of *dare* and *stare*, culminating in the establishment of *desti* etc. and *dessi* etc., *stesti* etc. and *stessi* etc. as the accepted type. *Dĕd'mus* and *stĕt'mus*, which regularly gave *demmo* and *stemmo*, were of course factors in the development; but they exchanged their *ę* for the *ę* of *femmo*. Again, on the model of *fe'*, *diede* (< *dĕdit*) was often shortened to *diè*, *dè;* whence *dienno denno diero* and a 1st pers. sing. *diei*. Imitating *dare*, the verb *andare* sometimes has *andiedi*, and *stare* has *stiedi* beside *stetti* (< *stĕtui);* conversely, *dare* adopts *detti* patterned on *stetti*.

10. Latin *fŭī fŭit* originally had a long *u*, which seems to have maintained itself in Vulgar speech, at least in the 1st person. *Fŭisti fŭistis* seem to have become **fŭsti *fŭstis;* in *fŭimus fŭerunt* the *u* may have varied in length; at any rate, the several forms influenced one another. The upshot in Italian is: *fui, fosti (fusti), fu* or *fue, fummo (fommo), foste (fuste), furon (foron)*. *Funno* comes plainly from *fue*. But what is the source of *fuoro* for *furo (n)*? *Fŭissem* > **fŭssem* > *fossi*.

INFINITIVES AND PARTICIPLES

198. The four common patterns of the infinitive usually remain in Italian: *amare, vedere, credere, udire*. Some verbs of the third conjugation, however, omit the next-to-last *e* (*porre, torre*). This syncopation probably started in the future: **ponerò *pon'rò porrò*, hence *porre*. Not all syncopated futures, though, led to a shortening of the infinitive: *vivrò*, but *vivere*.

In the present participle and the gerund, the only note-worthy feature is the reduction of *ie* to *e* (§§ 37, 2; 196): *-ientem -iendo* > *-ente -endo*. The *-nt-* form, having become adjectival or substantival (*intelligente, amante*) does not constitute a necessary part of the inflection.

199. In the perfect participle, Lat. *-ātus, -ītus, -ūtus* > It. *-ato, -ito, -uto*, the rare *-ētus* being lost. Lat. *-sus* and *-nsus* > *-so: cŭrsus* > *cŏrso, prehensus* > *prĕso*. Lat. *-tus* and *-ĭtus* > *-to: rŭptus* > *rŏtto, pŏsĭtus* > *pŏsto, volūtus* *vŏlvĭtus* > *vŏlto*.

Among these types there were many shifts in Latin and more in Italian. All first conjugation verbs took a perf. part in *-ato: crepare, crepĭtus* > *crepato*. The ending *-uto* spread to all the *-ui* verbs, which were greatly extended in Vulgar Latin: *habēre, habui, habĭtus* > *avúto; cadĕre* *cadĕre, *cadui* (> *caddi*), *casus* > *cadúto*. The *-so* and *-to* types were somewhat extended also: *abscondĭtus* > *ascoso ascosto, mōtus* > *mŏsso; quæsītus* > *chiĕsto, latus* > *tŏlto, vīsus* > *visto* and *vedúto*. In Sicilian, *-uto* is applied to all the fourth conjugation; and some of these Sicilian participles were not infrequently used by Tuscan poets: e.g., *vestuto* (Dante).

The practice of occasionally syncopating a perf. part. in *-ato* (as *pago* for *pagato*) seems to have arisen in the following way. At a time when, for instance, *canere* and its derivative *cantare* were used side by side, people might say *habeo cantum* and *habeo cantatum;* so *habeo ausum* or *ausatum, habeo acceptum* or *acceptatum, habeo usum* or *usatum.* Then, as the primitive verb was going out of use, the *cantum* (or whatever it might be) was taken to be an abridgment of the longer form; and new contractions were made on this model, such as *destato, desto.*

Tense Stems

200. We have seen (§ 190) that the Romance future is built out of the infinitive + *habeo* etc. In standard Italian, however, in the first conjugation, the *a* before the *r* became *e (amerò)*, except in the short verbs *darò, farò, starò* (where we do find also, but very seldom, *derò ferò sterò*). This is originally a central Tuscan phenomenon (§ 62); Siena and Lucca not only say *amarò* but carry the *a* into the third conjugation (*diciarò*).

In Old Italian *e* could be syncopated between two *r*'s (*dimorrò, liberrà*), hence such forms as *enterrò* for *entrerò;* next came doubling of a single *r*, as in *griderrà, presterrò*, used by Boccaccio, Sacchetti, Pulci; even *crederrò* (Boccaccio). In modern standard Italian there is no syncopation in the first conjugation, except in *and(e)rò;* but some dialects syncopate regularly (*drà, pagrà*). Verbs of the second and third conjugations syncopate whenever the infinitive does and often when it does not: *avrò, potrò, vedrò* (and dialectically *vendrà*); also, with assimilation: *rimarrò, varrò, verrò*, etc. Verbs of the 4th conjugation preserve their *i*, except sometimes *mor(i)rò, ud(i)rò*.

For *sarò, arò, porò*, see § 197.

The conditional always has the same stem as the future.

201. In Italian, as in Latin, the imperfect indicative (except *era*) has the same stem as the uncontracted infinitive: *aveva, diceva, faceva, poneva*. Italian, however, carried this identity into its imperfect subjunctive, which, being originally a pluperfect, had in Latin the perfect stem: *avessi, dicessi, facessi, ponessi;* cf. Lat. *habuissem, dixissem, fecissem, posuissem*. This process is evidently connected with the introduction of the same infinitive stem into three forms (the 2d pers. sing. and the 1st and 2d pers. pl.) of the perfect of strong verbs: *avesti, dicemmo, faceste, poneste*.

In weak verbs, of course, the infinitive stem and the contracted perfect stem were alike from the start: *amāre, amāsti, amāssem; sentīre, sentīsti, sentīssem*. To their example is added that of the verbs in *-dere*, which, as we have seen (§ 140), furnished a model for the weak inflection of the third conjugation: *credĭdĭsti > *creddęsti credęsti, credĭdĭmus* *credĭdmus > credęmmo, credĭdĭstis > *creddeste credeste; credĭdĭssem > *creddęsse credęsse.

Under these influences, one cannot tell exactly how, strong verbs assumed the infinitive stem in the aforesaid forms, before the beginnings of written Italian: *crebbi, crescesti, crebbe, crescemmo, cresceste, crebbero; crescessi,* etc. Exceptions are *essere, dare,* and *stare:* § 197, 9 and 10.

1. We have noted (§ 196) that *-iēbam* became *-ēbam* in the third conjugation: *faceva*. In the fourth it gave way to the old *-ībam: veniva.*

2. The weak perfects of course had the infinitive stem throughout: *amai . . . amaron, sentii . . . sentiron.*

202. We have noted, in § 140, the dissimilation of *habēbam* = *αβεβα* to *αβεα > avęa*. The same thing may have happened independently to *debēbam*. At any rate there spread from *αβεα*, or from *αβεα* and *deβęα*, an imperfect indicative type in *-ęa*, which was used beside the longer *-ęva* both in the second and in the third conjugation: *godęa, prendęa*. To match it, *-ia* was created for the fourth. Phonetically, *-ęa* should become *-ia* (§ 25, 3), but the influence of *-ęva* preserved *-ęa* in Old Florentine, and *-ia* was there used only for the fourth conjugation; in Siena and Arezzo *-ea* and *-ia* were confused; Sicilian has only *-ia*.

These forms occur only in the 1st and 3d pers. sing. Very rarely we find an *-ei* for the 2d: *credei* = *credevi*. For the 3d pers. pl., *-ean* and *-ian* were made: *vedean, venian*. There are no similar endings for the 1st and 2d pers. pl.: *credevamo, venivate*. The short terminations, once extremely common, are now literary and rather archaic.

The ending *-ia*, from *habebam*, was used also, in the south, to form the conditional (§ 190); and such forms as *daria, vorria, torrian, verrian* became very prevalent in poetry.

203. Of the strong perfects, the Latin reduplicating type disappeared, being replaced by one of the others: *cucurri > corsi, momordi > morsi*. The only specimens retained were *dedi* and *steti*, whose reduplicative formation was apparently not recognized; and even *steti* was in Italy generally supplanted by *stetui > *stetti*.

The three types kept are represented by *vidi, placui, risi.* Among these there were various exchanges, which resulted in extensive gains for the last: *morsi, posi, vinsi, valsi,* Old It. *volsi = volli.* The *-ui* class, which absorbed the strong *-vi* perfects, got sundry new recruits, but lost a couple of adherents to *-si: crebbi, conobbi; caddi, detti, venni,* Old It. *viddi; posi, valsi.* The *-i* class saved a few members, but lost more: *fui, feci, vidi; ruppi, stetti, venni, viddi, vinsi.*

Some strong perfects became weak throughout: *dovei, temei. Quæsivi,* on the other hand, became *chiesi.*

1. *Venni* is from *vēnui influenced by *tĕnui* while *tẹnni* gets its *ẹ* from *vēni*). *Viddi,* once current beside *vidi,* is from **vīdui;* Cellini has the odd form *vedde. Stetti* is from **stĕtui;* it induces *detti* beside *diedi.*

2. There is sometimes an influence of the perfect participle on the perfect: *mīsi mīssus* > *misi messo,* then *messi* beside *misi;* Cellini has *misse, misso.* He writes also not only *volse* but *volsuto.*

204. For certain changes in accentuation, see § 193: *credémo, facémmo, sentíssimo, avièno, sièno.* The 3d pers. pl. of the perfect may, in Classic Latin, accent either the penult or the antepenult, but more commonly stresses the former; in Vulgar Latin the accent is always on the antepenult: *fēcērunt fēcĕrunt* > *fẹcero.*

For the ending *-isco (finio* > *finísco,* etc.), see § 192.

1. For the occasional addition of *-ne* to final stressed vowels, see §§ 52, 170: *ène, fáne, háne, salíne.* Sometimes the *n* is doubled: *honne, sonne, fonne = fu.* The phenomenon belongs in eastern Tuscany, Umbria, and Rome. See *Zs.,* Beiheft XV, 59.

2. The group *ia* apparently tended to become *ie* before a consonant: *avía-lo* > *avielo, sia-ti* > *sieti, fiano* > *fieno, diami* > *diemi, stiavi* > *stievi.* For a subsequent shift of accent (*avièno, sièno,* etc.), see § 193, 1.

3. Inasmuch as final *o* can disappear inside a sentence, the *-mo* of the 1st pers. pl. was sometimes reduced to *m: andiamo presto* > *andiam*

presto. In poetry such a form may be used at the end of a phrase: *andiám!* An *m* thus made final was frequently assimilated to a following dental: *andianne, piglierenne, ripentianci, andiancene.* Hence probably arose such forms as *avén* (for *avęmo = abbiamo*), *faccián, potén* (for *potęmo = possiamo*), *vedián,* etc.; this *-ián* was used in Florence until the eighteenth century, and is still heard in Val di Chiana. From such *n*-forms, with a restoration of the *-o*, we get *avéno, faccián o,* etc., which are usual in Bologna and Romagna.

4. Most 3d pers. pl. forms have come to end in a movable *-o: aman amano, vedon vedono, sentiron sentirono,* etc. For the origin of this *-o*, see § 97 and § 97, 1; also § 205, end.

PERSONAL ENDINGS

205. The present indicative and subjunctive run much as one would expect, bearing in mind the gradual substitution of *-i* for *-a* and *-e* described in § 55:

amo	vedo	credo	sento
ama-e-i	vede-i	crede-i	senti
ama	vede	crede	sente
amámo-iamo	vedęmo-iamo	credęmo-iamo	sentímo-iamo
amate	vedęte	credęte	sentite
áman	vędon	crędon	sęnton
ame-i	veda	creda	senta
ame-i	veda	creda	senta
ame-i	veda	creda	senta
amiamo	vediamo	crediamo	sentiamo
amiate	vediate	crediate	sentiate
ámen-in	vędan	crędan	sęntan

The 2d pers. sing. *-i,* early borrowed from the fourth conjugation (*-īs>-i*) by the first and second, presently makes itself at home in the third. The first, having taken *-i* from the fourth and *-e* from the second and third, hesitates long between the two; and a result of this conflict is the substitution of *i* for *e* in the present subjunctive — first, no doubt, in the 2d pers. sing., then in all the singular and the 3d pers. pl. Petrarch, in the 3d pers. sing., wrote *-e* freely, in and out of the rime: *Zs.*, Beiheft XIII, 25. Forms like *tu ama* and *tu vede* are exceedingly rare; *tu crede*, on the other hand, is common in the early language, and so are *tu ame* and *che tu ame.*

For the loss of the *y* element in *vĭdeo, vĭdeam, vĭdeant, sentio, sentiunt, sentiam, sentiant,* see § 196. The 3d pers. pl. of the present indicative of the second conjugation is evidently made over on the model of the third conjugation: *vedon,* following *credon.* It is noteworthy that in the present indicative the 3d pers. pl. almost always adapts itself to the 1st pers. sing.; and with them goes the present subjunctive singular and 3d pers. pl.: *piaccio piaccion, piaccia, piaccian; cresco crescon, cresca crescan; vengo vengon, venga vengan; traggo traggon, tragga traggan; valgo valgon, valga valgan; voglio voglion, voglia voglian; finisco finiscon, finisca finiscan; posso posson, possa possan.*

Very puzzling is the extension of *-iamo,* which must have started with such forms as *habeāmus > abbiamo, sapiāmus > sappiamo, *siāmus > siamo, faciāmus > facciamo.* Thence, in preliterary times, it spread to the present subjunctive of all verbs, and a 2d pers. pl. in *-iate* went with it. It was used also by all verbs to make an imperative 1st pers. pl.: *udiamo, andiamo.* The strangest phase, however, is its introduction into the present indicative, which occurred largely in historical times. The starting-point was presumably the imperative. Inasmuch as the 2d person of that mood was at one time identical in form with the 2d person of the present indicative in nearly all verbs, it is perhaps natural that the identity should be extended to the 1st pers. pl.: *ama amate, vede vedete, crede credete, senti sentite,* hence *sentiamo,* etc., for both imperative and indicative. But why should the imperative rather than the indicative form have been chosen? Evidently there was something attractive in the ending *-iamo* itself; moreover, it afforded all conjugations a method of expressing the 1st pers. pl. idea in the same way. We may perhaps imagine *giamo < eāmus* coming to mean not only 'let us go' but 'we go,' inasmuch as *ite* has both indicative and imperative significance; then -*iamo* might creep, on the one hand, into other verbs in -*ire*, and, on the other hand, into the new synonym *andare* and thence into the whole first conjugation. In point of fact, the first and fourth conjugations yield their -*amo* and -*imo* more easily than the second and third give up their -*emo:* such forms as *amamo* occur sporadically in the thirteenth and early fourteenth centuries (for Guittone see *Zs.*, Beiheft XV, 9) and later turn up frequently in Boiardo; such forms as *udimo* are found in Guittone (*Zs.*, Beiheft XV, 10) and in Ristoro d'Arezzo; while *vedemo, credemo*, and the like are very common all through the fourteenth century. It is perhaps significant that *iamo* was in general adopted too late to palatalize a preceding consonant (*cerchiamo, paghiamo, prendiamo*), although it must be observed that the consonant is, by analogy, preserved from palatalization even in verbs in which the ending is original (*teniamo, vediamo, sentiamo, udiamo*).

The 3d pers. pl. may at any time add -*o*. This ending first developed in such verbs as *dĕdĕrunt* > *diędero, fēcĕrunt* > *fęcero, vīdĕrunt* > *videro*, and came to be regarded as an optional termination for nearly any 3d pers. pl. form: see § 97. For *hąnno, danno, vanno, fanno, stanno, enno, denno, ponno*, etc., see § 97, 2. The forms with -*o* are now looked upon as the normal ones, and those without *o* as apocopated.

1. *C* and *g* are not palatalized before *e* and *i* in the first conjugation: *cerche cerchi, cercherà; paghe paghi, pagherei.*

2. Boiardo uses -*ati* for -*ate* — probably a local contamination of singular and plural. Sacchetti has *andá* = *andate, pigliáve* = *pigliatevi.*

3. In the 3d pers. pl. there was a contest among -*ant*, -*ent*, and -*unt*. In Florentine and in the literary language -*an* held its own, and -*on* replaced -*en;* but in the vulgar speech of the city -*an* often supplants both -*en* and -*on* (*vendano* for *vendono*). In Arezzo, Pistoia, Lucca, and Pisa (as in some northern and southern dialects), -*en* displaced -*on* (*scriveno*). In Siena -*on* usurped the place of -*an* and -*en* (*cantono* = *cantano* and *cantino*).

4. Through the influence of the first conjugation and of such imperative-subjunctive forms as *abbi, sappi, sii,* an *i* was sometimes introduced into the subjunctive of the other conjugations: *che tu credi, ch'egli debbi, ch'egli facci, ch'egli vegni.* Occasionally an *-e* was used: *che tu ode.*

5. *Dare* and *stare* make their present subjunctive on the pattern of *essere:* § 197, 7. See also § 204, 2.

6. When *-i* was added to an Italian stem ending in an *i* pronounced *y,* the two *i's* combined: *picchiare, picchi; vegghiare, vegghi.*

7. Lat. *sum* > *son,* which frequently adds *-o* under the influence of all other verbs. Of the Latin synonyms *sŭmus* and *sŭmus,* Italian preferred the latter. *Somo* does occur very early, but *semo* was the regular form until it was superseded by *siamo.*

8. *Tenghiamo, venghiamo* are vulgar Tuscan forms modeled on *tengo, vengo.*

206. The imperative in the first and fourth conjugations keeps its Latin forms: *ama amate, senti sentite.* In the singular of the second and third, *-i* replaces *-e* as it does in the indicative; in Siena, however, we often find *-e* (*scrive*), which indeed occurs there even in the fourth conjugation (*sale*). The forms in the 2d pers. pl. are regular in all the conjugations: *amate, vedete, credete* (for the accent, see § 193), *sentite.* All borrow from the present subjunctive a 1st pers. pl.: *amiamo, vediamo, crediamo, sentiamo* (§ 205). Some verbs, which do not easily lend themselves to absolute command, take their whole imperative from the present subjunctive: *abbiate, sappiate, siate, vogliate,* and in Old Italian others still. In these there is a strong tendency to make the 2d pers. sing. end in *-i,* by analogy with the imperative of other verbs of the second, third, and fourth conjugations: *abbi, sappi, sii;* and sometimes these forms with *-i* are carried back into the subjunctive.

1. *Dare* and *stare* keep their Latin forms, *da date, sta state. Facere fare* and *dicere dire* have *fa'* < *fac* and *di'* < *dīc,* and from them construct *fate* and *dite. Andare* has, in imitation of these, *va* in the singular, but makes a plural *andate. Ducere durre* constructs *duci ducete,* while *traggere trarre* prefers *trai traete.*

207. From *-abam*, etc., *ēbam*, etc., and *-ībam* etc. (§ 201, 1) we should expect *-áva -áva -áva -avámo -aváte -ávan, -éva* etc., *-íva* etc.; and that is what we find, save that the 2d pers. sing. was very early differentiated from the 3d by substituting for *-a* an *-i* taken from the perfect: *facevi*, after *facesti*. Sometimes, instead, it used to have an *-e* borrowed from the present: *tu parlave*, after *tu parle*. In the 1st pers. sing., popular speech adopted, for clearness' sake, an *-o* drawn from the present; and this, in present day Italian, has become the usual form: *credevo*, after *credo*.

The 1st pers. pl. is subject to curious variations. Beside the popular *cantávamo cantávate* (§ 193, 1) we find, in Lucca and elsewhere, *gridávimo, credévimo, sentívimo*, etc. Moreover, there are hybrid formations such as *amavávamo, credevávamo*, whence, no doubt, Boccaccio's *avavamo avavate*. It is no wonder that popular speech has preferred *noi si aveva*. For the fall of the *-o* of *-mo*, and the change of *m* to *n*, see § 204, 3.

The second and third conjugation ending *-ea* and the fourth conjugation *-ia* have been discussed in § 202. For *ie*, *-ieno*, see § 204, 2.

1. *Essere* keeps its Latin imperfect *era*, but has in the 1st and 2d pers. pl. *eravámo eraváte*.

2. Some vulgar dialects use the 2d pers. sing. for the 2d pers. pl.: *voi aspettavi*.

3. In the 3d pers. pl., *-on* is occasionally substituted for *-an*: Cellini has *eron, usavon*. Cf. § 205, 3.

208. From *-āssem, -īssem, -īssem* we get *-asse, -ęsse, -isse:* *amasse, facesse, udisse*. Occasionally, in Old Italian, *-esse* and *-isse* were confused: Dante writes *venesse;* Boccaccio, *credissi*.

Inasmuch as *-em, -es, -et* all gave the same result, the three persons of the singular originally ended alike in *-e*. Early, however, the example of the perfect led to the introduction of *-i* in the 1st and 2d: *facessi facessi facesse*, after *feci facesti* *fece*. In the period of transition, *-i* sometimes slipped into the 3d pers.: *avessi, fussi, volessi.*

Of the shift of accent in the 1st and 2d pers. pl., mention has been made in § 193: *mandāssēmus *mandássemus>mandássimo, audīssētis *audíssetis>udiste* (in Lucca *udissite*).

In the 3d pers. pl., *-ent* would regularly become *-en* or *-eno: facesseno.* This occasionally became *-ino:* Cellini, *facessino.* Generally, however, it was exchanged for the *-ono* of the weak perfects: *facessono*, after *crederono.* Through the thirteenth and fourteenth centuries *-ono* (also *-eno*) was the usual form in Florence; in Arezzo and Lucca it is still current. But as early as the beginning of the thirteenth century, *-ero* was taken over from the strong perfect, and has ultimately prevailed: *facessero*, after *fecero.*

1. Occasionally the 2d pers. sing. is used, in popular style, for the 2d pers. pl.: Sacchetti writes *voi fosse;* Boccaccio, *voi credissi.*

209. In the perfect, the name ' weak ' is given to those types which keep the accent on the ending throughout; the others — those which in some persons accent the root — are called 'strong ': *amái, dovéi, credéi, sentíi* are weak; *vídi, piácqui, piánsi* are strong. It must be remembered that strong verbs adopted for the 2d pers. sing. and the 1st and 2d pers. pl. a stem from the ' weak ' system (§ 201): *piacesti piacemmo piaceste;* exceptions are *dare* and *stare* (*desti* etc., *stesti* etc.).

The strong endings developed thus: *-ī, -ĭstī, -ĭt>-i, -ęsti, -e; -ĭmus>ęmmo* (§ 201); *-ĭstĭs>-ęste; -ĕrunt>-ero* (§ 97). E.g., piacqui, *piacesti*, piacque, *piacemmo, piaceste*, piacquero; salsi, *salisti*, salse, *salimmo, saliste*, salsero. The 3d pers. pl. may drop its *-o* in imitation of the weak type: *fecer, dieder, vider*, after *amaron, crederon, sentiron.* Conversely, the weak type may copy the strong either by dropping *n* or by adding *o*: *amaron>amaro* or *amarono, sentiron>sentiro* or *sentirono.* From the latter arose a movable *-o*, attached at will to any

3d pers. pl.: *aman-o, amin-o, amavan-o; senton-o, sentan-o, sentivan-o;* etc. A further imitation of the *fecer* type changed *amaro* to *amar*, *sentiro* to *sentir*, etc. See § 97, 1. These shortened forms are common in poetry. Sometimes a strong verb assumed an ending *-eno* or *-ono* on the analogy of the imperfect subjunctive: *stetteno* (Cellini), *diedono*. For the forms with *nn*, see § 97, 2: *dienno, fenno, funno, uscinno, amonno;* and (with loss of *-no* on the model of *dan < dant*) *uscìn*. A cross between *amonno* and *amarono* is *amorono amoron amoro amor*. With syncopation we have *amarno, amorno, sentirno*. The forms with *o* for *a* belong to Tuscan, Umbrian, and Roman dialects, but were little used by the poets. *Amorno* is still common in the south.

In the weak, or 'regular,' type the first alteration is the loss of *v*, which in great part goes back to Classic times or even earlier. Between two *i*'s a *v* is likely to fall in Latin; hence *sentĭsti, sentĭstis* and *sentĭi, sentĭit*, for *sentivisti*, etc. So in the first conjugation *amāsti, amāstis, amārunt;* and, in vulgar speech, *amai* for *amavi, amát* or *amáut* for *amavit*. In the fourth, with retention of the characteristic vowel, *ĭ*, popular usage adopted *sentĭi, sentĭt* or *sentĭut, sentĭrunt*. The history of the 1st pers. pl. is not so clear; it seems to have generally modeled itself on the 2d pers. pl., becoming *amāmus, sentĭmus*, and ultimately, in Italy, to have doubled its *m* under the influence of such forms as *dĕdĭmus *dedmus > demmo, credĭdĭmus *credidmus > credemmo, fēcĭmus *fecmus > femmo:* so *amammo, sentimmo*. Vulgar Latin *-ai, -ĭi* remained as *-ái* and *-íi* in Italian: *amai, udii*. Vulgar Latin *-aut*, if monosyllabic, gave *-ò;* if dissyllabic, *-ao:* hence *amò* in most of Tuscany, *amao* is southern Tuscany and the south. Vulgar Latin *-ĭt* gave Tuscan *-ì*, while *-ĭut* gave southern Tuscan and southern Italian *-io: udì, udìo*. The endings, then, are *-ai, -asti, -ò* or *-ào, -ammo, -aste, -aron; -ii, -isti, -ì* or *-ìo, -immo, -iste, -iron*. The literary language eventually chose in the 3d pers. sing. the simpler forms (*amò, udì*). The perfect in *-ēvi* was extremely rare in Latin; as far as it was preserved at all in vulgar speech, it probably developed forms similar to the descendants of the *-āvi* and *-īvi* types.

The evolution of a new weak type in the third conjugation to match those of the first and fourth, has been touched upon in §§ 140 and 201. Compounds of *dare*, such as *perdĕre*, with a Vulgar Latin perfect in *-dḗdi* (§ 9, 3), would have developed phonetically thus: *perdḗdī* > *perdiẹdi*, *perdidĭstī* > **perddẹsti perdẹsti*, *perdẹdit* > *perdiede*, *perdĭdĭmus* **perdĭdmus* > *perdẹm-mo*, *perdidĭstis* > **perddẹste perdẹste*, *perdẹderunt* > *perdiedero*. Under the combined influence of dissimilation and of the 2d pers. sing. and the 1st and 2d pers. pl., the second *d* of the other three forms was lost; and they were made to conform to the pattern of *amai* and *sentii:* hence *perdẹi*, *perdè*, *perdẹron*. Subsequently the *e* became close, like that of the 2d pers. sing. and 1st and 2d pers. pl., and like that of the imperfect indicative and subjunctive. Relics of the open vowel are archaic *vendiè*, *vendiero*. This convenient inflection once established, it was extended to numerous verbs of the third conjugation and to some of the second: *battei, esigei, esistei, mescei, pascei, tessei*, etc.; *dovei, godei, potei, temei*. Some verbs take it in addition to a strong perfect: *fondei fusi, perdei persi, redimei redensi, rendei resi*, etc.

An alternative to *-ei*, *-è -eron*, for many verbs, is *-etti*, *-ette*, *-ettero*. This ending started with *stĕti* **stĕtui* > *stẹtti;* then came, by analogy, *dẹtti* for *diedi;* then *perdẹtti*, etc.; finally (with extension to verbs not compounds of *dare*) *dovẹtti*, etc. In Arezzo *-etti* was carried into the first conjugation: *fondette* from *fondare*. The Pisan and some other dialects create analogically an *-itti* for the fourth conjugation (*uditte*, etc.); such forms occur in the early poets: Boiardo, *moritte*, etc.

1. Occasionally the strong 1st pers. sing. has *-e* in imitation of the original imperfect subjunctive: *io vide*, after *io vedesse*. Rarely, in weak perfects, *-to* replaces *-ii*, with an *-o* taken from the present indicative (*udio* for *udii*, after *odò*); in the Sicilian poets we find also *-ao*, *-eo* for *-ai*, *-ei*.

2. In some old texts we find, in the 3d pers. sing., *-oje* for *ò* (*mandoje*). Neapolitan has *mandaje*. Either form is difficult to explain, as one sees no occasion for the development of a palatal glide: see S. Pieri in *Zs.*, XXX, 339. One may perhaps compare *sojo* for *suo* and *meje teje seje* for *me te se*.

3. In popular style, the 2d pers. sing. is sometimes used for the 2d pers. pl.: (*voi*) *lasciasti*, Sacchetti.

210. The construction of the Italian future and conditional was described in § 190, 1, 2.

As was there said, we usually have in the future greatly shortened forms of the present indicative of *avere: -ò, -ai, -à, -emo, -ete, -anno*. We find in the south, however, descendants of full *habeo* and of **ayo* (§ 197, 2): *ameraggio, ameraio*, with corresponding forms in the 3d pers. pl. We find also *-abbo* (§ 197, 2).

The Tuscan conditional, taking its endings from the preterit of *avere*, got: *-abbi, -ęsti, -abbe, -ęmmo, -ęste, -abbero*. But *-ęi*, borrowed from the perfect, was substituted for *-abbi* and sometimes crossed with it: *crederabbi*, then *crederęi* and *crederębbi*, whence *crederębbe crederębbero;* in the 1st pers. sing. *-ei* was finally preferred, and we get *crederei crederesti crederebbe* etc. In the 3d pers. pl. we find in Old Italian (beside *crederabbero*) *crederebbon-o*. Such forms as *crederebbi* are still used in Lucca. Beside *crederei* in the 1st pers., we sometimes find in the 3d *crederè*, which was especially common in Pisa. Some dialects carry the open vowel of *-ęi* all through the tense.

In most southern dialects the only native forms in the 1st and 3d pers. sing. and the 3d pers. pl. are *-ea -eano, -ia -iano*, coming from the imperfect indicative of *avere*. This *-ia* type was early introduced into Tuscany, and is still used in verse, as are the 3d pers. pl. forms *-ieno* and *-ièno*. Arezzo, like Umbria and Rome, had both *-ębbi* and *-ęa*.

1. In the 1st pers. pl. we occasionally find *-éssimo* (*avressimo*) borrowed from the imperfect subjunctive.

INDEX RERUM

The references are to paragraphs.

INDEX VERBORUM

This list does not include all words mentioned in the text, but it is meant to comprise all those for which search is likely to be made. The references are to paragraphs. Latin words are printed in heavy type.

essuto 197, 7
este = è 96
estrarre, 133
età 45, 2
etichetta 45, 2
etterno 100
Ettòr 10, 1
Eufratè 10, 1
Eunoè 10, 1
-evole 24, 1; 73
ex- 38, 3
exeo 10; 128, 2

fa 106, 3; 197
fabbro 100; 103
fabula 11
fac 185
faccenda 26, 1; 123
facci 205, 4
faccia <facies 156
faccio 196
face 196
facemmo 193
facere 185
facesseno 208
facessino 208
facessono 208
faciebam 37, 2
facondo 29, 6
Faenza 103
faesti 197, 9
faeva 197, 9
faggio 78; 107
fagiana 124; 129
fagiolo 79
fai 197
faína 107
falò 10, 2
famiglia 25, 4
fammi 94
fanciullo 25, 12; 133
fantasima 79; 130, Sm
fàne = fa 52
fante 40, 4
Faraò 10, 1
fare 71, 1

farnetico 45; 141
fascia 128
fastello 133
fata 157
fate 185; 193
faticare 108, 1
favola 103
fazzone 123
fè 52
fe' 52; 106, 3; 197, 9
febbraio 116; 118, 1
febbre 116
feccia 27
fedele 25, 10
Federigo 138
feminoro 161, 1
femmina 101
femmo 197, 9
fende 25, 9
fenice 45
fenno 97, 2; 197, 9
feo 197, 9
fermamento 36
fero 27, 3
festuga 108, K
feto 25, 10
fi' = figlio 51; 59, 1
fia 187, 3
fiaba 64, 2; 141
fiaccola 24, 5; 108, K
fibbia 113
ficatum 9, 4
ficcare 131
fico 155
fiedere 104, R; 138; 185
fieggio 151, 1
fieggo 151, 1
fiele 94
fiera 25, 2
Fiesole 27; 105
fievole 25, 2
figghio = figlio 125, 1
figgo 195
figliuoi 163, 6
filiggine 47, 4

filiolus 9, 2; 10
filius 11
filomena 138
filosofia 10, 2
fingo 25, 5
finice 45
finìo 77
finisco 192; 196
fiome 32, 2
fiore 89
fiorentino 36
fiorire 185
fir <fieri 187
Firenze 11; 26, 1; 36; 43; 161
firmare 45
fischiare 36, 1
fischio 113
fisiologi 163, 1
fiso 132
fistiare 113, 3
fiume 32; 89; 162
fiutare 49
Flegiàs 10,1
flemma 131
Florentiae 11; 36; 43; 161
Florentinus 11; 36
fo 197
foggia 31; 121
foglia 31; 154; 157
fola 33; 77
folaga 21; 29, 7; 68, 1; 73; 108, K
folgore 157
fondo 40, 4
fonte 30, 1
fora <forat 31, 1
fora <fuerat 37, 1; 189
formento 38; 141
foris 13
foron 37, 1
fortem 13
fossa 29, 5
fosse 2d p. pl. 208, 1
fossi 197, 10

Lightning Source UK Ltd.
Milton Keynes UK
UKHW021840041019
351026UK00008B/1699/P